WITH CHARITY
FOR ALL

WITH CHARITY FOR ALL

Welfare and Society,
Ancient Times to the Present

Merritt Ierley

PRAEGER

PRAEGER SPECIAL STUDIES • PRAEGER SCIENTIFIC

New York • Philadelphia • Eastbourne, UK
Toronto • Hong Kong • Tokyo • Sydney

29621

Library of Congress Cataloging in Publication Data

Ierley, Merritt.
  With charity for all.

  Bibliography: p.
  Includes index.
  1. Public welfare—History. 2. Charities—History.
I. Title.
HV16.137   1984   361'.9   84-11469
ISBN 0-03-000044-0 (alk. paper)

Published and Distributed by the
Praeger Publishers Division
(ISBN Prefix 0-275)
of Greenwood Press, Inc.,
Westport, Connecticut

Published in 1984 by Praeger Publishers
CBS Educational and Professional Publishing
a Division of CBS Inc.
521 Fifth Avenue, New York, NY 10175 USA

© 1984 by Praeger Publishers

All rights reserved

456789 052 987654321

Printed in the United States of America
on acid-free paper

PREFACE

The best method of caring for the poor has been the puzzle of centuries. The wisest thinkers have never developed it. The most experienced and practical workers have never agreed about it. When one thinks he has got it, it evades him like Proteus.

Dr. Henry B. Wheelwright
National Conference
of Charities, May 21, 1878

With Charity for All is a look across the ages at public provision for the needy, that which has evolved today into a veritable welfare society.

"Welfare" means those various governmental programs and services relating to the general welfare and condition of people. The significance of the title lies in the fact that the trend of public welfare is to be more and more inclusive. The Joint Economic Committee of Congress, in 1974, compiled a list of all existing Federal Income Security Programs and counted 91 of them, so diverse in nature that virtually every citizen is eligible for some form of public benefit at one time or another.

The tendency of social welfare to be "charity for all" is evident in a look at federal expenditures for half a century following the New Deal: In 1933, they totaled $1.3 billion; in 1983, $365.5 billion.* And yet, despite the enormous increase in expenditures, "Many of the nation's poor who need help don't get it, and many who do get it don't really need it," as Washington Governor Daniel J. Evans observed at the 1976 National Governors' Conference.

While current levels of spending may be unprecedented, there is ample precedent in times past—more, perhaps, than is generally recognized—for many of the social welfare programs that exist today. As far back as ancient Rome, there were rudimentary forms of food

---

*Federal Budget, Fiscal Year 1983, Estimated Outlays: Total of "Social Services"; "Health Care Services" (Medicare and Medicaid); and "Income Security."

stamps, medicaid, aid to dependent children, and work relief; there was also a profound concern about inflation, bureaucracy, and a declining ratio of those contributing to those receiving.

In colonial America public relief was extensive enough that a legislative committee was appointed (South Carolina, 1767) to determine why expenditures had increased 543 percent in 20 years. During the nineteenth century, the almshouse came into its own in the United States, but not to the exclusion of other forms of aid. New York City in 1870 had a Department of Public Charities and Corrections that included 32 separate agencies and institutions; Cincinnati, in the 1870s, what was virtually medicaid: a public physician in each ward to provide free medical care. In New York City, about the same time, it was estimated that 30 to 35 percent of the population was receiving free medical attention, some of it through private charity but most at public expense. Indeed, by the end of the century, public assistance was sufficiently taken for granted that W. W. Baldwin, president of the Charity Organization Society of Burlington, Iowa, in 1903 declared: "Willingness to accept support from the pauper fund is largely an inherited inclination and runs in families."

Yet, so little is generally understood of the development of social welfare over the centuries that *Congressional Digest* in January 1980 began an article on welfare reform by saying that, except for almshouses, "until well into this century the indigent, and others needing help, were generally cared for locally by neighbors, churches and other charitable organizations."

At a time when a bankruptcy-threatened social security system has revealed its own insecurity, and the cost of "charity for all" has contributed so substantially to federal budget deficits, a sense of historical perspective is more essential than ever. To that task, this book is dedicated.

M.I.

ACKNOWLEDGMENTS

Gratefully acknowledged is the advice and assistance of many who, in many ways, have been a part of this project. In particular: J. Mark Reifer, formerly Assistant Dean and Tutor in Politics and Economics, Wroxton College, England: page-by-page critique of the entire manuscript; William B. Widnall, for many years a representative from New Jersey, who, at the time he left Congress, was ranking minority member of the Joint Economic Committee of Congress: advice on relevant sections; Dr. Joseph Green, formerly Dean of the School of Business Administration, Fairleigh Dickinson University: review of sections of the manuscript; Donna Doyle, and Gretchen Bock, Alice Hecht, Robert Ierley, Bonnie Koopman, and Maureen Petrosky: their help, in many ways.

Illustrations

Chapter 1: American Numismatic Society. Chapters 2 and 3: Picture Collection, New York Public Library. Chapters 4 and 6: New York Public Library—Astor, Lenox, and Tilden Foundations. Mid-Chapter 4: Prints and Photographs Division, Library of Congress. Chapter 5: Center for Research Libraries, Chicago. Chapter 7: Prints and Photographs Division, Library of Congress (photograph by John Vachon, 1940, for the Farm Security Administration). Chapter 9: Washington *Post*, May 23, 1964 (reprinted by permission).

CONTENTS

PREFACE v

ACKNOWLEDGMENTS vii

1 *PANEM ET CIRCENSES*
   Athens and Rome: The Ancient World 1

2 SOME PROVISYON FOR THE POORE
   England: The Middle Ages through
   Elizabethan Times 21

3 EARLY POVERTY AMID EARLY PLENTY
   America: The Colonial Period 39

4 THE PUZZLE OF CENTURIES DEBATED
   From Old Poor Law to the Twentieth Century 51

5 A PLUNGE INTO THE WAVES
   The Federal Government Becomes a Relief Agency 87

6 TAKING AMELIORATIVE MEASURES
   Social and Economic Determinants 99

7 *NOVUS ORDO* BEGINS
   The Coming of the New Deal 133

8 *NOVUS ORDO* CONTINUES
   The Age of Social Security 151

9 *NOVUS ORDO* BROADENS
   The Present Era 169

A BRIEF EPILOGUE 197

SOURCE NOTES	199
INDEX	209
ABOUT THE AUTHOR	223

WITH CHARITY FOR ALL

1
PANEM ET CIRCENSES
Athens and Rome: The Ancient World

Coins of the Roman Empire proclaimed abundantia *(abundance),* liberalitas *(generosity), and* providentia *(foresight), reminding people of the state's interest in their welfare. Shown here (left to right) are coins of the reigns of Severus Alexander, Caracalla, and Maximinus I. As far back as the Roman Empire there were rudimentary forms of food stamps, medicaid, aid to dependent children, and work relief.*

He often rides a horse. A man of means, surely. Lesser folks ride mules, while poor people walk. He is able to get on and off the horse. A man of sound body, obviously. Yet this man is on "welfare," a supposedly indigent cripple.

The time is about 400 B.C., the place Athens, and the story a documented one. The man, whose name we do not know, was a recipient of *poleos argurion* ("city money"). Yet he was seen transporting himself by the ancient equivalent of an expensive motorcar, and some fellow Athenian, obviously angered at a seeming misuse of public charity, reported the man to the Council of Athens, which had responsibility as to qualification for public assistance. Thus the man came to be defended by the orator Lysias, whose "Oration on the Question of a Pension for an Invalid" preserves this story for modern times.

Lysias explained to the council that the horse was borrowed, and the man, though capable of riding horseback, was nevertheless crippled enough to require two sticks for walking and was thus handicapped at earning a living wage. Eloquently did Lysias plead the case in his client's name: "Providence has barred me from advancement in life, but you have done something to correct the balance. Do not undo it, I beg you."

Whether the man continued with poleos argurion is not known, but the story documents the existence of a prototypal welfare system in ancient times. It was a system curiously familiar in some ways, even if antique in others.

The extent of the public pension at this time in Athens was the same in all cases: one obol a day, which was precious little, although it was never intended for more than food. A laborer earned a drachma a day, the equivalent of six obols.

In time, the poleos argurion increased. Aristotle, in *Athenaion Politeia* about 325 B.C., recorded the allowance was two obols a day. The Council of Athens still determined which citizens were eligible for public assistance, but there was now also a means test (an applicant could be worth no more than 300 drachmas, or 1,800 obols) in addition to a judgment as to incapacity.

When the welfare program of Athens (such as described here) went into effect is not clear; nor is it clear how long it continued in this form. It is known that public pensions had been granted to veterans; the earliest such case was Thersippus, a wounded soldier for whom Solon arranged public support early in the sixth century. Subsequently, under Pisistratus, military pensions became part of the general law. By the fifth century, and Lysias's controversial client, civil pensions were likewise common.

That is to be inferred from the oration. Had the crippled man been a veteran, Lysias surely would not have missed the point in pleading his case.

Under Themistocles, early in the fifth century, with unemployment on the rise, there came about the ancient version of work relief, whereby the poor might have assistance by working for it, specifically aboard Athens' new fleet. This, Themistocles had under construction for use against the Persians as well as for seeking new food supplies abroad. Beyond these obvious purposes, the fleet also had the virtue of helping with what to do about the increasing number of poor.

Pericles, leader of the democratic party that took control in 461 B.C., enlarged upon the work of his predecessors, consolidating his power in the process. According to Plutarch:

> At the first, as has been said, when he [Pericles] set himself against Cimon's great authority, he flattered the people. Finding himself short of his competitor in wealth and money, by which advantages the other was enabled to take care of the poor, inviting every day some one or the other of the citizens in want to supper, and bestowing clothes on the aged people, and breaking down the hedges and enclosures of his grounds, that all, who would, might freely gather what fruit they pleased, Pericles, thus outdone in popular arts, by the advice of one Damonides of Oea, as Aristotle states, turned to the distribution of public moneys; and in a short time, having bought the people over — what with moneys allowed for shows and for service on juries, and what with other forms of pay and largess — he made use of them against the Council of Areopagus [the supreme tribunal], of which he was not a member.

Thus did Pericles secure his power and attain vast authority. His distribution of the public moneys included payment for service on juries (there were no judges) at a rate of two obols a day; and, in 458 B.C., salaries for the nine archons, thus opening that office to the lower classes, although the position had lost most of its importance by that time. More important was Pericles' use of public works employment on a massive scale. A notable example is construction (beginning in 447 B.C.) of a new Temple of Athena to replace an earlier one burned by the Persians. History knows it better as the Parthenon. Again, Plutarch:

> For as those who are of age and strength for war are provided for and maintained out of public funds, so, it being Pericles' desire and design that the untrained multitude that stayed at home should not go without their share of the public salaries, and yet not receive them for sitting still and doing nothing, to that end he thought fit, with the approbation of the people, to put them to work on vast projects

of buildings and public works that would take some time for completion, and would give employment to numerous arts, so that those people who stayed at home, no less than those at sea or in garrisons or on expeditions, would have a fair and just occasion for receiving the benefit and having their share of the public moneys.

The cost of Pericles' various programs must have been considerable. It may be appreciated in relative terms by the fact that the public payroll of Athens at this time was maintaining some 20,000 persons. According to Aristotle, in *Athenaion Politeia*, these included 6,000 jurymen, 1,600 bowmen, 1,200 knights, 500 members of the Council of Athens, 500 dockyard guards, 50 guards of the city, 700 magistrates at home, 700 of the same abroad, 2,500 heavy-arms troops, and 2,000 crewmen aboard 20 guardships and ships collecting tribute. Besides these, there were persons in other categories qualifying for public support, as listed by Aristotle: orphans, jailers, and those maintained at the Prytaneum, which served as a public table for dignitaries, individual citizens esteemed by the state, and children of those who fell in battle. In addition, of course, there were the disabled indigent—those receiving poleos argurion—of whom there is no record as to number.

There was also, at this time, the tradition of giving theater money to the poor, albeit on a somewhat limited basis. This was cash-in-hand with which to attend state festivals, although it was not uncommon for the money to go to other uses and thus be treated as a simple handout. The tradition began in the fifth century and was revived during the hard times of the fourth. In 358 B.C. it became institutionalized as the Theoric Fund, from which the poor were given two obols each from time to time for the theater, that amount representing the standard price of a seat. The fund was maintained with surplus revenue, but it effectively came to an end in 339 when Demosthenes diverted surplus funds to help pay for the war against Philip of Macadon.

All of these were benefits of Athenian citizenship. One that was not: a grain dole. There is no evidence of a regular distribution of grain at public expense in Athens, although such doles did exist elsewhere in Greece. Athens, however, did have occasional distributions; and when shortages drove the price of grain beyond the means of the many, the usual Athenian recourse was to an *epidoseis* (voluntary public subscription) to permit subsidization and thus keep the price within reach of the poor.

Even without a grain dole, Athenian provisions for the poor were the most comprehensive to their time. Indeed, to some, there seemed to be too many benefits—or too many eligible. In 445 B.C., the year Athens and Sparta ended a quarter-century of warfare with the supposed Thirty Years' Peace, the king of Egypt sent to Athens 40,000 bushels of wheat as a gift (this was apparently a time of scarcity, and perhaps even of famine, in Athens). The wheat was to be distributed among the citizens. This prompted an examination of the citizenship list, with the result that more than one-quarter of the claimants were stricken under a law of 451 stipulating that a person could not claim citizenship unless both parents were Athenians. According to Plutarch, some 5,000 persons were thus convicted of falsely posing as citizens, and were sold as slaves.

In still another way did Pericles thin out the ranks of those requiring public assistance, and this was by encouraging colonization abroad— that particular form of colonization known as the *cleruch*, whereby an Athenian could live on conquered land and yet retain the general benefit of Athenian citizenship. Besides reducing surplus population, this policy fostered a friendly inhabitation of strategic and often disaffected portions of the empire. To Cherso, Pericles sent 1,000 Athenians as planters who would share the land among them by lot; to Naxos, 500 more; to Andros, half that number; to Thrace, another 1,000; to Italy, still others. "And this he did," observed Plutarch,

> to ease and discharge the city of an idle, and by reason of their idleness, a busy, meddling crowd of people; and at the same time to meet the necessities and restore the fortunes of the poor city people, and to intimidate, also, and check their allies from attempting any change, by posting such garrisons, as it were, in the midst of them.

Pericles died in 429 B.C., two years into the Peloponnesian War. By the time the war was over, in 404, Athens was a changed place. Pericles' successors had none of the dignity and intellectual polish of the leaders of the glorious years, and took to appealing to the primitive passions of the masses. Repeated wars marked the early fourth century, and with these wars went political and social change. Although many of the aristocracy and the bourgeoisie remained prosperous, that portion of the population called proletariat was on the increase, along with unemployment and ever-more-frequent food shortages. Beggars became an increasingly more common sight.

Isocrates, pupil of Socrates, writing his *Areopagiticus* midway through the fourth century, perceived Athenian society to be crumbling and warned that it would not be shored up by stouter walls to protect against Athens' enemies. The enemy was within: it was the many living off the state instead of for it. "The lawgivers who instituted our ancient democracy," lamented Isocrates,

> did not intend a government which, while seeming moderate and popular, would turn out to be oppressive to those living under it. They taught the citizens to understand that liberty is not the same

as license to do what one pleases; that freedom is not the same as lawlessness. They detested and punished those who acted to the contrary, thus preserving the great body of the citizenry from the corruption of licentiousness. But most of all, they recognized that equality is perceived as of two kinds: on the one hand, it is construed as meaning that each is rewarded the same regardless of his due; on the other hand, that each individual is treated according to his service. The former they rejected as unjust. The latter, alone, they determined is properly to be called equality.

The Hellenistic era (323 B.C. through the time of Roman domination) produced a flowering of Greek culture throughout the known world and an abundance of wealth for the already well-to-do. For the poor there was only more of their own lot. Against the increase of wealth for the wealthy, the poverty of the poor grated the more. In the Hellenistic world as a whole there were occasional revolts and insurrections, but none to any effect. In Egypt, peasants went on strike a few times. In Greece, there was that peculiar, self-imposed remedy whereby the poor limited the number of poor by limiting the number of births, or, that failing, killing off the newborn by exposure. Alleviation of increasing poverty was at best temporary. Delos, about 300 B.C., began a regular distribution of free grain to the poor. Rhodes did likewise. Here and there in Greece there were limited redistributions of land and abolition of debt. But public policy managed neither to improve the lot of the poor nor to take to heart the lamentations of Isocrates. The proletariat became less and less a factor in policy; and by the time of Rome's domination of Greece, it proved to be no factor at all. What to do about the poor then no longer mattered.

ROME: THE REPUBLIC

Coriolanus. Whoever gave that counsel to give forth the corn o' th' storehouse gratis, as 'twas used sometime in Greece—

Menenius. Well, well, no more of that.

Coriolanus. Though there the people had more absolute pow'r, I say they nourished disobedience, fed the ruin of the state. . . . [Their] kind of service did not deserve corn gratis.

Shakespeare, *Coriolanus.* III. i.

Plutarch, who was Shakespeare's source for the tragedy of Coriolanus, observes that even in the earliest days of Rome there were those who saw in Greece a dangerous precedent. According to the legend, Coriolanus, in 491 B.C., was agreeable to a dole of grain provided the masses gave up a right to the tribunate. They declined. The intractable Coriolanus thereupon refused his assent to the free distribution of grain.

Whether or not the legend of Coriolanus is true, it is a matter of record that Rome had given some thought to its poor at an early date. The beginning was modest but was accompanied by the same cry of demagoguery, heard in Greece and often heard since, that the proponent of a given measure was less interested in the plight of the poor than in his own path to power. It was so, Livy tells us, in 486 B.C., when Spurius Cassius and Proculus Verginius had become consuls. Cassius proposed that half of the lands newly conquered from the Henrici be divided among the plebeians of Rome. There was an outcry among the senators, who challenged: . . . *largitione consulem periculosas libertati opes struere* (that the consul, through his largesses, was forming an influence dangerous to liberty). The other consul, Verginius, opposed the land reform measure, arguing that danger lurked in what appeared to be a gift to the people. Cassius in 485 was tried for treason (he was suspected of having monarchial ambition) and executed.

From time to time, land reform was again considered. Consuls and tribunes now and again would rouse the masses with, says Livy, *suo veneno, agraria lege* (their usual poison, a land law). The senate routinely shuddered. In Greece, even before Solon, there had also been cries for redistribution of land and abolition of debts, with the result that in 401 B.C. the Athenians introduced into the oath of those elected to the Heliaea, the supreme court, a clause prohibiting either matter from even being put to a vote. In Rome the same cry led to the *Lex Icilia* of 456 B.C., by which the Aventine Hill was assigned to the plebeians as a dwelling place. A century later, in 367 B.C., there came the Licinian Laws, which prohibited one individual from holding more than 300 acres of those state lands still left for occupation. More significant was the reform of Tiberius Gracchus, tribune in 133 B.C. He had stood for election as an advocate of "that old poison." With the support of the people, and recognition on the part of some patricians of the need to do something about the poverty of the many, he won passage of a law permitting confiscation of surplus land. A three-man commission, of which he and his brother were members, had the power then to redistribute such land in small holdings among the poor.

After Tiberius' death (he was killed by a mob when suspected of aspiring to be king), his brother, Gaius Sempronius Gracchus, carried on. Elected tribune in 123 B.C., he proposed, as related by Appian,

> that a monthly distribution of grain should be made to each citizen at the public expense, which had not been customary before. Thus, by this one policy measure, he quickly got the leadership of the people.

This distribution was not yet the dole as it existed at the time of Caesar and his successors, but rather, apparently, a subsidization program. Rome by this time had become an overgrown metropolis, and both employment and food supply fluctuated markedly. Under the *Lex Sempronia* of Gaius Gracchus, public granaries were established for the storage of grain, which was then sold throughout the year at a price as little as half the market value. Government distribution of grain may have existed since the earliest days of Rome, but it was sporadic at best until Gaius Gracchus institutionalized it. The impetus, however, was more likely precaution against scarcity rather than alleviation of poverty.

Even so, the *Lex Sempronia* in retrospect was the effective beginning of a public welfare system in Rome. It set a rate of *senis et trientibus*, or 6⅓ *asses*, per modius of grain (a modius was about two gallons), which was probably a bargain. Evidently they thought so then; it appears that peasants left the countryside in droves and crowded into Rome to take advantage of the cheap grain. All in all, there must have been a severe drain on the state's financial resources. According to Cicero, the grain program — which was not limited to the poor but open to all citizens, although only the needy were expected to take advantage of it — exhausted the treasury. Cicero made his point by telling of a man of consular rank, by the name of Piso, who had opposed the grain program from the start, yet one day was observed by Gracchus standing in a grain line with the poor. "How can this be?" asked Gracchus. Piso, according to Cicero, replied: "I was against your dividing up my property among all the citizens, but since you have done so, I am here to get my share."

Over the next few years, many got their share, but there is reason to believe the program lapsed sometime after the death of Gaius Gracchus. No further reference is to be found until 100 B.C. and the tribunate of Apuleius Saturninus, who carried through legislation reviving the Gracchian program. He sought to make it a far more substantial bargain, proposing a price of only 5/6 of an *as* per modius, about one-seventh of what it had been. That, protested the quaestor Quintus Caepio, would mean bankruptcy; members of the senate were vehement in their opposition. The old rate of 6⅓ *asses* most likely prevailed.

During the Social War (the *socii*, or Italian allies, struggling for citizenship, 90–88 B.C.) there were restrictions placed on the grain program, only to be lifted after the war. At the same time, some revision was made to the program to reduce the cost to the state. How, it is not clear — perhaps an increase in price, perhaps a reduction in quantity. Under Sulla, in 82, following a bloody civil war with the plebeians, there came reform of another sort: Sulla abolished the grain program. Nine years later the consul Cotta reinstated it, at the traditional price of 6⅓ *asses* per modius but with a limitation of five modii per month.

At the time of the First Triumvirate (Caesar, Crassus, and Pompey) in 60 B.C., grain was still being distributed at below-market prices, but the political turmoil of the time changed that. The support of the people was crucial to the Triumvirate, and the time-honored devices of land reform and grain distribution both figured into its strategy. First came a new land law, a moderate one known as the *Lex Iuliae Agraria*, which provided for the assignment of lands in Campania [Naples] to veterans of Pompey's eastern campaign and to poor citizens, particularly those with three or more children. The measure was passed in 59 B.C. by the Popular Assembly after the Senate refused to consider it. The following year, having made himself proconsul for Illyria and Cisalpine Gaul, Caesar left on his well-recorded travels to the north. Before departing, he saw to the election as tribune of a patrician-born rabble-rouser named Clodius, under whom the significant, final step was taken: With the *Lex Clodia*, grain was made free to all. A consequence of this, by the time Caesar was *dictator* in 46 B.C., was observed by Appian in describing the Rome of the day:

> The multitude of the city was mixed with all sorts of strangers. The freed men lived equal to the other citizens, the slave was dressed like his master, and except for the attire of senators, one mode of dress sufficed for the rest. Because of the grain distributed to the poor, which takes place in the city only, loiterers, beggars, and vagrants from all over Italy flocked to Rome. Besides, there were great numbers of soldiers who returned to Rome, and not as before, each to his own country.

How many resettled in Rome from elsewhere in Italy to take advantage of the grain dole* is not documented; nor is the number of slaves freed by masters who thus no longer had the responsibility of providing them with daily rations. It is known, however, that the number on the dole, then or soon thereafter, was about 320,000. Likewise documented is the effect on the Rome treasury, as related by Cicero in *Pro Sestio*. When the state stopped charging for grain (at 6⅓ *asses* per modius), its revenue immediately declined by nearly 20 percent. In making up that deficit, the state, in effect, had to commit 20 percent of its resources to maintaining the grain dole. The immediate cost was 70 million sesterces (280

---

*Slaves were not eligible for the dole or other forms of largess. As property of a master (*dominus*), however, a slave had to be fed and cared for to protect his usefulness, and was not likely to be in need of public assistance. The freeing of slaves was not uncommon, particularly during hard times to spare the dominus the cost of their maintenance. A slave then normally became a citizen entitled to the dole and other types of public assistance.

million *asses*) per year. Such an increase in spending might have caused alarm except for a happy coincidence: Cyprus, about that time, was added to the Roman province of Cilicia, and the wealth of its king became a part of the Roman treasury, enriching it by 7,000 talents. That offset the cost of free grain for the time being, and put off to another day the reckoning of how to pay for it year after year.

It is apparent that Caesar gave no thought to discontinuing the grain program. It would have been out of the question. He chose the course of reform and did basically what Pericles had done. He conducted a survey. "The survey of the people," wrote Suetonius,

> he ordered to be taken neither in the usual manner, nor in the usual place, but street by street, by the principal inhabitants. And he reduced the number of those who received grain from the public from 320,000 to 150,000. To prevent any tumults on account of the survey, he ordered the praetor every year to fill up by lot the vacancies [on the list of 150,000] occasioned by death, from those who were not enrolled for the receipt of grain.

Thus, with one edict, Caesar cut the list by more than half; and further, he decreed that the number stay at 150,000 permanently. Those left off the list could hope for better luck another year.

There was some consolation in another form of largess, the *congiarium*, which would become an increasingly frequent crowd-pleaser during the empire. Caesar ordered a congiarium on the occasion of a triumph celebrating his victory over the Gauls: grain over and above the usual amount, as well as olive oil and money (20,000 sesterces among the soldiers and 400 each among the people). Earlier in the day there had been a ceremonial procession, during which the axle of Caesar's triumphal car broke. The mishap occurred opposite the Temple of Fortune. A portent far from good, Caesar regarded it. The Ides of March, 44 B.C., were two years away.

The maximum of 150,000 for the grain dole is one that tended to remain something of a standard, although the number had a habit of creeping back up to 300,000 and more at frequent intervals, requiring that the list be pruned as Caesar had done. Congiaria, even more lavish, likewise remained a fixture of Roman politics in the centuries ahead.

ROME: THE EMPIRE

The Emperor Augustus (27 B.C. to A.D. 14) considered doing away with state distribution of grain, which at this time was not generally free but sold at a nominal charge substantially below market cost. He thought about it, then decided the dole might as well stay. If he abolished it,

Augustus reasoned, some other ruler, sometime in the future, would just reinstate it for political advantage. As Suetonius tells it, ostensibly quoting Augustus:

> I was much inclined to abolish for ever the practice of allowing the people grain at the public expense, for they trust so much to it that they are too lazy to till their lands. But I did not persevere in my plan because I felt sure that the practice would be revived some time or another by someone ambitious of popular favor.

Instead, in 2 B.C., Augustus re-fixed the number of recipients at 200,000, a limitation that, like Caesar's, would not hold.*

In time it was bread (*panis*) rather than just the grain that was doled out, and this constituted half of the classic formula by which Rome, under the empire, placated the multitudes. That formula, as recorded by Juvenal, was *panem et circenses*, commonly translated as "bread and circuses," although "spectator sports" may be the better modern-day equivalent of *circenses*. Even in Caesar's times, the games had been impressive enough, but Augustus surpassed these in magnificence, only to be outdone by his successors. The Circus Maximus, which in Caesar's day could hold 150,000, by the reign of Constantine could accommodate 485,000, including spectators on adjacent hillsides. In A.D. 248, despite civil war, anarchy, and economic crisis, Rome celebrated its 1,000th anniversary with games and spectacles that included, among others, 32 elephants, 30 leopards, 40 wild horses, assorted lions, giraffes, and hyenas, and 2,000 gladiators.

"The people of Rome," wrote Fronto in A.D. 165, "are kept in line above all by two things—the dole and the games." Suppose, then, there were not the games to keep the people entertained, nor the dole to keep them fed. Claudius (41–54) had a taste of "what then" during a particularly acute grain shortage, as accounted by Tacitus:

> Many portentous events happened this year. Birds of evil omen settled upon the Capitol. Frequent earthquakes occurred, by which many houses tumbled down, and in a panic afterward, infirm people were trampled. Certainly portentous was a failure of the crops, which resulted in famine. Now the complaints of the people were no longer confined to murmurs. In the forum, a crowd of people gathered around the Emperor, clamoring tumultuously and pressing upon him in a violent manner, driving him to the back of the forum, until at last his bodyguards forged a path for him through the incensed multitude.

---

*The population of the city of Rome at this time was about 1 million.

The dole, ever more munificent, and the games, ever more magnificent, had their intended effect of keeping the masses in line. But state benevolence was not without a price. The common citizen of the Roman Republic, who had wielded such influence through the Popular Assembly that it was under the banner of SPQR (the Senate and the People of Rome) that Caesar's legions marched, by the early years of the empire cared little that the Assembly was not much more than a formality; and he raised no protest when, under Tiberius, it was suppressed altogether. Hence satirized Juvenal of the plebeians of his day, that they

> For two poor claims have long renounced the whole,
> And only ask — the Circus and the Dole.

With such a workable formula the emperors did not meddle except to supplement the dole with additional programs as well as with more frequent congiaria. The latter, during the Republic, had included gifts of wine or oil on the part of magistrates, generals, and candidates for office. From Augustus on they became the exclusive province of the emperors. Augustus sometimes made donations of anywhere from 250 to 400 sesterces a person to gatherings of the poor ranging in size from 200,000 to 320,000 persons. Caligula (A.D. 37-41), otherwise to be remembered for senseless cruelty, once distributed 45 million sesterces in a single fit of kindheartedness. Nero (54-68), according to Suetonius, had "many thousands of articles of all descriptions thrown amongst the people for them to scramble for, such as fowls of different kinds, tickets for grain, clothes, gold, silver, gems, pearls" and so on. Domitian (81-96) entertained the people with extraordinary wild beast chases, and thrice bestowed congiaria of 300 sesterces each to the poor. By the time of Septimius Severus (193-211), it had been 250 years since Caesar's first disbursement of money on a grand scale to the people of Rome. In that time, it has been estimated, Roman emperors distributed 6 billion sesterces in the form of congiaria alone. The custom continued until after the time of Constantine, finally declining with the decline of Rome.

In the congiarium there is an element of Roman life that is without counterpart in the modern welfare system. It is wholly implausible to imagine the president of the United States scattering dollar bills along Pennsylvania Avenue, although some observers may profess to see at least a symbolic parallel in some modern-day programs. On the other hand, genuine parallels there are. Already observed, in Athens or Rome: a rudimentary unemployment compensation system, old age and disability benefits, public works employment, and relief in general in the form of the dole. Further to be found: food stamps, medicaid, aid to dependent children, and a welfare bureaucracy.

The use of *tesserae frumentariae* (the first of these parallels) systemized the distribution of grain and later of bread. A tessera was a ticket or token, either circular or rectangular in shape, of wood or lead or some other substance, with an illustration or legend signifying its use. Tesserae frumentariae came into use in connection with the distribution of grain during the time of Augustus (or perhaps even before that) and were used in exactly the same way as modern-day food stamps. The grain distributed to those on the list when Augustus was emperor required payment of a nominal price. But what of those too destitute to pay anything? They were given tesserae that entitled them to receive their grain at no cost.

How and where such persons received their "food stamps" at the time of Augustus is not clear, but it is documented for later times. During the reign of Trajan, the recipient on a certain day went to the Porticus Minucia, and there obtained (probably after standing on line) a token entitling him to a free ration of grain, apparently for one month. In time, however, the sale of grain at a subsidized price ended in favor of free grain for all, and tesserae were given to everyone. That such was the case is inferable from Seneca's observation that "the thief, the bearer of false witness, and the adulterer alike receive the public grant of grain, and all are placed on the register without any examination as to character."

Sometime before the reign of Aurelian (270–275) the distribution of grain was thought no longer adequate, and the state instead gave out loaves of baked bread. In the first half of the fourth century, a small payment was required. Under Valentinian I in 369, the bread became free but rules of eligibility were adopted. The number qualifying at this time appears to have been about 120,000.

Rome's equivalent of medicaid or medicare were the *archiatri populares* (physicians to the people), established by Valentinian I in 368. An imperial act provided for public physicians at public pay in 12 of the 14 districts of Rome, and directed these physicians to treat the poor in their districts. In the sixth century Justinian confirmed the provision of salaries for public physicians, which shows that the program was in existence at least until that time in the eastern empire.

How well this rudimentary public health service worked is not documented. It is evident these public physicians also took on private, fee-paying patients, so the effectiveness of the program in meeting the needs of the poor probably depended in large measure on the conscience of the individual physician. The act of Valentinian establishing archiatri populares exhorted those so commissioned "honestly" to attend to the needs of the poor rather than spend their time "shamefully" on the rich. Regardless of what income it produced, the position of public physician was ample in its perquisites. Archiatri populares were classified under Roman law with professors of rhetoric, philosophy, and liberal arts; and in common with these, doctors and their families enjoyed certain privileges: they were exempt from property taxation; they were not required to provide accommodation for soldiers and officers of justice; they were not subject to being hauled before a magistrate without due process.

Even this program had its antecedents. More than a century and a half before Valentinian, the Emperor Septimius Severus (193-211) included in his congiaria free medicine for the poor. And there is evidence that in ancient Greece provision was also made for the public pay of certain physicians, albeit not on the scale instituted by Valentinian.

Today there is AFDC—Aid to Families with Dependent Children. Rome had its *alimenta*. State assistance to children began under Augustus as part of an attempt to increase the birth rate and thus keep Italian stock predominant in the empire. Various laws encouraged marriage and the bearing of children. Augustus opened the distribution of congiaria to boys under age 11. Nerva (96-98) instituted the alimenta, which had the twofold objective of dealing with a lagging birth rate and declining agricultural production. Under Nerva's program there was public assistance to poor children coupled with low-interest loans to sustain small farmers who were going out of business. From the emperor's own treasury, the *fiscus*, working capital was made available to those municipalities throughout Italy wishing to participate. From these funds there were loans issued to farmers at 5 percent interest, which was less than the prevailing rate. A loan was limited to a small fraction of the value of a farm but secured by the whole, which had the effect of virtually assuring payment. As the loans were paid off the interest accrued in a separate fund. It was from this fund that maintenance allowances were paid to the needy children of the municipality.

There is, unfortunately, little information as to how well the program worked. One of only two municipalities for which a record exists is Veleia, north of the Po River. To Veleia, Trajan (98-117) gave a capital fund of 1,044,000 sesterces. Out of the revenue from this fund, 245 boys were to receive 16 sesterces each per month, and 34 girls 12 sesterces each. In addition, one illegitimate boy was to get 144 sesterces a year and a like girl 120. The total of these allowances for a year is 52,200 sesterces, which is exactly 5 percent of 1,044,000, corresponding to the stated interest.

While details are otherwise scarce, it is clear the alimenta established by Nerva were held in high regard by his successors. Trajan, Hadrian, Antoninus Pius, and Marcus Aurelius (98-180) progressively extended the alimenta. Hadrian put the program on a permanent footing by appointing a *praefectus alimentorum* to oversee the distribution of grants from the treasury, thus establishing an ancient prototype for the modern welfare bureaucracy. He also decreed that assistance continue until the age of 18 (for a boy) and 14 (for a girl). Trajan extended the concept of alimenta from the farm country to the city by setting up a special distribution of free grain to 5,000 poor children in Rome. This and other such benevolence Trajan called to the attention of his people in a relief sculpture on a triumphal arch he built along the Appian Way in Benevento, in southern Italy. The sculpture shows a group of appreciative parents with their alimenta-supported children. The arch still stands — a monument not only to the ancients' social consciousness but to their public relations savvy as well.

The alimenta, however, had nowhere near the longevity of the arch. Commodus, who succeeded Marcus Aurelius in 180, was too extravagant for such an enterprise; in exhausting the treasury on concupiscent living he dried up the source of funding. Attempts early in the third century to keep the alimenta going were unsuccessful and the program went bankrupt.

Child assistance was revived during the reign of Constantine (306–337). The Theodosian Code records an act of 315 that sought to restrain infanticide by holding out a promise of help to impoverished parents. The law provided that parents unable to support their children make known their plight to authorities; the state then, "without delay," would undertake assistance in the form of food and clothing paid for by the imperial treasury. A similar law of 322 pledged like assistance as a means of countering the selling off of children by poverty-stricken families.

There is an interesting footnote to the establishing of the alimenta. Nerva was concerned about the cost, and instead of piling another program atop those existing, he appointed a five-member commission — the *quinqueviri* recorded by Pliny — to reduce governmental expenses. Their work produced little in the way of results. A few sacrifices and a horse race here and there were discontinued, but nothing else is recorded in the way of a cost-saving measure.

Work relief, already seen in Athens, was likewise employed by the Romans. That relief of the needy was indeed a factor in undertaking public construction projects is to be judged from an account of the Emperor Vespasian (69–79) as recorded by Suetonius:

> Someone offered to convey some immense columns into the Capitol at only a small expense by means of a mechanical contrivance. He [Vespasian] rewarded the man very handsomely for the invention, but said he would not use it, explaining, "I must have work for the poor."

Thus a contrivance apparently in the nature of a hoisting mechanism was rejected in favor of manual labor, which was considerably more expensive but of usefulness beyond the moving of immense columns.

A very great amount of that labor went into the construction of Rome's most conspicuous public works project, the Colosseum, begun by Vespasian in 69 and completed by Domitian in 82. Although otherwise a frugal emperor, spending relatively little on games and congiaria, Vespasian delighted in public construction on a grand scale. Perhaps chief among the builders was Claudius, who spent freely and duly depleted the treasury. One of his projects was the draining of the Fucine Lake, 50,000 acres in area, to create a new imperial estate. It was an undertaking that kept 30,000 men at work for three years.

A QUESTION ANCIENT AND MODERN

Before turning to the later years of the empire, it is appropriate here to consider one other parallel with modern times, and that is the question of equitableness in the distribution of benefits. Should thieves and profligates of all description be accorded the same benefits as the law-abiding poor? It is not necessary to attempt an answer here, but simply to observe that the ancients were troubled by the question of equitableness no less than many in modern times. Isocrates was troubled. So also, in Rome, was Seneca. But Stoic philosopher that he was, Seneca saw another side. From *De Beneficiis*:

> "The gods," you may say, "bestow much, even upon the ungrateful." But what they bestow they had prepared for the good, and the bad have their share as well, because they cannot be separated. . . . The thief, the bearer of false witness, and the adulterer alike receive the public grant of grain, and are all placed on the register without any examination as to character; good and bad men share alike in all the other privileges which a man receives, because he is a citizen, not because he is a good man. God likewise has bestowed certain gifts upon the entire human race, from which no one is shut out. Indeed, it could not be arranged that the wind which was fair for good men should be foul for bad ones, while it is for the good of all men that the seas should be open for traffic and the kingdom of man be enlarged; nor could any law be appointed for the showers, so that they should not also water the fields of wicked and evil men.

It was Seneca who once characterized the history of Rome, up to his own day, by analogy to the ages of man: Under Romulus, Rome had its infancy; under the kings, its childhood; with the Punic Wars, it reached its manhood; and by Seneca's time, the first century A.D., it had attained adulthood. That was as far as Seneca could go. It would take another, later in time, to perceive when Rome had reached the next stage of life. That "other" was Lactantius, writing his *Divinae Institutiones* about 315. At the time tutor to the son of Constantine, Lactantius saw Romulus's infant now in old age and declining fast:

Nor should it appear strange to anyone that a kingdom founded with such vastness, and so long increased by so many and such men, and strengthened by such great resources, shall nevertheless at some time fall to ruin. For there is nothing achieved by human strength that cannot equally be destroyed by human strength, since the works of mortal men are mortal.

Dio Cassius had thought he had seen the decline coming earlier—on the death of Marcus Aurelius and the succession of Commodus in 180—writing in his *Roman History* that as of that time Rome had ceased to be a kingdom of gold and had become one of iron and thus vulnerable to rusting away.

Whether the decline of Rome began with the utterly extravagant and licentious Commodus, or at some other point in time, if a certain point is even possible to determine, it is a fact that the span of time between Dio Cassius and Lactantius—the third century—was one of perpetual crisis: civil war, economic chaos, and the gradual disintegration of Roman society. The emperor became absolute; the Senate supine, so far as any real power was concerned. The army, bound up in the civil wars, loosened its defense of the borders. Society became polarized, the middle class virtually disappearing. Taxation turned ruinous. The land tax by Justinian's time was more than a third of gross product and drove farmers into the cities; the government, faced with increasing shortages, sent them back to the abandoned farms and made them *coloni*, hereditary serfs assigned forever as farmers. The state made other occupations compulsory and then hereditary—at first work concerned with state revenue but eventually labor of every kind. Society was then a regulated one, and the instrument of regulation was the bureaucracy.

The bureaucracy began with the emperors following Augustus and developed gradually, in time eliminating the Senate from any administrative role and concentrating power entirely in the hands of the emperor. The bureaucracy, in superseding local authority, also made local government powerless. Probably the worst of its features, and the most corruptible, was its army of *agentes in rebus*, or secret police, of whom there were countless thousands watching over the people, making sure there was no trouble (for example, over payment of taxes or adherence to compulsory work). The agentes in rebus, who might arrest anyone considered dangerous to the emperor, came into being by name under Diocletian, but, in their role as secret agents and spies, they existed earlier under the name of *frumentarii*. The frumentarii were originally grain supply functionaries, and both those in civil and in military service went by the same title. Whether the later empire's secret agents were descended from the civil or the military frumentarii is not certain. Beyond question, however, is the enormous cost of maintaining the bureaucracy, which, coupled with the vast number on the dole, made it seem, according to Lactantius (*De Mortibus Persecutorum*, about 320) that, "There began to be fewer men who paid taxes than there were who received benefits."

Inflation, caused primarily by the debasement of currency, was the dominating factor in the economy of Rome during the third century. Prices of all goods mounted steadily. Grain is perhaps the best example here. In the mid-second century A.D., wheat sold for about eight *asses*, or half a denarius, per modius, which was not much above the subsidized price of 6⅓ *asses* per modius set by Gracchus in 123 B.C. Over the century and a half between, let us say A.D. 150 and the end of the third century, the price had gone up more than two hundredfold and was fixed (most likely on the low side) at 100 denarii, or 1,600 *asses*, per modius. The prices of rye and barley were less.

As for currency, debasement had begun with Nero in the first century as a means of accommodating his extravagant expenditures. Nero reduced the weight and lowered the precious metal content of the standard silver coin, the denarius (equal to four sesterces), thus reducing its value by perhaps 5 or 10 percent, but allowing more to be minted. Faced with financial difficulties, later emperors resorted to the same expedient. By the middle of the third century the denarius had lost about 75 percent of its value, and eventually 98 percent, the coin then having but a slight silver wash over base metal. Only a sackload had any value by then, and that is how the government eventually issued them—the sacks (called *folles*) themselves circulating unopened as currency. (From the Latin came the English word "folly.").

Diocletian, at the end of the third century, tried to rein in Rome's runaway economy with a revision of the tax structure and the introduction of new coinage, but without success. Early in 301 he turned to a more drastic remedy, and one unprecedented in Roman history: a wage-and-price freeze. In his *Edict on Prices*, Diocletian observed that it would be better to have voluntary restraint but that the greed of "uncontrolled madmen" of "unlimited avarice" left no choice but to impose restraint. Thus Diocletian issued his edict setting maximum prices, coupled with maximum wages, on virtually all goods and services throughout the civilized world, with death or exile as the penalties for violation. The measure touched all alike, freezing the price on everything from beans and lentils to turtledove and peacock meat; from cabbage to endive; from river fish to sea urchins; from cheap domestic wine to imported Egyptian beer. Wages were likewise frozen: artists at 150 denarii per day, stone masons and carpenters at 50, camel drivers and sewer cleaners at 25. Costs were also prescribed with fine precision: so much for a three-pronged fork, so much for a two-pronged.

The result was that goods either decreased sharply in quality or disappeared entirely from the marketplace. In time, no one could afford to pay attention to the edict; it was ignored and goods again became plentiful, at prices higher than ever.

One effect of the prolonged period of inflation was the demise of the alimenta. The economic climate was not a good one for long-term mortgages, and without them the unique subsidization of allowances for poor children was doomed. When child assistance was revived under Constantine, the cost now had to come entirely from the imperial treasury.

As for the cost of Rome's equivalent of welfare generally, there is only scattered data. Plutarch provides the information on the republic. In his biography of Cato he places the cost of the grain dole in 62 B.C. at 30 million sesterces. As to the reign of Augustus, it is possible to estimate the cost of the dole at 60 million sesterces per year (assuming 250,000 recipients), making it the second largest public expenditure in an annual budget of about 400 million sesterces, of which the largest share, probably some 240 million sesterces, went to the military. (Revenues were an assortment of taxes, import and export duties, rents on public lands, and provincial tribute, the last accounting for some of the provisions issued to the poor—grain from Africa, and pork later in the third century from the provinces of southern Italy.)

It is not realistic to attempt even a guess at the cost of assistance to the poor during the later years of the empire. One difficulty is that assistance was more diverse; another is that during the third century taxes came to be raised in kind. The value of currency had dropped so low that the emperors declined to collect taxes in money and instead demanded produce and commodities with which to pay the army and the bureaucracy. Inherently wasteful and inefficient though it was, this system generally remained in effect until the end of the empire in the West.

Nevertheless, it is a certainty that the cost of assistance to the poor, whatever its form, continued to increase, and that paradoxically the economic precariousness of the times did not, for some years, manifest itself on those who relied on public support. The dole continued, and indeed those in the city on public support probably fared much better than the population as a whole. A review of their situation during the economically troubled third century shows why.

Under Septimius Severus (193–211), free distribution of olive oil was begun on a regular basis, presumably to those on the list receiving the free bread. The oil was distributed from shops known as *mensae oleariae*, of which there were some 2,300 in Rome. The program continued at least until the latter fourth century.

Severus Alexander (222–235), reigning during relatively stable times, kept the dole and congiaria intact while concentrating public generosity on public baths, completing the vast *thermae* begun by Caracalla

(211-217). The public baths, of course, were exceedingly popular among the masses.

Under Aurelian (270-275), inflation was particularly great. One of his predecessors, Gallienus (253-268), had issued new coins—a billion of them—that were nearly worthless, thus leaving the state and countless individuals on the brink of bankruptcy. Aurelian issued new coins, alleviating the financial crisis but not managing to halt inflation. Despite the gloomy economy, he was able to raise the level of assistance to the poor. He made the distribution of bread daily rather than monthly, and also instituted the issue of free pork in season. The pork was given out for five months of the year at a ration of five pounds per month, an arrangement that continued at least until 419. It is estimated that 20,000 pounds of pork were given out each day.

Aurelian also considered the free distribution of wine to the poor, but heeded his praetorian prefect who cautioned that Aurelian then by rights ought also to give fowl and geese to go with it. In the fourth century, however, Valentinian I did provide wine at a subsidized price 25 percent below market cost. Aurelian, meanwhile, also instituted the regular distribution of salt, which had been given out on an occasional basis as far back as the time of the republic.

Such provisioning of the poor continued past the time of Constantine but from there on it is not possible to document with any degree of certainty. The decline of Rome, meanwhile, is well recorded. Inherent is the basic economic unbalance that is bound to come with so great a proportion of the population idle and thus dependent on the rest. But there will be no attempt here to assess that as a cause of decline relative to other factors. The largest drain on Rome's resources was maintenance of the army and the huge, corrupt bureaucracy that increasingly regimented the lives of the citizens of the empire while taking from their pockets even larger exactions to finance that very subjection. No doubt there were some among Rome's citizens who welcomed the barbarians.

The accepted date for the fall of Rome is 476, when the German warrior Odoacer deposed the last emperor, Romulus Augustulus. A few years later Odoacer was in turn defeated by Theodoric, king of the Ostrogoths, who took for himself the title of governor of the Romans.

Thus fell the empire in the West—though not all of its customs. It is recorded by the historian Procopius that Theodoric summarily "ordered that the needy gathering about the Church of St. Peter the Apostle should forever be supplied by the treasury with 3,000 measures of free grain a year."

2

SOME PROVISYON FOR THE POORE
England: The Middle Ages through Elizabethan Times

Fear of disorder was a factor in Rome's panem et circenses, *and has continued as a factor in social legislation to the present (President Johnson's warning to Congress, during the upheaval of the 1960s, that "the clock is ticking"). It was something of the same during Tudor times. Rogues and vagabonds were the impetus for modern poor law. Society set out to suppress them, but found it could not do so without also doing something about the legitimately needy.*

> Six cnihtef... in pore men ʒuyse... ʒo to
> þe kingef dole afe hii weren on-hole.
>
> Six knights . . . pretending to be poor men . . . go to the king's dole as if they were infirm.
>
> Layamon's *Brut*
(c. 1200)

By the witness of Layamon, the first prominent Middle English poet, it is evident that some measure of poor relief existed during the Middle Ages. Here, in this brief excerpt from *Brut*, a chronicle of the early history of Britain, we see that a form of dole existed at court. Indeed, from time to time, there was more than this; and even though feudalism was, in a sense, one great welfare state, there were various acts for relief of the poor in England during the Middle Ages that appear remarkably enlightened in retrospect.

To begin: The year is 928. Athelstan, grandson of Alfred the Great, is king of the English. He is a flaxen-haired man, of average height but of powerful build, strong-looking despite somewhat bent shoulders—so far very much the Anglo-Saxon king. But Athelstan rules with a sense of humanity not notable to the kings of his time. To churches, he makes gifts of books; to foreign scholars, he offers a home at court; to criminals promising amends, he sometimes grants pardons; and to children under fifteen, he grants exemption from the death penalty—it's too cruel a punishment in their case.

It is not surprising, then, that King Athelstan's reign produced the first relief law in England, an act passed during a council at Greatlea in Hampshire in 928. In marked contrast with other laws of the same council (for example, having one's hands nailed to the mint house door as punishment for corrupting the coin of the realm), King Athelstan's Ordinance stands out as a model of humaneness:

> I, Athelstan king, make known to all my reeves within my realm . . . that I will that ye entirely feed one poor Englishman, if ye have him, or that [if] ye find another. From two of my *feorms*, let there be given him one amber of meal, and one shank of bacon, or one ram worth four pence, and clothing for twelve months every year. . . . And if the reeve omit this, let him make compensation with thirty shillings, and let that money be distributed to the needy who are in the farm or manor where this remains unfulfilled, in the witness of the bishop.

An amber a few centuries later was equal to four bushels; if so also in 928, the monthly ration thus prescribed was about three times that of Rome's allotment of five modii of grain per month. Regardless of the quantity, King Athelstan's Ordinance was a public relief act, and the first such in English history, in that a feorm was to all intents and purposes a feudal equivalent of state revenue. The word in Anglo-Saxon usually meant "farm, purveyance, or food," but it was also used to represent a portion of the produce of the land due the lord by his vassals according to terms of the feudal charter. The act thus set up a means for distributing a share of the equivalent of public revenue to the needy.

King Athelstan's ordinance was perhaps the only act corresponding to a poor relief law, as such, during Anglo-Saxon times, but it was by no means the only one relating to the poor. Another of the same period exempted poor widows from paying a tax on property. Under King Edgar (959–975) there was a law decreeing that every man, "rich or poor, should have the benefit of a just decision at law," an act doubtless greater in its intent than in its effect and yet a forerunner of *in forma pauperis* legislation that will be seen occasionally in later times. The reign of Ethelred (978–1016) produced several laws relating to the poor. One of them simply decreed that the people comfort and feed the poor. Another ordered that anyone breaking a three-day fast preceding the feast of St. Michael pay a fine that went for poor relief.

There was, of course, help available through the church; and yet other Anglo-Saxon laws, secular not ecclesiastical, had a bearing thereto. Edgar, in 970, made payment of tithes mandatory and set a penalty so severe—forfeiture of nine-tenths of the defaulter's property—that compliance was virtually guaranteed. What is significant is not the penalty but the fact that it was secular authority assuming responsibility for the collection of church revenue, and thus, by extension, for support of the poor. The parish structure of the church had been developing, and even by the time of Athelstan it was at the parish rather than diocesan level that the helping hand was extended. Church revenue consisted principally of tithes, scots, and plow-alms (a penny per year for each plow), in addition to which was collected the Peter's pence that went to Rome. In 1014, during the reign of Ethelred, the distribution of the tithe was established by law, the poor now receiving their share by statute rather than by custom:

> Respecting tithe: The king and his witan have chosen and decreed, as is just, that one third part of the tithe which belongs to the church go to the reparation of the church; and a second part go to the servants [clergy] of God, the third to God's poor, and to the needy ones in thraldom.

A manorial system, feudal in effect, existed in England during Anglo-Saxon times, but it was not the all-encompassing feudalism of France. In England, for example, there remained some free land holdings, and the law allowed a man to abandon his lord with his consent. Englishmen might have been bound to their lords technically, but they were free to seek new ones, a measure of freedom of no small significance. "Let no lord obstruct it," decreed Athelstan, "once he has received what is due him."

The Conquest gave England the Norman version of feudalism, absolute in its domination of life and society. All land in England, even that belonging to the church, became the property of William and was allocated on feudal terms. Subjection also became hereditary, so that villeins might no longer change lords as it suited them. Below the aristocratic class — likewise now imported from Normandy — freedom largely disappeared. Serfdom was now the dominant condition of the great mass of the population.

In such a society there was no significant problem with the poor. Each man was bound to his task, be it that of laborer, herdsman, shepherd, blacksmith, or wheelwright; and bound to his manor, a virtually self-sufficient place. Except for a call to arms or an occasional famine, the life of medieval man was largely untouched by outside events. And because a master was necessarily responsible for those subservient to him, the disabled (whether out of sickness, old age, or other cause) had a continuing source of subsistence — in effect, benefits of a welfare state.

Aid to the poor from the local parish thus dropped substantially during this time, even though there undoubtedly continued to be vast numbers of poor, notwithstanding the self-sufficiency of the manorial system. We can assume a lapse in the practice of giving a one-third share of parish tithes to the poor because the practice was reinstated by statute in 1391, albeit for "a convenient sum" and not necessarily for one-third.

During the fourteenth century the feudal system declined in England. Ties binding lord and villein loosened. Some tenants and feudal vassals were relieved of their feudal obligations in return for a monetary payment. At the Battle of Poitiers in 1356, soldiers of the Black Prince fought not out of feudal duty but for promise of pay and a share of the spoils. Elsewhere, wheelwrights and blacksmiths began working for wages. Towns were abuilding, and that meant an increased mobility of the population.

Evidence of this mobility — and of a corresponding increase in the number of visible poor as feudalism declined — may be seen in some of the laws adopted in London. One, dated 1359, observed that the city had become a haven for vagrants from throughout the kingdom, and that these vagrants had chosen to go begging in order to have "ease and repose, not wishing to labour or work for their sustenance." This furthermore had the effect, according to the law, of wasting alms intended for the legitimately needy: Thus, all those able to work but still inclined to beg should leave the city by a certain date or be punished. Some of the hale found a way around the law by "counterfeiting" themselves, apparently in such ways as rubbing rat poison and other caustics on their arms and legs to produce ugly (but sympathy-inspiring) lesions. A law adopted in 1375 expressly included counterfeit disablement among prohibitions for which penalties were provided.

Who were these beggars, now of such great concern? They were both the beneficiaries and victims of the decline of feudalism. In earlier times they would still have been bound to and protected by their lord, a buffer against so many of life's perils. As they gained their freedom — and many in the latter fourteenth century still had not — serfs found they had given up the security that had been the manor. Most adjusted to it; others did not and, now lacking the protection of a liege-lord, turned to begging or thievery. In his epic work, *The State of the Poor* (London, 1797), Sir Frederic Morton Eden made a classic observation:

> It is one of the natural consequences of freedom that those who are left to shift for themselves must sometimes be reduced to want. Dr. Johnson's remarks on marriage and celibacy may perhaps be applied with propriety to freedom and servitude: the one has many pains, the other no pleasures. The decrease of villeinage seems necessarily to have been the era of the origin of the poor.

Meanwhile, there was a natural calamity that came to have an effect on how the state would deal with those who could not, or would not, support themselves: the Black Death. After ravaging the Continent (50,000 had died in Paris, 100,000 in Venice), the plague struck England in the summer of 1348. Between one-third and one-half of the population fell victim. The dead had to be buried in layers in deep pits. Landowners fled their holdings and went wandering the countryside. Flocks ran wild. Untilled land remained untilled. Crops went unharvested, rotting for lack of reapers.

Because of an extreme scarcity of labor, competition became intense for those who survived the scourge. Farm owners and other employers, now desperate, gave in to ever higher demands for wages — often twice what had been the case before. Laborers, realizing they had the upper hand, became not only exorbitant in their wage demands but particular about where and when to work. With the old ways of feudal obligation still fresh in mind — and indeed often still in force in the southeast of England — that was plainly not a tolerable situation.

The most immediate result was the Ordinance of Laborers (Edward III, 1349) ordering laborers to work for wages and prices that prevailed before the Black Death. Furthermore, the ordinance sought to increase the available work force by making beggars go to work. This it did through the simple expedient of making it illegal for anyone to give them alms. It was an interim measure pending the return of Parliament, which, in 1351, passed the first Statute of Laborers. This reaffirmed wage restrictions and added provisions restricting laborers to working in their own villages. In conjunction with the ordinance of 1349, it was a heavily repressive measure, with more than just a flavor of the old feudal order.

It did not work. Laborer and employer alike found it more expedient to ignore. Nonetheless, the law was significant and may be cited as the first step toward the English welfare system of modern times. The Statute of Laborers of 1351, coupled with the 1349 ordinance, was the first law to deal with beggary and the transiency that goes with it, and thus the first to try to do something about the postfeudal poor. At the same time, and paradoxical to the repressiveness that made the statute hated among the masses, it was a law that gave something of great significance to the masses — recognition. Even though the statute tried to preserve something of the old feudal order, it necessarily had to recognize the existence of a free labor force, something wholly at odds with the very concept of feudalism.

Thus was the door opened to agitation for political change, culminating in the Peasants' Revolt of 1381. It was stirred by the likes of John Ball, a maverick priest who, wandering about the countryside, warned that all would not be well in England (in the words of the chronicler Froissart)

> tyll every thyng be common; and that there be no villayns nor gentylmen, but that we be all unyed [united] toguyder, and that the lordes be no greatter maisters than we be. What have we deserved, or why shulde we be kept thus in servage? We be all come fro one father and one mother, Adam and Eve: whereby can they say or shew that they be gretter lordes than we be?

Spurred on by Ball, Wat Tyler, Jack Straw, and others, a mob of peasants, perhaps 60,000-strong, marched on London, but to no avail. The revolt ended when young King Richard II met the insurgents face-to-face and, seeming to take their cause to heart, prevailed on them to turn back. A week later he let them know what he really thought of their cause. "Serfs ye are," the young king told them, "and serfs ye shall remain."

In law, serfs they remained. In literature, and particularly in the ballad, they found escape. The ballad had come to England in the twelfth century. Sung and resung, and often embellished as it made the rounds of the common people, it recorded an event of general significance or some aspect of life (work, love, tribulation) common to all. A whole series of ballads, perhaps as many as 40 of them, celebrated a folk hero who was the personification of the Peasants' Revolt. From at least as early as the fourteenth century, he did battle with that most visible symbol of authority, the sheriff, and sought to change the social order through transfer of wealth from the rich to the poor:

> And to the end of time, the Tales shall ne'r be done,
> Of *Scarlock*, *George a Greene*, and *Much* the Millers sonne,
> Of *Tuck* the merry Frier, which many a Sermon made,
> In praise of *Robin Hood*, his Out-lawes, and their Trade.
> An hundred valiant men had this brave *Robin Hood*,
> Still ready at his call, the Bow-men were right good,
> All clad in Lincolne Greene, with Caps of Red and Blew,
> His fellowes winded Horne not one of them but knew,
> When setting to their lips their little Beugles shrill,
> The warbling *Eccho's* wakt from every Dale and hill.
> From wealthy Abbots chests, and Churles abundant store,
> What often times they tooke, they shar'd amongst the poore.

Another lengthy work of poetry of the same period was the allegorical *Vision of Piers Plowman*, presumably of William Langland (c. 1330–1400). Certainly a very popular work in its own day, judging by the number of manuscript copies of it, and beyond question one of the great literary accomplishments of the Middle Ages, *The Vision of Piers Plowman* sought to redress social grievance not by upheaval but through a deeper acceptance of the Christian faith. Neither the rich nor the poor were free of admonition. As for the poor who turned to begging:

> *He shal soupe swetter• whan he it hath deserved.*

He shall eat sweeter who has earned his supper.

[And the rich:]

> *For, how hit evere be ywonne• bote hit be wel dispended,*
> *Worldliche wele is wicked thynge• to hym that hit kepeth.*

Worldly wealth however got, unless it be well spent,
Is a wicked thing to him who is its keeper.

A MORE SYSTEMATIC APPROACH

Two centuries hence, and the reign of Elizabeth I, there had been a noticeable change in how England provided for its needy. English poor law was now evolving, and a relatively more sophisticated system existed, as described in 1577 by *Holinshed's Chronicles*, Shakespeare's principal source for many of the historical plays:

> There is no commonwealth at this day in Europe wherein there is not great store of poor people, and those necessarily to be relieved by the wealthier sort, which otherwise would starve and come to utter confusion. With us [in England] the poor is commonly divided into three sorts, so that some are poor by impotence, as the fatherless child, the aged, blind, and lame, and the diseased person that is judged to be incurable; the second are poor by casualty, as the wounded soldier, the decayed householder, and the sick person visited with grievous and painful diseases; the third consisteth of thriftless poor. . . . For the first two sorts (that is to say, the poor by impotence and poor by casualty, which are the true poor indeed, and for whom the Word doth bind us to make some daily provision), there is order taken throughout every parish in the realm that weekly collection shall be made for their help and sustentation — to the end they shall not scatter abroad, and, by begging here and there, annoy both town and country. . . . Such as are idle beggars through their own default . . . having sound and perfect limbs . . . they are all thieves and caterpillars in the commonwealth, and by the Word of God not permitted to eat, sith they do but lick the sweat from the true labourers' brows. . . .

It is evident from this account in Raphael Holinshed's chronicle that there was now a more systematic approach in dealing with the poor. All poor were not alike. That had been understood to some extent in earlier times — for example, the London ordinance of 1359 ordering vagrants out of the city so alms for the legitimately needy would not be wasted. It was now expressed in a well-drawn distinction between those who were poor by circumstance and those who were poor by choice (assuming that all vagrants were lazy and didn't like to work). Here and there the understanding went deeper, even to concluding that economic causes were at the root of at least some idleness.

Many of the idle were agricultural workers, victims of enclosure in particular. Enclosure — the setting aside of arable land as pasture, and even as parks and hunting preserves — was prevalent early in the reign of Henry VIII. There had been a period of inflation, along with a rise in population, following the death of Henry VII in 1509. Landlords sought a better return on their land by converting it to pasturage, and going into sheep-raising to take advantage of increasingly attractive prices on wool. The result was unemployment for many agricultural workers who then flocked to the city looking either for work or for alms. The connection between enclosure and a rise in vagrancy was argued at the time, notably by Sir Thomas More in *Utopia* (1516):

> The increase of Pasture, said I, by which your Sheep, which are naturally mild, and easily kept in order, may be said now to devour Men, and unpeople not only Villages but Towns. [And of those displaced] what is left for them to do, but either to steal and so to be

hanged (God knows how justly), or to go about and beg? And if they do this, they are put in Prison as idle Vagabonds; while they would willingly work, but can find none that will hire them.

Laws against enclosure were passed early in the reign of Henry VIII, and Cardinal Wolsey, the lord chancellor, had charge of enforcement. Happy to have a cause against the rich who had never accepted him as one of their own, Wolsey pulled down hedges and reopened fields but never fully ended the practice. There was another round of economic distress in the 1540s, and, with wool prices increasing, enclosure was once again on the rise. For this and for other reasons, unemployment and vagrancy also increased markedly.

Some of those now begging on the streets had earlier found a haven and hospitality ("abbey alms") at monasteries. For years, monasteries had been tending to the poor at their gates—food, drink, lodging, a little money—despite the prohibition against giving alms to able-bodied beggars. The monasteries could do it with impunity because they were outside the jurisdiction of civil government, although it is true the civil authorities, the justices of the peace, were lax about enforcing antibegging laws anyway. The extrajurisdictional nature of the monasteries ended with the Act of Supremacy (1534). Five years later came the dissolution, some factor in which was the charge that the monasteries ostensibly were adding to the poor problem through their indiscriminate charity to able-bodied beggars—that the monks thus were doing as much to increase poverty as to relieve it.

Many of the poor were victims of the sixteenth century's notoriously unstable economy, and, in particular, of those recurring and staggering waves of inflation cumulatively known as the Price Revolution. In 1600, at the end of the Tudor century, prices were generally five and a half times what they had been in 1500. Heavy taxation, to pay the cost of war, also contributed to the increase in vagrancy. After all, to be a vagrant was to be free of paying taxes. Some of the unemployed were discharged soldiers and sailors home from the wars. After the defeat of the Spanish Armada in 1588, for example, there was a noticeable upturn in vagrancy.

A substantial number of the poor, whatever their origin, belong in a special category: the professional rogue. These were itinerant beggars and vagabonds of all sorts, the legendary and notorious vagrants of Tudor times immortalized in nursery rhyme:

>   Hark, hark,
>   The dogs do bark,
> The beggars are coming to town
>   Some in rags,
>   And some in tags,
> And some in velvet gown.

These were the beggars who, roaming from place to place, struck fear into many a heart, especially in remote farms and villages. By contemporary reckoning, there were 24 orders of them, the likes of: rufflers (thieving beggars), priggers of prancers (horse thieves), jarkemen (counterfeiters of licenses and official papers), and doxies (prostitutes), as they were called in their own cant. Some were experts at black art (lock picking) or conny-catching (swindling), but many were also professionals at begging. In his *Caveat for Cursetors* (London, 1566), Thomas Harman told of a "counterfeit crank" who pretended to be an epilepsy victim, a fit object of pity and thus of alms:

> He was naked from ye wast upward, saving he had an old jerkin of leather, patched, that was lose about him. . . . An old felt hat he caried in his hand, to receyve the charitye and devotion of the people, for that would he hold out from him, having his face from the eyes downward all smerd with fresh bloud, as though he had new fallen, and bin tormented with his paynefull panges. . . . About xii of the clocke, hee wente on the backsyde of Clementes Inn without the Temple barre, there is a lane that goeth into the Fieldes, there hee renewed his face agayne with freshe bloud, which he carried about him in a bladder, and dawbed on fresh dyrte upon his jerkin, hat and hosen. And so came back agayne unto the Temple, and begged off all that passed by. The boyes behelde how some gave grotes, some sixe pence, some gave more: for hee looked so ougley and yrksomly, that every one pitied his miserable case that beheld him.

At the end of the day, Harman and a friend followed the beggar home and watched him count out the day's proceeds of more than 14 shillings. At prevailing wage rates, it would have taken an honest laborer at least a month to earn the same amount. With the likes of such rogues, Tudor legislation came to deal harshly, at times even savagely.

The Tudor era began, however, with an easing of existing laws on vagrancy, both for reasons of humanity and economy. Since the mid-fourteenth century, there had been no basic change in public provision for the poor. The first Tudor, Henry VII, continued to draw a distinction between able-bodied and impotent poor, but provided that vagrants be brought to heed "by softer meanes [than] by such extreme rigour," and lowered the penalty for begging to three days and nights in jail for the first offense. It had heretofore been indefinite imprisonment.

A humane consideration in light of the statute's reference to "extreme rigour": Yet the statute also had a motive of economy, inasmuch as it spoke of "the great charges that shulde growe to his [subjects] for bringing of vagabondes to the gaols . . . and the long abiding of theym therein." In other words, sending vagabonds to jail and throwing away the key was an expensive proposition, particularly when it seemed to have little effect.

Another enactment of the reign of Henry VII—one evocative of King Edgar in 962—was a law of 1495 intending free legal aid to the poor. It stipulated that

> every poor person or persons . . . shall have, by the discretion of the Chancellor of this realm, for the time being writ or writs original and writs of subpoena according to the nature of their causes, therefor nothing paying to your Highness for the seals of same, nor to any person for the making of the same . . . and in like wise the same Justices [of the King's Bench] shall appoint attorney and attorneys for the same poor person and persons. . . .

Two years earlier, Henry VII had established a standing committee of the King's Council to hear poor men's causes and those of the king's servants, but this committee, which was the forerunner of the Court of Requests, followed the king about. It would seem that the 1495 act was intended to make some degree of legal assistance obtainable to those who could not avail themselves of the committee. There is no record as to whether the earlier *in forma pauperis* legislation of King Edgar had any effect, but it is evident that something came of the law of Henry VII. The *Vitellius Chronicle* of 1502 reported that the mayor of London had conducted sessions of a Court of Requests on divers afternoons, the result of which was that many poor people had "their maters sped without spence of money."

Just as charitable were the vagabond statutes of Henry VII in general. But there were not yet the hordes of wandering beggars so notable to the reign of Henry VIII; otherwise, there could not have been such leniency. There was nowhere near such leniency in years to come. Enclosure, rising prices, increasing population, widening unemployment, and in many cases a personal choice as to way of life—all these contributed to a sharp increase in vagrancy during the early years of Henry VIII. Indeed, there came to be

> great and excessyve nombres . . . by the occasyon of ydelnes, mother and [root] of all vyces [whereby] spryngeth contynuall theftes, murders, & other haynous offences & great enormytes to the high displeasure of God, the [inquietation] & damage of the Kyng's People & to the marvaylous disturbance of the Comon Weale of this Realme.

Such "marvaylous disturbance" was confronted in 1531 with a statute (from which the above is quoted) taking a far tougher stand on vagrants and able-bodied beggars. In the words of a contemporary rhyme:

A Stockes to staye sure and safely detayne,
    Lasy lewd Leuterers that lawes doth offend:
Impudent persons, thus punished with payne,
    Hardly for all this, do mean to amende.

A whyp is a whysker that will wrest out blood,
    Of backe and of body, beaten right well:
Of all the other it doth the most good.
    Experience teacheth, and they can well tell.

WHIPS HERE, ALMS THERE

The statute of 1531 took out the whip and put it to use, even for a first offense. It provided that a vagrant be tied naked to the end of a cart, and be beaten while dragged throughout town "tyll his Body be blody by reason of suche whyppyng." For those perceived as needy and legitimate poor, on the other hand, there was approval to continue begging, provided — and this was something new — they obtained a license to do so. Eligible beggars were now assigned areas in which to beg and issued licenses in the form of a letter from a justice of the peace bearing the name of the beggar and his authorized territory. The system did not work well, however. It was cumbersome and nearly impossible to control; and justices of the peace were relatively (since 1501) new to administrative responsibilities for the poor law.

In 1536 there was supplementary legislation, which, with the 1531 law, represents the essence of English poor law as it existed over the coming centuries. The act of 1536 carried over the earlier provisions for dealing with vagabonds but concentrated primarily on what to do about the poor. The distinction between legitimate poor and idle vagabond already having been made, and idle vagabonds having been dealt with, this law focused on those who were begging out of necessity. It established, in effect, that the legitimate poor should not have to beg, that society should see to their needs. Using the parish as the basic unit of jurisdiction (and here it is a political rather than ecclesiastical subdivision), the act directed the gathering of alms so

> the pore impotant lame feble syke and disseased people, beyng not able to worke, may be provided holpen and relieved, so that in no wise they nor none of them be suffered to go openly in begging; [and that the hardy] stronge ynough to labour may be daily kepte in contynuall labour, whereby every one of them may gette theyr owne substaunce and lyving with their owne handes.

With minor changes in language, that is the substance of English poor law as it continued over the next several centuries and as it came to America during colonial times.

Noteworthy about the same law is a provision recognizing that children growing up in poverty and ignorance tend to perpetuate a cycle of poverty. Even if somewhat crudely, the poor law of 1536 sought to break that cycle by providing that children between the ages of five and fourteen share of the alms collected and receive such training — vocational education, so to speak — as might keep them at work and thus off the charitable rolls when they reached adulthood.

Doubtless, such a program looks better in the language of a statute than it ever turned out to be for the mass of impoverished children begging along filth-laden London streets or elsewhere in England. Tudor relief laws, on the whole, were administered in a notoriously negligent way. Certainly it was so of the vagabond statutes. In some cases, local officials were probably overzealous in their enforcement; in most cases, they were more like the bumbling constable Dogberry in Shakespeare's *Much Ado About Nothing* (III, iii):

> *Dogberry.* . . . You are thought here to be the most senseless and fit man for the constable of the watch; therefore bear you the lantern. This is your charge: you shall comprehend all vagrom [vagrant] men; you are to bid any man stand, in the prince's name.
>
> *Second Watch.* How if a' will not stand?
>
> *Dogberry.* Why, then, take no note of him, but let him go; and presently call the rest of the watch together, and thank God you are rid of a knave.

There was a substantial increase in the number of unemployed and destitute, many of them former agricultural workers, pouring into London in 1549 and 1550. The latter year, authorities rounded up and expelled all they could find, but the hordes drifted back in, with the result that by 1552 there was such evident distress that something had to be done. Young King Edward VI, age 15, the son of Henry VIII, summoned Nicholas Ridley, the bishop of London, who had preached that too little was being done for the poor. What ought we to do? asked the king. Bishop Ridley suggested a course of action be devised by conferring with those closest to the problem, and he called together a committee, eventually 24 in number, that included the lord mayor, two city aldermen, and six commoners. It was this committee that devised the classification ("poor by impotence," "poor by casualty," and "thriftless poor") outlined in *Holinshed's Chronicles*, as well as a plan of implementation, which went into effect, at least in part; that is a matter of record. Wrote the chronicler John Stow in 1552 (*Annales*, London, 1592):

> The 23 of November, the children [of the poor, who were regarded as "the seed and breeder of beggary"] were taken into the hospitall at the Grey friers called Christs hospitall [for care and training], to the number of almost fower hundred. And also sick and poore people into the hospitall of Saint Thomas at Southwark, in which two places, the children and poore people should have meat, drinke, lodging, and cloth, of the almes of citie.

On Christmas Day, 1552, according to Stow, as the mayor and aldermen rode to St. Paul's Cathedral, some 340 children of Christ's Hospital, all dressed alike in russet outfits, the boys in red caps and the girls with kerchiefs, lined the street to show their appreciation.

As for the thriftless idle, the answer was seen in a disused royal palace known as Bridewell, which was converted so that the healthy beggar might be "chastised and compelled to labour, to the overthrow of the life of idleness." Bridewell continued as a workhouse, apprenticeship foundation, and house of correction until 1864, its very name becoming a generic term for workhouse in the United States as well as in England.

A law enacted in 1552 is significant for its title: "For the Provisyon and Relief of the Poore." The state, in developing its policy toward the poor, had set out primarily to suppress vagabondage, but found it could not do that without also doing something about the legitimate poor. Earlier statutes had generally been of such titles as "For the Punishment of Vagabondes." By 1547 the needy were beginning to share the focus: "An Acte for the Punishment of Vagabondes and for the Relief of the poore and impotent P[e]rsons." Now, in 1552, there came the statute devoted entirely to the needy. It was a law providing for appointment of collectors in each parish to canvass inhabitants and make sure that all were making regular, weekly contributions (whether church-goers or not) for relief of the poor, as had been asked earlier on a voluntary basis.

It was a cumbersome way of doing things, one that would have to be improved upon. Yet this poor law of 1552 is otherwise interesting in that it sought, probably for the first time, to help the poor in accordance with the specific needs of each. It distinguished, as it were, between full and partial disability:

> . . . and after such sorte that the more impotent may have the more helpp and such as can get parte of their livinge to have the lesse, And by the discretyon of the Collector to be putt in such labor as they be fitt and hable to doo, but none to goo or sitt openlie a begging. . . .

"Such labor as they be fitt and hable to doo": doubtless an earnest provision of an earnest law, and yet one to which little practical thought had been given. Two decades later it was still to be resolved, as is apparent from a debate in the House of Commons on April 13, 1571, on a bill further restraining vagabonds (who, being idle, could easily be drawn into the religious revolts). From *The Journals of All the Parliaments of Queen Elizabeth*:

> Mr. Sands endeavoured to prove this Law for Beggars, to be over sharp and bloody, standing much on the care which is to be had for the Poor; saying, that it might be possible with some travail had by the Justices, to relieve every man at his own house. . . .

The concept of relieving the poor in their own homes, as opposed to a workhouse, was new. London had been experimenting with it, as had the County of Worcester. It might now be considered as a matter of national policy, had Mr. Sands his way, but that was still a few years off.

More immediate, as ever, was the perceived need for legislating vagrancy out of existence. A bill considered by Parliament in 1572 sought to do more about vagrants by defining as vagrants more of the population. So inclusive was it that it would have encompassed poor scholars at Oxford and shipwrecked sailors trying to get home. Compromise eventually exempted these and such mainstays of Elizabethan life as minstrels, actors, and exhibiters of bears and trick animals. For those adjudged vagrant, however, the penalty became more severe, which perhaps can be best appreciated by an example from the records of the Middlesex Sessions June 9, 1575:

> True bill, that Thomas Maynerde, Oswald Thompson and John Barres (having at the Justice Hall in the Old Bayle, on 18 March 17 Eliz. [1575], before Sir James Hawes knt. Mayor of London, and William Fleetwood esq. J.P. [Justice of the Peace], been flogged severely and burnt 'per le gristle dextre auricule' [through the right ear] with a hot iron of a thumb's circuit, according to the form of the statute of 14 Eliz. entituled 'an Acte for the Punysshement of Vacabondes and for the relief of the Poor and Impotent'), being over eighteen years old, and fit for labour, but masterless and without any lawful means of livelihood, were again on the said day of June wandering as felonious vagrants at St. Gyles's-in-the-Feilde and elsewhere in the said county. Putting themselves "Guilty," without chattels, the three incorrigible vagrants were sentenced to be hung.

As so often happens when penalties are perceived to be overly severe, the law was not universally enforced. It did not put an end to the ranks of vagabonds. Its defect, and the defect of all such legislation to date, was that, short of sending a man to the gallows, the law did nothing to stop able-bodied vagabondage because it did nothing about an able-bodied man's not working. The law could deal with those who refused to work, in those cases where the law was enforced, but what of those who simply could not find work?

That dilemma was finally being faced. In a sense, it had been faced a few years earlier in the Statute of Apprentices (1563), which was the culmination of piecemeal legislation trying to deal with a period of economic distress early in the reign of Elizabeth. The statute attempted strict control over labor, not only as to wages but as to place and kind of employment as well. In effect, it required that every able-bodied man be apprenticed to some particular trade or craft, which is to say that every able-bodied man must work. Work was a legal obligation. Yet, if a man could not find work? In 1576, even if in a rudimentary way, Parliament got to that: For really the first time, it allowed that the pauper and the vagrant might be one in the same, in some cases. This was the statute (18 Elizabeth) setting the poor to work in their own homes. It required that wool, hemp, iron, flax, and other such raw materials be provided in every city or town for the poor to work on at home, spinning wool into yarn, for example. The products of their labors would then be sold by the city or town, and the proceeds of these sales used to pay the poor according to "the desert of their work." For those unwilling to take part, a house of correction was to be built in each county. Essentially the workhouse of later times, the house of correction would see to the labor of the lazy with whips and chains, albeit to a regular ration of food, as well.

That, basically, is how matters remained through the end of the century, when Parliament at last chose to assemble in one law the many that had been spawned through years of experimentation. It was the Parliament that opened late in 1597 and continued into 1598, and included such distinguished men in public life as Sir Francis Bacon, barrister, essayist, and later lord chancellor; Sir Edward Coke, renowned jurist and former speaker of the House of Commons; and Sir Walter Raleigh, not long returned from his only expedition to the New World. Raleigh was Commons' chairman of the conference committee that resolved differences in the poor law between Lords and Commons.

The legislation of 1598 (39 Elizabeth), the most comprehensive to date though it included very little that was new, provided for the annual appointing of overseers of the poor to have responsibility for the needy within each parish; for setting poor children to work as apprentices; for putting the adult poor to work in their homes on wool and hemp and the like; and for relieving the aged and infirm through financial assistance and through the building of hospitals. The cost of this comprehensive program came, as before, from a parish tax called the poor rate. (Voluntary alms had become compulsory in 1572). Rich parishes could be assessed over and above their needs to help poorer ones. At the county level, there was provision for almshouses and hospitals supported by a county poor rate, which would also go for relief of prisoners.

All in all, the poor law of 1598 essentially continued what had developed over the preceding decades. Reenacted in 1601 as 43 Elizabeth — the legendary "43rd Elizabeth," as it was known for years to come — this same basic legislation continued as English poor law into the twentieth century, meanwhile emigrating to America with the first colonists.

3

EARLY POVERTY AMID EARLY PLENTY
America: The Colonial Period

Although there was some incidence of begging in Colonial America, public provisions for the needy, often modeled word-for-word on English poor law, existed in all the colonies. These provisions were extensive enough that the South Carolina legislature in 1767 appointed a committee to determine why the cost of poor relief had increased 543 percent in 20 years.

Charleston, South Carolina, is still called Charles Town midway through the eighteenth century. It is one of the five largest cities in the colonies (after Philadelphia, New York, Boston, and Newport), and the only one of them in the South. It is perhaps the loveliest, with its many wrought iron gateways, and gardens of wisteria, tamarisk, magnolia, oleander, and crape myrtle. For its many prosperous residents, life is good: the best English wares, coffee from the West Indies, domestic mutton, fresh fish, lots of good Madeira wine. There are three newspapers with the latest (only a month or so by boat from Europe) news, and a theater and horse racing for diversion. The people of Charles Town are friendly, and, by reputation, notably warm and gracious to travelers.

Amid the plenty there is also poverty. The plight of Charles Town's poor is less well recorded for posterity than the good life of its gentry, yet the poor are there: widows and children of departed soldiers and seafarers; poverty-stricken immigrants—French Huguenot, German, and Irish in particular; and the indigenous chronic poor, of which every community has always had its share.

South Carolina's State House is at Broad and Meeting Streets, a few blocks from the docks that are the source of Charles Town's prosperity. It is here the Commons House of Assembly meets. If we choose to look in on the 6th of April, 1767, we find it is poor relief that is being discussed—not its institution, but rather its reform. Someone has been keeping a check on costs and has found that in 20 years the public budget for relief has gone up 543 percent. A legislative committee, appointed to study the increase and make recommendations, on this day submits its report: a proposal for a four-point program of reform.

It is thus apparent, from what we know so far, that there were provisions for relief of the poor in colonial America, and that, in their ever-increasing costs, they bore a trait in common with later (not to mention earlier) times. These provisions were brought over to the English-speaking colonies, sometimes word-for-word as they had existed in England. South Carolina's poor law was sufficiently institutionalized early in the eighteenth century that a newcomer by the name of Thomas Nairn could write matter-of-factly (*A Letter from South Carolina*, London, 1718):

> Tho' we are so happily situated, that no body is obliged to beg or want Food, yet the Charity of the Inhabitants is very remarkable, in taking suitable Methods to prevent any Persons falling into extream Necessity. For Commissioners are appointed by Act of Assembly, to take Care of the Poor, and necessary Helps are settled for that End; though there are few Occasions to make use of this

Provision, unless towards the Widows or Children of such Strangers, who die before they are comfortably settled

The "few Occasions" would become considerably more numerous by midcentury, and the poor law would broaden accordingly. South Carolina's basic law, like those of other colonies, dated from the seventeenth century. In this case, it was "An Act for the Poore," adopted in 1694 and reenacted in 1695, that provided for commissioners to supervise the distribution of funds to the needy. These funds initially came from private charitable contributions, but were supplemented by a fixed public appropriation of £10 per year and in 1698 by provision for a tax comparable to the poor rate paid in England. The commissioners were directed to find or make work for the able-bodied, and to bind children into apprenticeship.

In 1712, in response to "the necessity, number and continual increase of the poor" (in the words of the act), the law was changed to give administrative responsibility to parish vestries, these really constituting the local government. At the same time, a three-month residency requirement was set for those seeking aid; and, for those qualifying for continuing support, provision was made for compelling relatives to the extent of grandparent or grandchild to contribute.* Persons failing the residency requirement were to go back whence they came, and, refusing, to be punished as vagabonds. In 1736 the colony approved the building of a workhouse in Charles Town, and it was in use at least by 1744. Meanwhile, the fixed public subsidy in 1713 was raised from £20 to £70, and then, finally to £200 in 1758.

Such were the basic provisions for dealing with the poor in South Carolina when a legislative committee, in 1767, undertook to determine the reasons for a "vast increase" in cost. The committee, headed by Henry Laurens, later president of the Continental Congress, found among other things: (1) that the increase, in part, could be explained by a "too easy means of gaining a settlement . . . so as to entitle such persons to relief" or, in other words, a tendency on the part of those administering relief to be too liberal through an "inattention" to residency requirements; (2) that some of the increase was attributable to an influx of needy, especially German, Irish, and French Huguenot immigrants, drawn to the province by a 1735 act (no longer in effect) promising assistance to newcomers; (3) that there was a reason unique to the times—hardship upon some as a result of the "late stagnation of Trade and Business occasioned by the British Stamp Act."

---

*A common provision of the poor laws of the various states into the twentieth century.

So much for reasons. What should be done? The committee recommended, in effect, an emphasis on indoor (almshouse or workhouse) as opposed to outdoor relief (monetary or in-kind assistance). A workhouse, the one in use by 1744, still existed, but it had long since become a common receptacle for debtors, paupers, derelict seamen, petty offenders, runaway slaves, and prisoners of war. The committee said two other institutions should be built and operated in conjunction with it: a poorhouse, for only the needy who could not work; and a house of correction, which would siphon off from the workhouse fugitive seamen and slaves and the like.

A year after the Laurens committee submitted its report, the Commons House followed its essential recommendation — an emphasis on indoor relief — by approving construction of a new poorhouse and hospital. The House also added something of its own: It increased, from three months to one year, the residency required for public relief.

How these measures worked is not recorded in detail, but it is clear that the cost of relief declined, at least initially. There are figures available for Charles Town (and they represent by far the largest part of all such costs in South Carolina). Expenditures had totaled £6,515 the year before the Laurens committee went to work; by 1775 they were down to £3,000. The cost was up again in 1776, but the Revolutionary War understandably produced a great deal of dislocation and an increased demand for public assistance. That was true in other colonies, and would have been no less true in South Carolina since it was the target of a British invasion in June 1776.

In peacetime the decline in cost, even allowing for a change in the value of currency, was more marked. The Charleston *Columbian Herald* in 1785 reported relief expenditures for the year at £1,300 — only £100 more than in 1747. Nonetheless, poor relief was still the largest single expenditure in the municipal budget.

THE POOR: COMING AND GOING

In its incidence of poor amid plenty, colonial South Carolina offers an interesting analogy to the modern-day United States. But no one colony is wholly descriptive of them all; as a lot, they were diverse in culture, religion, government, and economy. In poor law they were far more alike than dissimilar, and yet there were certain differences, making it appropriate now to look at colonial America generally.

There are, however, two factors that should be considered first, two unique influences on the composition of the poor: the frontier in America and the poor law (as applied to vagabonds) in England.

As for the frontier, it was thought to be a great natural asylum. The poor could be diverted there, thence to find opportunity, or otherwise at least disappear as a social problem from the seaboard states. Charles Pinckney, at the Federal Convention of 1787, suggested the vast territory to the west ought to prevent, for a considerable time, "the increase of the poor discontented." The frontier probably did lessen the degree of poverty that might otherwise have existed during colonial times as well as during the early years of the new republic. It did not eradicate the poor problem in the colonies. Furthermore, particularly in the early years, the frontier was often only a temporary dwelling place, thanks to Indian tribes that did not take kindly to being dispossessed from their heretofore permanent dwelling places. Many early settlers fled back to the seaboard as refugees. Notable was the time of King Philip's War (1675-76), before which Newport had too few paupers to count and after which it was spending £800 for relief of refugees from the frontier, many of whom remained as permanent charges. Boston had an even more significant influx during the 1670s—to such an extent that the province had to supplement the efforts of local government. There were also those who returned from the frontier as failures, and, failing in the towns of the East as well, sought public assistance.

As for the poor law: Applied with increasing zeal to vagabonds and the like in England, its contribution to the ranks of the poor in America was even more significant. The English government systematically shipped over the undesirables among its own people—a motley assortment of political prisoners, religious nonconformists, delinquents of all sorts, and common criminals. Vagabonds and miscreants of all kinds, it was supposed, would be well suited to the wild and primitive conditions of the New World. Deportation might, in fact, do them some good, it was argued; and if not, at least they were gone. The practice began in the earliest years of the colonies and is nowhere so clearly stated as in a proclamation of James I in 1617 for rounding up "the most notorious and lewd persons . . . notorious and wicked offenders . . . the most notorious ill livers, and misbehaved persons . . . " in Northumberland, Cumberland, and Westmoreland counties, and sending them off to Virginia, so that they might "no more infect the places where they abide within this our Realme."

In *The Present State of Virginia* (London, 1724), the Rev. Hugh Jones, late of the faculty of the College of William and Mary, wrote that, in general

> the Servants and inferior Sort of People, who have either been sent over to Virginia, or have transported themselves thither, have been, and are, the poorest, idlest, and worst of Mankind, the Refuse of Great Britain and Ireland, and the Outcast of the People.

No wonder, by 1769 and the eve of revolution, Samuel Johnson was given to remark of Americans: "Sir, they are a race of convicts and ought to be content with anything we allow them short of hanging." And no wonder, there were those in the highest echelons of the British government, including some of its most eminent generals, who thus foresaw the prosecution of the war in America as little more than the rounding up of disorderly vagabonds — a miscalculation of the most profound effect on history.

It is not surprising, then, that early American poor law followed English precedent in setting stiff penalties for vagrancy and idleness. At the same time, colonial law followed English precedent generally, and certainly so with regard to poor relief in its broadest application. Notable is the colony of Rhode Island, whose first General Assembly quite expeditiously adopted this as part of its first code of laws for the colony in 1647:

> It is agreed and ordered, by this present Assembly, that each Towne shall provide carefully for the reliefe of the poore, to maintayne the impotent, and to employ the able, and shall appoint an overseer for the same purpose. See 43 Eliz. 2.

A common form of assistance during the seventeenth century was the boarding of needy persons with better-off families at some agreed-upon recompense paid out of the town treasury (as also came to be the case in England). The town of Newark, New Jersey, in 1690, for example, paid one John Gardner 2s.6d. a week for the care of one Richard Hore.

As the number of needy increased, it occurred to officials there and in other towns that it would be cheaper simply to give a small allotment and let the recipient make a home for himself or herself, much in the manner of modern-day welfare. This, in fact, came to be the common form of public assistance in the eighteenth century. Some almshouses did appear, in major cities and towns, and likewise workhouses for the able-bodied (in practice, one institution usually served both purposes), but in many localities the cost of construction and subsequent operation made the allotment a preferable alternative.

Virtually all assistance was locally administered and paid for through local taxes. There were, however, exceptions now and again that set a precedent for later times. The exigencies of war contributed to such an instance. Early in the Revolution, Newport, already ravaged by the British, found it difficult to keep up with relief and appealed to the General Assembly of the colony. The Assembly sent £200. Subsequently, other towns appealed for similar aid, and in the course of six years the General Assembly made not only cash grants but distributions of food and firewood to various towns in Rhode Island. In Massachusetts, as early as 1675, there was provincial aid in response to suffering from the war against the Indians.

The number of poor receiving public assistance in the early years was certainly small, but kept increasing as time went on. Boston, by 1690, had a hard core of poor, many of them refugees of the first two Anglo-French wars, as well as the Indian wars. In 1700 Boston spent £500 on relief; in 1715 the amount was £2,000. The poor also became a serious problem in eighteenth-century Philadelphia as it went through successive waves of immigration. There was less of a problem at the time in New York, and the least of one in Newport among the principal cities and towns.

In August 1751 Boston's assessors reported that there were 1,153 widows entitled to public support — a number, together with dependent children, representing some 7 percent of the population. At the end of the Revolutionary War, Philadelphia is said to have had some 1,600 families on relief, or about 20 percent of the population of the city and its suburbs. Defining "poor" as having no land and a cash income of nothing to only a few pounds, the number of poor in the new United States at the time of the war may have been as high as 40 percent of the population (of white population, 20 percent), according to estimates based on probate records.

With the number of those on relief increasing, there was a tendency throughout the colonial period for public assistance to be administered in a continuously more repressive way. Even in the early days, however, could that be so. Boston selectmen, in 1636, forbade any inhabitant entertaining a stranger for more than two weeks without permission, lest that stranger become both needy and permanent. In 1647 Peter Stuyvesant ordered that no stranger stay more than one night in New Amsterdam without first having his name recorded (obviously for the same reason as in Boston).

The Puritan work ethic played an inhibitory role. It was often difficult to separate the legitimately needy from the able-bodied lazy, to be sure, but when it could be done there was plenty in Scripture to show why it was right to have *The Idle-Poor Secluded from the Bread of Christian Charity by the Christian Law*, to quote the title of a published sermon of the Rev. Charles Chauncy, great-grandson of Harvard's second president and Boston's most influential clergyman of his day. The sermon was preached and printed in 1752, to further the aims of the Society for Encouraging Industry and Employing the Poor. One can imagine the many Charles Chauncys of New England, Bibles in hand, summoning the wrath of the Almighty on the giving of public support to any but the neediest, with the likes of:

> In the sweat of thy face shalt thou eat bread.
>
> Genesis 3:19
>
> For even when we were with you, this we commanded you, that if any would not work, neither should he eat.
>
> II Thessalonians 3:10

If one did not work, neither might he eat. It may not always have come to that, but the poor whose plight evoked little or no sympathy could expect to get aid only with the most grudging approval of authorities. And then there was often an attempt to shame the would-be recipient out of receiving aid by branding him as a pauper and holding him up to public scorn. Virginia, in 1755, required of everyone receiving relief that he "shall, upon the shoulder of the right sleeve of his or her uppermost garment, in an open and visible manner, wear a badge, with the name of the parish to which he or she belongs, cut either in blue, red, or green cloth. . . . " For failure to wear such a badge, the penalty was a public whipping, or either reduction or forfeiture of relief. Maryland, by a provincial law passed in 1773, ordered recipients of relief in Baltimore each to wear the letters "PB" (Pauper Baltimore) in red or blue cloth on the right sleeve. New Jersey in 1774 specified a large "P." That alone would be the most common insignia.

Furthermore, paupers largely forfeited civil and political rights. They could be jailed as debtors or auctioned off as servants. Children were commonly indentured as apprentices. In 1774, for a pauper who had moved away and then returned to town, New Jersey ordered a whipping of 10 to 15 lashes just for coming back.

The principal right usually forfeited was that of suffrage. In general, colonial suffrage laws restricted paupers from voting. One way was through a property requirement, the ownership of at least 50 acres being a common requirement in colonial times. In other cases there was the stipulation that taxes be paid in full, which many paupers obviously could not manage to do. In addition, some colonies provided for the waiving of taxes as a form of relief, thus eliminating from the voting the beneficiaries of relief in that they were not then taxpayers. William Penn's "Great Law" of 1682 provided for suffrage on the part of those paying scot and lot, the old form of parish tax, thus ruling out those who did not or could not pay.

The first constitutions of the new states (there were eight adopted in 1776) generally set property requirements for voting. New Jersey, which specified that a voter be worth at least £50, required only an oath to that effect, leaving considerable room for abuse. Oaths were routinely filed by many of lesser means, leading William Griffith in his *Eumenes*

(Trenton, 1799) to complain that New Jersey's vote was being thrown away on "every vagabond in the country." (New Jersey and several other states, beginning with Virginia in 1830, eventually eliminated all such possibility by constitutionally prohibiting paupers from voting, while others specifically provided that almshouse confinement have no effect on eligibility to vote. Such restrictions were generally removed by amendment, or as new constitutions came into being, later in the nineteenth century or in the twentieth century.)

FORERUNNERS OF MEDICAID

For the sick poor of colonial times it was easier to have sympathy, and there were surprisingly frequent responses to their needs. Yet lack of sympathy—even cruelty—there was as well.

Of the latter sort of response there is the example of one Sarah Hinks in 1715. Sarah Hinks, a poor woman whose residence was Salem, had been staying in Boston at the home of a friend for more than two weeks. It troubled authorities that she was expecting a child almost any day, which meant both she and the child might become a charge to Boston's relief rolls. Sarah Hinks was asked to leave Boston for Salem immediately. Heartless as it may have been, it was no more than the routine application of settlement laws, whereby the taxpayers of a town were spared the financial burden of a pauper who was not one of their own. The Hinks case is akin to the "passing on" process in both England and America, whereby the burden of the poor laws could be evaded altogether by endlessly routing a pauper from one jurisdiction to another.

On the other hand, there were also instances when colonial authorities could be beneficent beyond call. In New Kent County, Virginia, in 1774 a poor man named Richard Sentale was ailing. Authorities arranged for him to stay, at public expense, at a spa on the New River. In 1762 a woman on relief gave birth in New York's poorhouse. The attending physician—at a handsome fee of £7, paid out of public funds—was Dr. John Bard, one of the most eminent doctors in the country and later the first president of the New York State Medical Society. Ordinarily, his patients came from the best and wealthiest of families.*

The use of public funds to pay physicians for treatment of the poor was a fairly frequent occurrence in colonial times. It is reminiscent of the

---

*In New York City in 1874, several soup kitchens, privately financed with a grant from New York *Herald* publisher James Gordon Bennett, served soup expressly prepared by the *chef de cuisine* of Delmonico's Restaurant using ingredients that included "choice rib and shoulder" cuts of beef (*Frank Leslie's Illustrated Newspaper*, March 7, 1874).

archiatri populares of the Roman Empire but is probably more accurately equated with the lesser scale and less systematic approach that characterizes the use of publicly paid physicians in ancient Greece.

Usually the colonial doctor was paid outright for his services; sometimes he received compensation in the form of exemption from taxes, as is evident from this account in the records of Boston's selectmen for November 29, 1671:

> Upon the Motion of Doctor Daniell Stone to pay for Chirurgery & phisicke administered to severall poore of this towne the select men see cause to abate him his rate this yeare for what is done for the time past; & doe further now agree with him for 12 monseths next comeinge from the first of March next, to take care of the poore of this towne as to phisicke & Chirurgery, for which he is to have 20s. out of the towne treasury & to be rate free the next yeare.

In many cases the public funds paid not for a physician but for a lay practitioner, usually a midwife. In Georgia there was a public midwife who was paid a crown by the colony for each birth. As of 1737, when recorded in a diary, she had earned 128 crowns.

Sometimes a sick person was lodged, at public expense, in the home of a doctor or lay practitioner for the duration of an illness or infirmity. Whatever the case, there seems to have been no firm public policy in dealing with the medically indigent. Each locality had its own way of doing things. Sarah Hinks was sent packing so that the residency laws of Boston might be enforced to the letter. In East Hampton, New York, in 1697, when a poor sick woman wandered into town, authorities routinely warned her to leave, then changed their minds and boarded her with various residents at public expense. Subsequently, they sent her for treatment by two notable physicians in nearby towns. In 1700, when last recorded, she was still getting free care. Nor were manifest symptoms of serious illness necessary. One Edward London of Providence in 1693 had become dependent out of "imbercillity" and "decrippedness." Thoughtful authorities arranged to have him boarded at public expense with townspeople (apparently on a rotating basis), and in such manner he spent the rest of his days.

Provision for the medically needy began in the earliest years of the colonies. New Netherlands had its *sieckentroosters*, or "sick-comforters," the first of whom arrived in the Dutch colonies in 1624. The sieckentrooster was a church official charged with seeking out the sick and poor and seeing to their needs. The cost was borne by voluntary church collections but was sometimes supplemented by compulsory public levies.

Care of the sick, like treatment of the poor, was often crude, but nevertheless reflected the Elizabethan principle of responsibility toward the helpless. In time, that responsibility became institutionalized. The Philadelphia Almshouse (eventually to become Philadelphia General Hospital) was opened in 1729 and had doctors available for the medical needs of inmates. In 1751 Pennsylvania Hospital was built with the proceeds of a fund-raising drive organized by Benjamin Franklin. It was the first general hospital in America, and as such was open not only to Philadelphians but to strangers from far and wide. In the case of the poor, care was free, doctors handling such cases without fee. The other major hospitals with colonial origins—Bellevue in New York and Massachusetts General in Boston—were outgrowths of the infirmaries in early poorhouses.

Doctors sometimes also furnished free care on an outpatient basis, as is evident in this advertisement in the Charleston *Columbian Herald*, September 14, 1786:

> The poor families in the city of Charleston, who may at any time stand in need of medical assistance, and are so distressingly circumstanced that they are unable to purchase it, are hereby informed, that by calling on Dr. Ladd, at the house of Mrs. Theus, No. 87, Church-street, the really poor man will find a medical friend —ready to assist him with prescriptions, advice, and in particular cases with medicines, gratis. . . . The pleasure of doing good is the most elevated and refined of all the pleasures, and the only enjoyment that can reconcile us to the woes and miseries inseparably annexed to human life.

Virginia, in 1769, established the first public mental health hospital in America. Located in Williamsburg and known later as Eastern State Hospital, it was committed by an act of the legislature to the care and the maintenance of those who fit the existing definition of insane: "Ideots, Lunatics and other persons of unsound minds."

Still another form of assistance to the poor was help with fuel. An early example was Newport in 1747: The town council ordered the supplying of firewood at public expense to each of four widows in town, apparently because the winter was a severe one. During the Revolutionary War, something of the same was done on a much broader scale in Philadelphia. The Council of Safety, on January 1, 1777, directed the overseers of the poor to procure 100 cords of wood then standing on the commons and make it available to needy families. The severity of the winter of 1784 in Philadelphia resulted in a public subscription that raised £1,500 to purchase 500 cords of wood for 5,212 people, among whom were 2,696 children and a woman 102 years old. On the other hand, in Newport in 1767, an intended distribution of firewood to the poor at public expense apparently came to nought, and a letter to the Newport *Mercury*,

December 14, 1767, laid the blame squarely on "our wise-headed Politicians."

All this, generally speaking,* was the development of poor relief in America through the time of the Revolution. Once independence had been achieved, and the 13 former colonies had settled down to working the kinks out of their new state governments, poor relief was often considered equal to schools and roads as a function of local government. Observed Jeremy Belknap's *History of New-Hampshire* (1792) on government under the constitution of 1784:

> Every township in New-Hampshire is a distinct corporation, having a power of choosing all town officers, which are named in the laws, and of raising money by taxes for the support of ministers, schools, bridges, highways, the maintenance of the poor, and other public purposes.

There were also those who saw a need for reform — indeed, "a reform, which all agree should long since have been made. . . . " The comment is from a contributor to the New Hampshire *Mercury*, March 8, 1786, who took note that relief costs were "much increased" and proposed a Society for Promoting Industry to put the able-bodied to productive labor. The idea was hardly new, as he himself recognized. Well, said he, sounding like reformers before and since,

> if the plan should be objected to as uneligible, it is earnestly wished that some person capable of the task would offer one more suitable for producing a reform, which all agree should long since have been made, that every stranger that comes into town may not have his first salutation from a beggar.

A month later the Portsmouth, New Hampshire, overseers of the poor, newly elected, pledged a reform of the system, asking the public's patience while it was carried out (as if to concede it would not be a simple process). The reform was not spelled out in detail, but appears to have focused on doing a better job of separating the legitimately needy from their able-bodied fellows — and "to use all proper economy in the matter" (*Mercury*, April 12, 1786).

---

*Auctioning off a pauper to the lowest bidder for care was another form of relief sometimes applied.

4

THE PUZZLE OF CENTURIES DEBATED
From Old Poor Law to the Twentieth Century

Although the nineteenth century was the age of the almshouse, generally speaking, there was continued debate about the preferability of "outdoor" assistance, one form of which was the soup kitchen. This one was in New York City. From Frank Leslie's Illustrated Newspaper, *March 7, 1984. Other forms of outdoor assistance at this time included cash allotments (Iowa, as one example), free fuel (Cincinnati, for instance), and free medical care (among others, New York, where, in 1877, between 30 and 35 percent of the population benefited from an early form of medicaid).*

If a broad generalization may be made about poor relief in the United States through the early nineteenth century, it is this: The predominant form of relief alternated, more or less by centuries, between indoor and outdoor assistance.

In the seventeenth century a common (though by no means exclusive) form of relief was the boarding of the poor or the indigent sick with some family in the community at public expense. That represents a form of institutional, or indoor, relief. During the eighteenth century it was commonly supposed that direct payments to the poor were more efficient. The Virginia House of Burgesses, for example, spurned the governor's recommendation for construction of county workhouses, countering that the poor could be relieved "an Easier way" — through direct payments.

Thus one might wonder if the nineteenth century means a return to the institution. For various reasons — economy, efficiency, and the lessening of administrative abuse and political favoritism — it does; the institution, whether known as poorhouse or almshouse or by many a euphemism, becomes predominant in the nineteenth century, although outdoor relief will be found as well, often in competition with the poorhouse.

NINETEENTH-CENTURY REFORM

The ascendancy of the poorhouse was accompanied by that circumstance common to change — reform. Four examples in the early to midnineteenth century stand out: Boston, New York State, Philadelphia, and Chicago.

Boston

The 1820s were a time of reform generally in Boston. The old watch and constable system gave way to a reasonably modern and efficient police force (and this before Sir Robert Peel and the London "Bobby"). Urban mass transportation (nineteenth-century style) came into vogue to relieve streets so clogged with horses and buggies that no one could go very fast on his own. More to the point was a change at the root of all other progress, and that was a change in government. On May 1, 1822, Boston became a city instead of a town. In so doing it abandoned forever its nostalgic town-meeting form of government for the up-to-date: a mayor and city council.

The third decade of the century was likewise a time for reform of poor relief. In 20 years the cost of state-administered relief had risen almost 150 percent in Massachusetts (from $28,100 to $72,663), and local expenditures must have increased proportionately. It was not wholly on the basis of cost, however, that the city of Boston set out on reform. Local politics was also a factor.

The driving force, Josiah Quincy, later president of Harvard, would have been Boston's first mayor under city government but for losing the Federalist nomination. Failing the mayoralty, Quincy kept his hand in municipal affairs as chairman of a committee supporting construction of a new house of industry. Boston at this time had its Leverett Street almshouse, built in 1800 in response to an earlier call for reform. It was now written off as a "large and expensive pile of buildings" where the vagrant and dissolute were jammed together with the "unfortunate and honest" poor. It had a population of somewhat more than 400 (considerably more in winter), and represented the major portion of a poor relief program that was costing Boston more than $32,000 a year (from which could be deducted $12,378 in state aid, which still left the town with $20,000 in expenditures).

Quincy's committee recommended construction of a new and presumably more efficient house of industry that would allow for distinction between the "poor by reason of misfortune" and the "poor by reason of vice," the latter meaning principally "poor by reason of alcohol" in the opinion of the committee. The house of industry, which would put the able-bodied poor to work in agriculture, was soon under construction on a 63-acre site in South Boston, south of what is now the naval base. The original appropriation (approved at the final town meeting March 28, 1822) was not enough, however, and work stopped early in 1823.

Long before this, the overseers of the poor, who would have no jurisdiction over the new house of industry, made known their displeasure. They were elected in 1822 with the city's first mayor, John Phillips. The new city council, successor to the town meeting that had approved construction of the house of industry, was considerably less enthusiastic about the project and saw a way out by turning the new facility into a house of correction. The city council would then have another facility into which everyone alike might be thrown, as in times past, and would save itself the cost of building a new jail as well.

A month later the legislature got into the matter by vesting in Quincy's house of industry committee legal authority over operation of the new facility corresponding to the authority the overseers had over the Leverett Street almshouse. Meanwhile, nothing came of the council's change of plan because nothing more came of the project. At the end of the first year of city government, the house of industry stood uncompleted.

On May 1, 1823, Boston began its second year of city government with a new council and Quincy as mayor. He wasted no time on his favorite project and got work going again with an appropriation of $8,000. Up to now the cost, including land, had run $40,100. By July 28th the new home of Boston's "poor by reason of misfortune" was ready for them, and all that remained was for the city to move them from Leverett Street to South Boston—an easy boat ride.

It turned out otherwise. Quincy later explained part of the reason: The inmates

> had imbided gross and unfounded prejudices against the House of Industry, in addition to the dislike which paupers, accustomed to be supported in comparative idleness, naturally felt towards an institution in which work was to be required of them.

That was one thing, but no one took the wishes of the inmates very seriously. What had to be dealt with were the overseers, and they flatly refused to cooperate, contending they had no authority to transfer the poor to some new-fangled institution. Then they backed off a bit, agreeing to the transfer of some—41, they decided—of Leverett Street's ablebodied. The house of industry committee, although hardly satisfied, agreed; it was better than letting the new building stand empty.

When the time came for transfer of the inmates, however, the overseers, instead of handing their charges over directly, called them into the almshouse office one by one, and offered each a discharge. Twenty-one declined the offer, choosing the house of industry. The others, according to Quincy, decided "they did not go into the almshouse for work; that if they wanted to work they would get it out of doors."

Subsequently, the city council, which so far had only *asked* the transfer of the inmates, voted to *tell* the overseers that all able-bodied poor be sent to South Boston. Later in 1823 the council broke ground for a house of correction at the South Boston site, thus providing for a separate facility for the vagrant that was also separate from the jurisdiction of the cantankerous overseers. The Leverett Street "pile of buildings" was sold in 1825, and, with transfer of the remaining inmates, the overseers were left with no one to oversee.

It is fair to say that Quincy himself regarded his efforts on behalf of the poor—efforts that embraced the most up-to-date conceptions of poor relief—as the most important work of his mayoralty. In his *Municipal History of the Town and City of Boston* (1852), he began each chapter for the years of his mayoralty with the continuing saga of almshouse reform.

A biography written by his son took pride in noting that Alexis de Tocqueville visited a facility for juvenile offenders that was also built by Quincy and pronounced it a model worthy for France to copy.

New York State

The impetus for reform in New York in the early 1800s was also that two-headed one so frequently encountered: cost versus efficiency. The cost was clear; but how effective was relief in meeting the needs of the poor? That was open to question, not least of all on the part of the Humane Society of New York, which in 1809 issued a report deploring the "extreme poverty and misery, which have so much increased among our labouring poor."

And yet it was not a matter of skimping. Relief was the largest single item in the New York City budget. Even at the turn of the century it was 23 percent of the whole, as evidenced by the city budget for 1800:

Almshouse	$ 30,000
Contingencies	29,450
Watch (police)	25,000
Street lighting	15,000
City contingencies (in addition to above)	7,500
Roads	7,500
Bridewell (workhouse/jail)	5,000
Streets (in addition to "Roads" above)	5,000
Maintenance of prisoners	3,000
Wells and pumps	2,500
	$129,950

In 1823 the state of New York launched the most thorough and systematic study of the operation of poor laws ever undertaken in the United States up to that time.

It is not that there was a shortage of ideas. The Humane Society, in 1809, had laid the blame for pauperism squarely on intemperance (which was plausible since New York City at the time had 3,500 retail/tavern licenses and Philadelphia 190). The Society for the Prevention of Pauperism in 1819 cited the influx of recipients from elsewhere in the state, and even from Canada, as constituting the principal demand on relief rolls. Governor De Witt Clinton, in his annual message of 1818, meanwhile laid responsibility on the relief laws themselves:

Our statutes relating to the poor are borrowed from the English system. And the experience of that country as well as our own, shows that pauperism increases with the augmentation of the funds applied to its relief.*

There was thus plenty of opinion. But how, really, did the poor laws work; and if not well, why? That is what a committee headed by Secretary of State John V. N. Yates set out to determine. Its key findings, in a report to the legislature in 1824:

> . . . even in China the laws of the empire have made provision [for support of the poor]. All this is certainly no slight proof, that the total want of a pauper system, would be inconsistent with a humane, liberal, and enlightened policy.

And yet

> our poor laws are manifestly defective in principle, and mischievous in practice, and that under the imposing and charitable aspect of affording relief exclusively to the poor and infirm, they frequently invite the able bodied vagrant to partake of the same bounty, are propositions very generally admitted.

The "best manner" of improving the system might be gathered from the experience of other jurisdictions. Therefore, "the adoption of the poorhouse plan, in every county, is recommended by the proposed bill. . . . Its advantages over every other system for the support of paupers, are manifest."

The Yates committee based its findings on the results of questionnaires sent to officials throughout the state, this material totaling 150 pages of documents that formed an appendix to the report to the legislature. The returns showed that the various localities of the state were administering poor relief principally in four ways: (1) the almshouse; (2) outdoor, or home relief; (3) the contract system, whereby care was contracted out; and (4) the auction system, by which the lowest bidder was paid to care for the town's poor. The state at this time had 30 almshouses.

In essence the Yates committee's recommendation was simple: Make indoor relief, meaning the almshouse, the predominant form of

---

*A not uncommon complaint; it appeared, for example, in the Boston *Independent Chronicle*, April 8, 1784: "The burden of supporting the poor has been the subject of complaint with almost all civilized nations; and strange as it may seem, the number of indigent objects has usually increased in proportion to the provision made for their relief." See also Benjamin Franklin, p. 118.

assistance; and, in the interest of economy and efficiency, make the county rather than the town the principal administrative unit.

Legislation of 1824 implementing recommendations of the committee did that, in effect; but it allowed so many exceptions that many counties remained without almshouses. Even so, the principle was clearly established in law. With subsequent amendments, state law came to provide that even disorderly persons and children found begging in the streets be committed to almshouses, and that every inmate able to work be required to perform some labor.

Philadelphia

Philadelphia in 1827 named a committee to visit almshouses in other cities (Baltimore, New York, Boston, Providence, and Salem) and, though it would have surprised reformers elsewhere, the committee reported back that "on a careful consideration of what has been stated, your committee cannot but admit the mortifying fact, that every system they have examined is superior to our own."

What the committee recommended was essentially restriction as to assistance offered the poor. It amounted to no more than a variation in wording on what others had concluded:

> It is an axiom abundantly confirmed by experience, that in proportion to the means of support, provided for the poor and improvident, they are found to increase and multiply.

In other words, reduce the benefits and reduce the number of beneficiaries. This meant that the overcrowded almshouse would decrease in population, and that classification of inmates would be possible—the aged and infirm "who have never forfeited their title to respect" thus separated from vagrants, drunks, and petty criminals. Keep charity for the deserving, as so oft repeated. Above all, make sure public charity is not too pleasant. "Public establishments," said the committee, quoting a Boston report of 1821, "become thronged, as will never fail to be the case, whenever Alms House support is better than, or even equal in its kind, to the support to be obtained by labor." Collaterally, the committee advised that outdoor relief, if given at all, be restricted to firewood and provisions, and that "no money in any case be given."

Chicago

Chicago, after the Great Fire of 1871, was a city rebuilding, and thus got a reputation as the place to be. Countless of the unemployed from other parts of the country poured in expecting to find easy work. Many found they were only adding to the ranks of the jobless.

The ranks of the poor swelled accordingly. By 1874 there was a virtual state of emergency. With both the poorhouse and the county hospital overflowing, the county agent was giving outdoor assistance, at one point, to more than one-tenth of the Cook County population.

Keeping pace with the increased demand for services was a demand for reform. A new county agent took office promising just that. "Promises have been made before," snarled the Chicago *Tribune*. This was a time they were kept. County Agent McGrath, in one year's time, cut relief costs from $230,000 a year to $90,000. "Dumbfounding," said the *Tribune*. What McGrath did, in particular, was to require strict control over eligibility, thus weeding out the likes of the woman whose five children were found, on double-checking, to be staying the same age, or even getting younger from year to year, to keep their mother permanently on public assistance.

THE WEST

Elsewhere, during the early to mid-nineteenth century, there was not yet the call for reform; poor relief was still in its formative stage. Such was the case in the great American West.

The U.S. frontier of the nineteenth century is popularly recalled as a colorful place, abounding in freedom, initiative, and individualism—the land of the strong, the brave, and the hardy beating down the wilderness.

At the same time, the poor were there too—the dependent poor. In St. Clair County, Illinois Territory, in 1809, poor relief accounted for almost 20 percent of the county budget. In Mississippi, when it became a territory in 1799, a poor law was promulgated prior to laws regulating highways and establishing ferries.

It stands to reason that there were people of modest means, often very modest, settling the frontier. Many had little or nothing to lose and everything to gain. In the Kansas Territory, public lands were available for $1.25 an acre. The Emigrant Aid Company estimated that $100 was enough on which to get started. A pioneer named Elijah Iles, in his *Sketches of Early Life and Times* (1883), said many of the early settlers of Kentucky and Tennessee arrived without a dollar, but, by raising corn and selling it to those who came later, they were enabled to buy their own land.

Some pioneers got rich. Some stayed poor, and often personal initiative had nothing to do with it. The climate was frequently an enemy. Although the pioneer by common depiction was a robust and healthy individual, he was also mortal. Disease was a companion on the trip westward. Smallpox and jaundice were common among adults, cholera among children. In summer it was the lucky family that was spared recurrent attacks of shaking chills and burning fever. In winter the unexpected severity of the season turned common colds into pneumonia, and pneumonia into death statistics. In the frontier outpost of Indianapolis in 1822, of some 1,000 living there, 900 fell ill in a fever epidemic. To make matters worse, doctors everywhere were scarce.

Poor to begin with, or poor through the adversity of frontier life, there were those on the westward migration of society who had to turn to public charity for help. They found the poor law had migrated with them across the continent, as once it had across the sea:

> the necessary Releife of the lame ympotente olde blynde and such other amonge them beinge poore & not able to worke.
>
> England, 1597
(39th Elizabeth)

> the necessary reliefe of the Same Impotent, old blind and such others, being Poor and not able to work &c.
>
> Colony of New York, 1695

> relieving such poor, old, blind, impotent and lame persons, or other persons not able to work.
>
> Northwest Territory, 1795

> relieve, support and maintain its own poor, such as the lame, blind, sick and other persons who from age or infirmity are unable to support himself or herself.
>
> Missouri Territory, 1814

> [relieve] its own poor; such as the lame, blind, sick and other persons who, from age or infirmity, are unable to support himself or herself.
>
> Oregon Territory, 1849

Occasionally, a reluctant legislature might drag its feet until prodded into action. Indiana's constitution of 1816 made it the duty of the state's General Assembly to provide poor farms "as soon as circumstances will permit." As of 1825 nothing had been done, and Governor James B. Ray, on December 8 of that year lectured his lethargic legislators:

> The uniform silence of our legislature on this subject, is sufficient to induce a belief that this benevolent provision has not yet received that consideration to which it is entitled. . . . It is the poor and needy that can justly claim more of our deliberations than the affluent, whose wealth sets legislative interposition at defiance.

In response to the governor's chiding, the legislature did something: It passed a law requiring county clerks to report on local relief expenditures, presumably so such data could help to determine the number of poor houses needed. There were then 53 counties in Indiana; 14 county clerks responded. That led Governor Ray to another lecture, on December 8, 1826:

> I view it as our constitutional, yea, moral duty, to interfere in this business. And I hope we will pause, ere we conclude that our existing laws in this respect, are not a deep blot upon the fair escutcheon of our country's fame. Do they speak the spirit of the age, which is pregnant with relief for the poor, the unfortunate, the weak, the miserable? There are those who think they do not.*

Although the age, in retrospect, may have been less pregnant than it appeared at the time, the trek of civilization westward carried with it varying degrees of concern about the poor. Iowa, Nebraska, and California provide examples.

Iowa

> In Iowa, we have no outdoor poor law, and hundreds of worthy but indigent persons, in families, have suffered untold privation and misery, by reason of the want of such a law.
>
> *Iowa State Register*
> April 8, 1868

It was incorrect that Iowa had no provision for outdoor relief. There had been a law since 1851, but in practice it amounted to nothing. The legislature finally passed a new law, and it was on behalf of this legislation that the *Register* was commenting. The new law set a maximum allowance of $2 per week per person for those qualifying for support— those, in the judgment of relief authorities, who should not be sent to the poorhouse.

In debate on the measure in the Iowa House of Representatives, March 25, 1868, Representative John A. Kasson said it was the intent

---

*Governor Ray declared his age "pregnant with relief for the poor." A country legislator named William Crafts, four years earlier, echoed much the same feeling as he laid the cornerstone of an asylum in Columbia, South Carolina, one day in July 1822: "Welcome be this day and this solemnity, which . . . in the cause of humanity . . . assures every individual among us of the guardian sympathy of the State."

of the measure to give families the choice of being supported outside at $2 a week per person, or of going to the poorhouse. If this meant that poorhouses would be deserted, he said he hoped God would hasten the day—to which several other members are reported to have responded, "Amen." In fact, however, the law applied only to incorporated cities of the first class; and Iowa's poorhouses continued to thrive, along with the others around the country.

Public assistance of $2 per week defies judgment without some objective measure of what it meant at the time. It appears to have been a very reasonable amount. Eggs sold for 15¢ a dozen, flour for 6¢ a pound, and dressed turkey for 10¢ a pound on the Des Moines and Jefferson markets in the spring of 1868. Accordingly, a market basket for a family of four with a combined allowance of $8 per week might have held

> 2 lbs. of flour, 2 lbs. of cornmeal, ¼ bu. of corn, 2 lbs. of rice, 2 dz. potatoes, 1 lb. of brown sugar, 2 dz. eggs, 1 lb. of butter, 1 lb. of dried apples, 2 lbs. of bacon, 2 lbs. of ham, 2 lbs. of dressed turkey, 3 chickens, 2 lbs. of codfish, 1 lb. of mackerel, and ½ lb. of coffee. . . .

and used only $4.04 of the allowance, leaving the rest for local fresh vegetables, milk, rent, fuel, clothing, and incidental expenses (medical needs were provided for separately). For a short period of time, at least, it would seem to be a viable allowance.

Nebraska

> If you have ordinary health, determination, self-reliance, energy and ambition, come West.

So exhorted an immigrant guide to Southern Nebraska in 1870. And come they did. During the 1860s alone, the white (as opposed to Indian) population soared by 330 percent.

With increasing population went the need for poor relief, which, with statehood in 1867, was focused on the poorhouse or poor farm. A *History of the State of Nebraska* (Western Historical Co., 1882) included detailed accounts of the life of the period, and those relating to relief offer a notably clear look at conditions that were largely typical of the Midwest, and indeed most of the country outside of the big cities, in the middle to late ninteenth century. Some examples:

> *Douglas County (Omaha)*: The county poor farm consists of 160 acres of "the most fertile land in the vicinity and occupies perhaps the

finest site along the Missouri." Having a poor farm, instead of a poorhouse in the city, is considered a mark of progress. Before the farm, Douglas County paupers were limited in their accommodations to ill-furnished rooms in an "old and dilapidated shanty." The new facility, built in 1869, is a two-story brick building accommodating 40 persons. In 1882, there are 36 inmates, some of them insane. The annual appropriation of the county is $3,500, to which is added the proceeds of the farm.

Lancaster County (Lincoln): "Fortunately, the condition of Lancaster County is such that few need to be thrown upon public charity. She, however, has made the usual provisions, erecting a two-story frame building for a poor house, ten years ago. The poor farm of 240 acres and buildings upon it are situated five miles northwest of Lincoln on Oak Creek." As of 1882, there are 20 inmates at the poorhouse, as well as a few families receiving outdoor relief. The county population is 28,090.

Dodge County (Fremont): In 1882, only "seven or eight families" are permanently supported by the county, "which speaks well both for it and its people."

California

> California, land of wonders!
>   El Dorado of the earth!
> Like Minerva, 'mid the nations,
>   Full grown at thy birth.
>
> *Daily Alta California*
> San Francisco
> September 21, 1851

One year old in 1851, the state of California was already well along in establishing provisions for the poor. Other states and territories provided poor relief—at the *local* level. California began at the state level and, one year into statehood, had presaged the development of state direction of welfare a quarter-century later.

The impetus for poor relief was one and the same with the cause of California's early surge of growth—the gold rush. Hometown of the bonanza was San Francisco, whose population zoomed from perhaps 800 in 1849 to as many as 35,000 at the height of the rush a few years later. There were those who got rich, and countless more for whom luck ran the other way.

For many down-and-outers, the misery was often short-lived. The city had no public health measures to speak of and was generally filthy:

mud everywhere, rats, cholera. Sickness, instead of riches, had often been the find of prospectors in the field, where the damp, the long hours, and the absence of medical facilities conspired to make the worst of even a minor malady. The ill, so often also penniless, poured back into a city already rampant with illness. Many died in the streets; some hid themselves in bushes, awaiting the end. Interments at San Francisco's three cemeteries, many of them indigent burials, totaled nearly 6,000, or about one-sixth of the population, between 1850 and 1854.

The city sought some recourse for the indigent sick through arrangements with private infirmaries. The most notable one was operated by eight Sisters of Mercy; its contract with the city, however, was cancelled in 1857 for nonpayment, a situation resulting from the municipality's tangled finances. The sisters continued their own private ministrations.

Even before the city's short-lived agreement with the sisters, it was clear to many in authority that some broader public provision was needed for the ill who had no means to care for themselves. Thus, in 1851 there was established the State Marine Hospital at San Francisco, a state institution intended from the start as a refuge for the indigent sick. Legislation establishing the hospital thereby recognized the regional nature of the problem and the need for a solution transcending local resources.

The State Marine Hospital, using rented quarters in the former American Hotel, served its purpose well. During 1852, its first full year of operation, it admitted 2,283 patients, of whom only 51 paid. The most frequent reason for admission was intermittent fever, of which 538 cases were recorded. Other complaints typical of time and place included syphilis and gonorrhea, 60, and gunshot wounds, 23.

Publicly funded medical care was not to be unbounded, however. The hospital was in its third year when the legislature began questioning in earnest (a few members had from the start) the substantial outlay of public funds inherent in the project. State expenditures for the fiscal year ending June 30, 1852, were $925,695, making the appropriation for Marine Hospital better than one-tenth of the state budget. An omen came in the form of a decision by the State Assembly to postpone "indefinitely" a bill that would have allowed the poor to prosecute suits at no cost. More to the point was a report of the Assembly Committee on State Hospitals in April 1853, recommending flatly that the state get out of the hospital business and leave care of the medically needy to the counties. At this time there were now three state hospitals—facilities at Sacramento and Stockton in addition to State Marine—with aggregate admissions (1852) of 5,480. The committee's principal argument turned on those benefitted. The state hospitals, according to the committee, tended to serve only their immediate areas rather than the state as a whole. "For two years, . . ." said the report, the State has tested the operation of this system; and experience has taught us that with each year additional requirements and demands for funds on the Treasury have been created, without producing a corresponding benefit to our citizens. Each citizen contributes equally to the support of the Hospitals, but few actually receive benefits from them.

The committee's recommendation: a system of county hospitals operated with state aid. That notwithstanding, another committee, the Special Committee on the State Marine Hospital, argued on humanitarian grounds:

The great end of a charity like this—the care and healing of the sick—is completely achieved, and the Hospital should be regarded by the State, as it really is, one of the proudest monuments of the humanity and generosity of the citizens.

The hospital was saved, but two years later the legislature again raised the question of keeping its proud monument in the face of continually increasing costs. By now, the hospital had outstanding indebtedness of $83,707 against an annual budget of $115,000. Furthermore, for its quarters (the old American Hotel) the hospital was paying rent of $1,400 a month—due six months in advance by its lease—which the committee [on State Hospitals] discovered was $1,000 a month more than had been offered to other parties, leading the committee to recommend the "abolishment of the whole concern."

When a bill abolishing the hospital came before the Assembly in March 1855, there was no longer any argument to the contrary, and the bill passed 64-0. The State Marine Hospital was duly abolished, following the precedent of Sacramento and Stockton State hospitals, which had closed at the end of the 1854 fiscal year.

In time, however, the state's charitable impulse found a new channel: subsidization of private charity. In 1860 this totaled $23,000 and included the San Francisco Ladies Protection and Relief Society ($5,000), the San Francisco Sisters of Mercy ($5,000), the Roman Catholic Orphan Asylum of Los Angeles ($1,000), the San Francisco Orphan Asylum ($6,000), and the Roman Catholic Orphan Asylum of San Francisco ($6,000). There also came to be new areas of public concern, in particular, support of public schools ($84,956 in 1860) and maintenance of a state insane asylum, many of whose inmates were undoubtedly indigent ($84,436 in 1860). These various appropriations ($192,392, including $23,000 in aid to private charities) added up to very nearly as much ($210,307) as the state spent on State Marine, Sacramento, and Stockton hospitals in fiscal 1853, the last year before embarking significantly on

The almshouse was more often than not a cheerless place; and although conditions varied widely, it was "over the hill" even at its best. This was Richmond, Virginia's, as it appeared in the 1860s. Photograph from the Matthew Brady Collection.

support of public schools and an insane asylum. What the state thus saved on hospitals for the indigent, for what it perceived to be valid reasons, it turned and used elsewhere for other purposes perceived to be more appropriate for the expenditure of public funds.

By the 1870s poor relief in the United States was fixed in the form in which it would remain until the dramatic and fundamental changes of the twentieth century. It was characterized by a predisposition to indoor assistance—the almshouse—although the debate went on; by a sharpening interest in public works employment, through which the poor would work for what they received; by an increasing awareness of medical care as an appropriate channel of public concern for the poor; and by a vagrant problem more noticeable perhaps than at any time since Elizabethan England.

What follows is thus a more detailed view of the late nineteenth and early twentieth centuries through a closer look at: indoor versus outdoor relief; work relief; medical aid to the poor; vagrants, vagabonds, and tramps; and the almshouse.

INDOOR VERSUS OUTDOOR RELIEF

> The best method of caring for the poor has been the puzzle of centuries. The wisest thinkers have never developed it. The most experienced and practical workers have never agreed about it. When one thinks he has got it, it evades him like Proteus.
>
> Dr. Henry B. Wheelwright, of
> Newburyport, Massachusetts,
> at the National Conference
> of Charities, May 21, 1878

The great debate continued through the century. Was it better to spend public funds on the poor in the form of institutional care (the poorhouse, or indoor relief) or to assist the needy outside of the institution (outdoor relief, or relief administered at home).

Was it better for the poor? Was it better for the state?

It was a controversy that mirrored one in England earlier. There it had been chiefly over the so-called Speenhamland Act of 1795, which provided for a system of relief: (1) supplementing the wages of those who were employed but making less than needed for a basic standard of living; or (2) seeing to a man's employment, if jobless, by subsidizing his wages directly through an employer. The amount of subsidization was generally based on the price of bread and the number of children in the family.

For a generation, the Speenhamland system dominated the administration of poor relief in England, and yet, in all, it was a failure. Its flaw was not long in being discovered. If one were a prospective beneficiary, one could increase the size of his allowance by increasing the size of his family. If one were an employer, one could reduce wages to a starvation level (and thus increase profits), and let the government make up the difference. Wherever the allowance system was in effect, there was a tendency for it to be utilized to the maximum. Wages were lower, which meant increased spending for allowances, which in turn meant higher taxes, and these were passed on to the consumer in the form of higher prices, which reduced the value of the allowance.

Resentment grew. For this and related reasons, there came the Poor Law Amendment Act of 1834. The commissioners who drafted it declared the Speenhamland system to be a "great and fatal deviation from our previous policy. The 43rd Elizabeth never contemplated, as objects of relief, industrious persons. It made no promises of comfort and happiness."*

In the years prior to 1834 the cost of relief had risen dramatically. Between 1784 and 1818 alone the poor rate went up three times as fast as the population. The reform act of 1834 therefore made sweeping changes, notably in stifling outdoor relief and in reinstating the workhouse test (no relief unless received in the workhouse). A sequel in 1844 flatly forbade relief except in the workhouse, but nevertheless allowed for exceptions in case of sickness or bodily infirmity—exceptions that would perpetuate the cycle of controversy in England as also in the United States.

In Massachusetts the abolition of outdoor relief was considered but not carried out. The State Board of Charities in 1871 made a survey of municipalities. It found, on the basis of returns from 160 towns and cities, that there was a widespread concern about abuses of outdoor relief but a consensus that it could be kept under control. Indeed, suggested residents, it would work a hardship on the poor. According to the board's report,

> it was thought, that however great the disadvantages of out-door relief, it would be impracticable, oftentimes, particularly in the cities, to exclude it entirely. The almshouse, unless built of mammoth proportions, it was feared would not hold all the paupers.

Sometimes it was argued that rural areas rather than the city raised the strongest claim upon continuance of outdoor relief. "I do not think we can get along with either in-door or out-door relief alone, exclusive of the other," Henry W. Lord, of Michigan, told the 1878 Conference of Charities.

> For instance a fisherman is drowned, or a man is killed in a mine, and his family thrown into distress and want, and there is no poorhouse perhaps within 75 miles. In these cases relief must be afforded at once, and it must, from the nature of the circumstances, be outdoor relief.

---

*In moving the Poor Law Amendment Act in Parliament, the Lord Chancellor of England (Lord Brougham, generally recognized as an ardent supporter of liberal legislation and a champion of the poor) declared there was nothing more futile than "that in defiance of the ordinary law of nature, the human lawgiver should decree, that all poor men have a right to live comfortably, assuming to himself the power of making every one happy, at all times—in seasons of general weal or woe—and proclaiming with the solemnity of a Statute, 'Henceforth let human misery cease. . . .'"

Similarly, Thomas F. Ring, overseer of the poor in Boston, defending outdoor relief in the city at the 1881 Conference of Charities:

> I think it would be cruel in the extreme to abolish all out-door relief, because as an overseer of the poor in Boston, I have seen so many cases where a little judicious charity has kept the family together and has kept away the stigma of the almshouse; cases where a little help has retained mother and children under their own roof.

In some states at the time, outdoor relief was provided by law — Ohio, for example. In Wisconsin the state took care of those judged permanently poor (indoor relief), and the towns provided outdoor relief to those considered to be only temporarily in need. In the southern states outdoor relief existed only in the form of private charity.

Opposition to outdoor relief, meanwhile, was common. A frequent complaint was that it tended to perpetuate itself. Argued Professor Francis Wayland of Yale in 1877:

> Its direct and unavoidable tendency is to encourage the pernicious notion that the State is bound to support all who demand assistance; a notion which leads the recipient of relief administered in this way to accept it without gratitude and use it without discretion. The State represents to the professional pauper a vast, intangible body, which, somehow, owes him a living.

And, speaking in 1903 at a convention of the County Supervisors of Southeastern Iowa, W. W. Baldwin, president of the Charity Organization Society of Burlington, Iowa, lamented the equivalent of the "welfare cycle" that would be discovered, seemingly anew, later in the twentieth century. Said Baldwin: "Willingness to accept support from the pauper fund is largely an inherited inclination and runs in families."

Some criticism of outdoor relief had nothing to do with social policy. It was rather a manifestation of a lack of confidence in government. The late nineteenth century was a time of widespread corruption in public office. Opinion of government being low to begin with, opinion of anything administered by government was low — not least of all the administration of public assistance funds, which were ready-made for diversion to partisan purposes. Often expressed was the contention that outdoor relief should be restricted to private charity and thus be kept insulated from public corruption. Furthermore, it was argued that relief was accepted more sparingly when it was known to have come from private sources; or to put it another way, that a recipient, inclined to overstate his needs, was more likely to heed his conscience knowing that someone else had *given* him what he received rather than paid it in taxes.

In theory, outdoor relief had been generally abandoned early in the nineteenth century with the ascendancy of the almshouse. New York effectively abolished it with the reform act of 1824. Three years later, New York revived it on what was intended to be only a very limited basis: that is, in case of a person too sick or disabled to go to an almshouse. "Temporary," of course, meant different things to different people. And so, over the years, outdoor relief continued—and this was true, generally, throughout the country—leading Seth Low,* president of the Brooklyn Bureau of Charities, to conclude, in 1881, that "any poor person, disabled or not, has virtually a right to look for relief from the public poor master."

Although Ohio generally retained outdoor relief statewide, Cincinnati had abolished it by 1880 except for free medical care and the distribution of free coal during ten weeks of winter. The distribution was handled by six disbursers, who, at $600 a year each, were not underpaid for their services. Of the six, three were saloonkeepers and ward politicians, and this led the Rev. Charles W. Wendte of the Associated Charities of Cincinnati to puzzle over an anomaly: "Strange as it may seem, a man will thus ruin the father by selling him drinks, and at the same time help the mother and children with the city's relief."

Brooklyn in 1877—when it had 46,350 on outdoor relief and 1,071 in its almshouse—abolished outdoor aid. The following year, when the city gave out only free coal and nothing else in the way of outdoor assistance, Brooklyn's almshouse increased by only 35 inmates (out of a potential of 46,350 applicants) and the privately supported Society for Improving the Condition of the Poor had a net decrease of 1,079 (to a total of 21,458). In other words, reported Seth Low: Even though there had been "an improvement in the times," which had something to do with the results, it was clear Brooklyn didn't need outdoor relief. Philadelphia, in 1879, also abolished aid to the poor in their homes—likewise with no significant increase in the number of poor asking for almshouse support. Said Low, an outspoken opponent:

> The experience of Brooklyn and Philadelphia proves beyond controversy, that in those cities private benevolence is equal to the burden of such outdoor relief as may be actually needed. . . . An overseer of the poor in one of New York's smaller cities is reported to have said, "Outdoor relief is as catching as the small-pox." Not only so, it is almost as disastrous, certainly in the cities, to the families who catch it.

In Boston, where per capita expenditures for poor relief rose 57 per-

---

*Seth Low was later president of Columbia University and a reform mayor of New York City.

cent between 1866 and 1876, a Commission on the Treatment of the Poor came to the same conclusion as had been reached by officials in other cities: Abolish outdoor relief. Said the commission in an 1878 report:

> When the assistance, which ought to come from personal sympathy and be accompanied by friendly counsel, is distributed by officers of the law, the recipient soon learns to demand it as a right, gradually comes to rely upon it, without any sense of duty or obligation, and is dissatisfied both with what wisdom denies and goodness lends.

Boston, however, did not abolish outdoor relief—an exception among the major Eastern cities. During the last quarter of the nineteenth century, New York, Brooklyn, Philadelphia, Baltimore, and Washington, for example, all discontinued or virtually abolished assistance to the poor in their homes. The New York City charter of 1897 (incorporating Brooklyn as a borough) explicitly prohibited the use of public funds for outdoor relief, except to the adult blind. In 1903, out of a poor relief budget of $1.8 million, all but $50,000 went to almshouse relief.

WORK RELIEF

> It is not the purpose or object of the City Government to furnish work to the industrious poor. . . . We can't tear down the City Hall so as to furnish work for the unemployed.

Thus, in 1874, did Mayor William Havemeyer of New York give his opinion of work relief for the jobless. Yet public construction had long since found its place in the scheme of things. Indeed, we may recall that it had already found a place in the ancient world: under Pericles, the Parthenon; under Vespasian, the Colosseum.

In more recent times work relief had become a demand of the unemployed and met with varying degrees of acceptance on the part of the body politic. Economic stagnation caused by the embargo of 1807 resulted in a rally of unemployed sailors and others in New York. The call was for public action. The city responded with a three-point program that included work relief, in particular the leveling of Inclenberg Hill (Murray Hill), a project that did not materialize because of bad weather. Pennsylvania, in the wake of the depression of 1819-21, built $2 million worth of bridges and turnpikes.

Nevertheless, it was not until late in the century that public works projects became common, Mayor Havemeyer to the contrary. The tide was running against him. Two months before his unequivocal rejection of work for the poor, there was a mass meeting of some 800 working men representing various trades. The meeting resulted in a unanimous vote in favor of a series of resolutions that included demands: that the city council and city department heads, for the purpose of relieving "the necessities of the unemployed, place more work on the market"; that "the Controller approve of the contracts for public improvements now in his hands"; and that the city ask the federal government for a loan of $10 million "for the purpose of labor." Furthermore, to quote an account that appeared next day in the New York *Times* (November 16, 1873):

> Mr. Thompson, of the Working Men's Association, made an address, in which he demanded temporary employment for the working classes during the Winter, and perpetual employment in the future; and if this were refused, "there will be a revolution." [Cheers] They did not ask for soup-kitchens. Such charities are degrading to their manhood. [Cheers] Mr. Robert Crowe, of the tailors, said that citizenship was a farce, except they could demand work. He called upon the City authorities to construct an underground railroad, from the battery to Harlem, and asked that Comptroller Green should join Mr. Van Nort in accepting proposals for opening streets, grading, paving &c. He feared, however, that such work will not be done until the politicians find the working men's votes missing from the ballot-box.

A minor concession was made by the New York City board of aldermen in December 1874. The board directed that, when buying stone for macadam, preference be given to stone broken with hand labor rather than steam power, provided the quality was equal and the price competitive.

The depression of 1893–97 represented the first extensive use of work relief and public works employment. ("Work relief" may be considered more ad hoc in nature, smaller in scale, nearer to the subsistence level in pay, and more suitable for the unskilled; "public works," the contrary; but the distinction has often been blurred and the terms frequently interchanged.) The city of New York in 1894 embarked on a $1 million public works program that put to work 2,000 of the city's jobless. In 1895, two-thirds of the cities of Massachusetts and one-third of its larger towns undertook public works projects. About the same time, other cities large and small throughout the country turned to public works and work relief—among them Detroit, Dayton, St. Louis, Chattanooga, Burlington, and Helena.

Yet advocacy of public employment, even at the end of the century, was by no means universal. On the one hand, it could be argued that work relief served a useful civic purpose over and above the relief of individual hardship, while at the same time possessing the virtue of making the man relieved work for what he got. It was thus seen as separating the truly needy from the deliberately idle. Furthermore, there was this value: Public works could be stepped up in times of unemployment and cut back in more prosperous times. Economist John B. Andrews, in *American Labor Legislation Review*, June 1915, characterized public employment as a "sponge" that sopped up workers in the slack season and loosed them as jobs became plentiful in the private sector.

On the other hand, some argued that public employment was only an artificial remedy. The New York Association for Improving the Condition of the Poor, in its annual report for 1875, contended: "As well might it be affirmed, that the water in our Croton [Reservoir] would be increased by multiplying the drafts upon it." The New York State Commission on Employers' Liability and Other Matters, in its *Third Report on Unemployment* (1911), declared flatly:

> In periods of great emergency such provision is often necessary, but all experience seems to show that its administration is fraught with great difficulties and the relief it affords is paid for in wide-spread demoralization.

During the winter of 1914–15, nearly 100 U.S. cities carried out emergency public works programs: digging sewers, laying water mains, improving roads, building schools, repairing public buildings. Idaho, in 1915, passed legislation establishing for every resident (provided a residency of six months or more) a right to 90 days of public employment a year, at 90 percent of his usual wage if he had dependents and 75 percent otherwise. The law was repealed in January 1919.

By 1919 public works relief had clearly become widespread public policy. The U.S. Department of Labor encouraged it, sending telegrams to all governors inquiring what they planned to do in the way of public construction during the period of demobilization. Were that too subtle a message, each telegram ended tersely: "We are withholding the mailing of important papers pending your reply."

In actuality, not a great deal of encouragement was needed from the federal government. State and local public works were increasing on their own in the postwar period, in part because they were needed and in part because work had been deferred during the war years. In 1921, another depression year, many cities set new records for public works spending. Pipes were going under, drains down, roads across, schools up — all over the country. In the last quarter alone, the sale of public bonds totaled $560 million. The federal government, which had so far limited itself to exhortations to state and local governments, in the autumn of 1921 took direct action on unemployment when Congress passed a special $75 million appropriation to aid the states in construction of roads. It was the only such appropriation prior to 1932.

Meanwhile, there came an increasing degree of federal involvement with creation of the U.S. Employment Stabilization Board under Hoover in 1931. It was the board's job to use the sponge, planning ahead so far as possible to keep public improvements "under such control as may enable speeding-up of such expenditures during periods of dull business, and slowing down during prosperity, in order that a reserve of employment may be built up."

Before there would be such prosperity as to allow for a slow-down, there was only more massive public expenditure. Under Roosevelt there were launched the largest public works efforts ever undertaken by government to that time. In 1933 alone, the federal government appropriated $3.3 billion for public works.

MEDICAL AID TO THE POOR

Medical care of the poor in the nineteenth and early twentieth centuries was surprisingly broad in scope in some of the major cities and hardly distinguishable from colonial times elsewhere.

As an example of the latter, there is an item from the New York *Evening Post,* February 11, 1824:

> *Cow Pox*—The Physicians of New Haven, greatly to their credit, have taken on themselves the task of visiting every home in the place, for the purpose of performing a thorough vaccination. The poor are attended for nothing.

Care of the poor gratis, it may be recalled, was a frequent occurrence in the colonial period (as well as in later times) although in other cases the community paid a physician for caring for a resident too poor to get medical attention on his own. It was generally on a case-by-case basis and, with certain exceptions (for example, the woman in New York's poorhouse in 1762, whose child was delivered by Dr. John Bard, the society doctor), such provisions were notably modest.

Considerably more extensive was the care of the medically indigent in many of the major cities. At the 1877 Conference of Charities there was a report on medical relief in New York City by Theodore Roosevelt, philanthropist, father of the president, and then a member of the New York State Board of Charities and vice president of the New York State Charities Aid Association. Roosevelt reported that there were then between 30 and 35 percent of the population of the city receiving free medical care; and furthermore, 80 percent of these—one of every four persons in the city—were people able to pay and yet receiving such care as charity. Roosevelt quoted a New York *Tribune* article (April 13, 1877) that reported this dialogue at a meeting of the New York Public Health Association:

"Our five dispensaries and medical hospitals are shamefully imposed upon. Applicants for relief and medicines are, in a majority of cases, far from being objects of charity, but in order to save a few dollars, they pretend to be paupers," said Dr. Ward. "Yes, that is a fact," said a physician attached to a free dispensary. "It was only yesterday that a fashionably dressed man, who gave his occupation as a broker, called at our institution for treatment, explaining that times were dull on Wall Street, and that he thought it well to economize in the way of a doctor's bill."

Added Roosevelt, of his own observing:

On the slightest pretext, malingerers seek entrance to some hospital, and, having obtained it, spend their time in passing from one to another, and when convalescent, have become so demoralized by their long life of idleness that they do not willingly return to their former habits of self-supporting industry.

As for these facilities—which is to say, indoor relief—there were, at the time, three in particular in the city: Bellevue Hospital, the first public hospital in New York, established in 1735 as an infirmary for the almshouse, and a separate institution as of 1825; New York Hospital, a semipublic facility operated with a public subsidy, which was opened in 1791 and intended mainly for the sick poor but also open to others; and New York Dispensary, a private, nonprofit facility established in 1790, which cared for the sick poor not taken in by the almshouse or New York Hospital. There were also smaller dispensaries operated with private funds. Outdoor relief, according to Roosevelt, included housing, food, fuel, and medicine, paid for by public or private funds. Medical and surgical attendance was contributed by the physicians free of charge.

It appears the poor—and a good many of means—made liberal use of the free medical care furnished by New York at this time. At the same Conference of Charities, another New York delegate, Charles Barnard, complained:

It is a common impression among a large class of people in New York that dispensaries are, like the fire department, a city institution, supported by the tax-payers, and that any one may demand medical aid, precisely as he would call the firemen in case of need.

Barnard cited a survey, by a committee of the New York Society for Improving the Condition of the Poor, covering 152 persons who had received free medical care. The survey disclosed that:

- 82 turned out to be earning between $3 and $20 a week, at a time when $7.79 was the average for New York State trade and manufacturing jobs (1870 Census);
- 58 had given wrong addresses ("it is thought," said the committee, "the majority desired to deceive, wishing to get help for which they were able and unwilling to pay");
- 12 were without means, and entitled to the free care they had received.

Chicago, at this time, offered primarily institutional care. The city had 11 dispensaries, all funded at least in part by public appropriations, which provided free medical care to the indigent. In addition, in the one ward in which there was no dispensary, there was a public doctor to visit the poor in their homes. The city itself maintained only one medical charity, the city smallpox hospital, which, in reality, was nothing more than a pest house. The principal public facility was Cook County Hospital, established in 1865, which served both city and county. It was under the control of the Board of County Commissioners, a prototypal Cook County institution that had a reputation for sparing nothing on contracts and everything on administration. Fifteen years after the hospital's inception, according to Dr. Roswell Park, it was a vast facility on ten acres of land that still could accommodate only 250 patients and was notable for a medical board of publicly appointed members who had got there by some "disgraceful wire-pulling." (Dr. Park was a distinguished local physician who later was president of the American Surgical Association and one of the doctors attending President McKinley in Buffalo in 1901.)

In Massachusetts, according to Dr. Henry B. Wheelwright, of Newburyport, speaking at the 1878 Conference of Charities, state and towns together were supporting 4,100 sick paupers — 16,000 to 20,000 persons in terms of families — most of them in their own homes. For the period of twelve and a half years ending December 31, 1877, the state relieved 26,690 indigent sick at a joint state-town cost of $458,000. With dependents included, this represented some 100,000 persons, or one in every 15 of Massachusetts' 1870 population of 1,457,351. The Massachusetts system made use of doctors paid by the public; and it was not uncommon, said Wheelwright, to find the doctor "who doses from habit, the more energetically as he catches a glimpse of the town treasury."

For a look at Cincinnati at this same time, there is a contemporary report by Dr. William H. Taylor, later dean of the faculty at Miami Medical College and the first president of the American Association of Obstetricians and Gynecologists. Cincinnati maintained a public hospital, an infirmary, and an insane asylum, financed by a municipal tax. There were also private hospitals and four dispensaries operating with private funds. The city's medical mainstay for the poor, however, was its remarkably comprehensive outdoor program providing for the relief of sick indigents in their homes. Each ward had a district physician who was paid by the city and who served under the supervision of the board of police commissioners. Any impoverished citizen was entitled to call upon the services of the district physician and be treated, at home, free of charge. Pharmacists were also designated by ward to dispense medicine and surgical appliances at no cost.

In 1877 there were 4,464 patients treated under the Cincinnati program, in the course of which physicians made 22,961 visits. The cost, including physicians' salaries, medicine, and surgical appliances was $11,137. Besides this program the city had Cincinnati Hospital, established in 1822, for those who could not be treated at home. Its charity patients in 1877 numbered 3,954. The city infirmary, meanwhile, cared for the chronically ill, who averaged 559 daily in 1877. How many of these were charity cases is not clear. Overall, including those in city institutions, Cincinnati at this time was providing publicly funded medical help to 10,000 persons a year, or one in every 30. Medical charity in the aggregate, including that from private sources, went to 20,000, or one in 15.

Cincinnati's comprehensive program had one problem according to Dr. Taylor: "a liability to extravagance in the use of medicines"; otherwise, it seems to have worked well. The district physicians were usually junior members of the profession interested in both the wide experience and the reputation for community service inherent in the position. They also served as district sanitary inspectors.

VAGRANTS, VAGABONDS, AND TRAMPS

>"Pointer Frank, 9-19-88, B.S."
>"No. Fatty."
>"Ole Kid, left E.H.S. 3-11-89."

The American vagabond of the late nineteenth and early twentieth centuries was a reincarnation of his colorful sixteenth-century predecessor: a cut from the same rag that wrapped the ruffler, prigger of prancers, tinker, and doxie of earlier times. He even had his own updated cant, which, reflecting the supposed advance of civilization, had now become a written language — at least on fence posts and the like. Thus to be found one day in 1890 on a fence at a small railroad station in Oregon were the inscriptions quoted above, which may be deciphered as:

>"Pointer Frank. September 19, 1888. Bound south."
>"Fatty, northbound."
>"Ole Kid. Left all right. Headed south. March 11, 1889."

immorality has become reprehensible to the community at large." Such definitions, of course, easily pass the test of credibility.

While there was little or no difference as to population or function from one such institution to another, there was as to name. One and the same, basically, were all of the following: almshouse (the name by which it was most frequently known in New England and some of the Eastern states); poorhouse (more common in the Middle West); county infirmary (the legal name at one time in Ohio); county asylum (legal name in Indiana once); county home (Maryland); county hospital (California); county farm (New Hampshire); home for the aged and infirm (Washington, D.C.); city home (Richmond); and workhouse (here and there). Whatever its name, its reputation was the same; and generations grew up (as the expression had it) with "a reverence for God, the hope of heaven, and the fear of the poorhouse."

The first real poorhouse (it was called a workhouse, which was its intended function) was in Bristol, England, and was established in 1697 by act of Parliament. The poorhouse, or almshouse, came to America during the colonial era but found sparing use until the nineteenth century, the Age of the Almshouse.

Not all almshouses were bad. E. S. Abdy, a fellow of Jesus College, Cambridge, visiting the United States in 1833 and 1834, found a good one in Providence: the Dexter Asylum, which was established by private philanthropy and then turned over to the town council for operation. Abdy recorded these observations:

> The buildings were completed in 1828; and the average number of poor in the establishment is 100 of both sexes; the female being rather more numerous. The superintendent took me over the house, and shewed me the rooms, which were clean and in good order; the kitchen being well-furnished with an excellent range and other apparatus for cooking. . . . [The superintendent] was very civil in answering my queries, and remarkably clear-headed and sensible in his opinions on the subject of pauperism. The comforts to be found there, he said, were often superior to what a hard-working mechanic could obtain in his own house.

The same standard was deemed to have been met at the Sanilac, Michigan, poorhouse. According to a state report published in 1873 (State of Michigan, *Abstract of Annual Reports of County Superintendents of the Poor*, 1873):

> The food is prepared in the ordinary way, as farmers generally do, over a cook stove; three meals a day, consisting of wheat and corn bread, potatoes, pork, beef, mutton, butter, milk, tea, coffee, sugar, apples, vegetables, etc., and occasionally cakes and pies; we intend they shall live equal with the common farmer.

put me on the town." So fared the subject of Will Carleton's 1873 poem about the poorhouse. Less well recalled is a sequel, in which a no-good horse-thief son, just out of jail, narrates how

> One blowin', blusterin' winter's day,
> With a team an' cutter I started away;
> My fiery nags was as black as coal;
> (They some'at resembled the horse I stole);
> I hitched, an' I entered the poor-house door—
> A poor old woman was scrubbin' the floor;
> She rose to her feet in great surprise,
> And looked, quite startled, into my eyes;
> I saw the whole of her trouble's trace
> In the lines that marred her dear old face;
> "Mother!" I shouted, "your sorrows is done!
> You're adopted along o' your horse-thief son,
>   Come *over the hill from the poor-house!*"

They came, and they went. Almshouse population, in fact, fluctuated widely. In winter it was a refuge for vagrants, in other seasons for the temporary down-and-out. For many, however, the trip "over the hill" was one-way, and the melodramatic sequels were few, if not entirely in the poet's imagination.

To those for whom it was a last refuge, and a permanent one, the almshouse was far more often than not a dismal last stop on life's journey. It was generally a cheerless place, a receptacle into which might be dumped all the luckless of all ages, of both sexes, of decent health and ill, of reasonable sanity and certified madness, whose common bond was inability or unwillingness to care for themselves. In short, the almshouse was an ironic twist of a definition of home by a later and greater poet: "a place where, when you have to go there, they have to take you in."

Robert Frost was talking about another kind—the home with the "lamp-flame at the table"—and yet it is a definition that works equally well for the poorhouse. Among those who, when they went there, had to be taken in, were the "insane, feeble-minded, and epileptics; blind and deaf mutes; sufferers from chronic diseases; persons with criminal records; prostitutes; mothers of illegitimate children; orphans and deserted children." So reported the Pennsylvania Commission on Old-Age Pensions on conditions in the state's almshouses in the early twentieth century.

The Virginia State Board of Charities supplied this official description: "a catchall for the dregs of society, where anything may go and live in comparative idleness." And the New Hampshire Board of Charities: " . . . the habitation of the tramp when he is no longer disposed to travel; the drunkard when he can no longer keep the peace; the thief when his crime is not startling enough to demand iron bars; and the person whose night lodging provided the vagrant, next morning, work until 11 A.M. breaking stone. The city averaged five guests a night. Less than 30 miles away was Hartford, which provided no-work, no-strings-attached free lodging in police headquarters. Hartford averaged more than 100 guests a night.

In New York, shortly after the turn of the century, a charity organization surveyed nearly 2,000 beggars and concluded the chances were two-to-one that a begging man, taking up his street corner post, already had money in his pockets.

Speaking at the 1909 meeting of the New York State Association of County Superintendents of the Poor, Onondaga County (Syracuse) Superintendent H. D. Nottingham echoed the familiar: "Indiscriminate giving, free lodging houses and bread lines promote instead of prevent pauperism and vagrancy." In apparent evidence, he cited this: In New York, during the winter of 1905–06, some 27,000 beggars standing on Bowery bread lines were offered jobs; 307 of them accepted.

Some impact, however, did industrial society have on vagabondage, as further reported by Nottingham at the 1909 conference: As to "the army of tramps who are roaming through the country . . . the only agency that has reduced the number, so far as we know, is the railroad train." According to the Interstate Commerce Commission, there were, at the time, 5,000 persons killed annually on the nation's railways, of whom three-fourths were trespassers, or in other words, vagrants.

THE ALMSHOUSE

> Over the hill to the poor-house —
> I can't quite make it clear!
> Over the hill to the poor-house —
> It seems so horrid queer!
> Many a step I've taken
> A-toilin' to and fro,
> But this is a sort of journey
> I never thought to go.
>
> What is the use of heapin'
> On me a pauper's shame?
> Am I lazy or crazy?
> Am I blind or lame?
> True, I am not so supple,
> Nor yet so awful stout;
> But charity ain't no favor,
> If one can live without.

She was seventy, a widow, the victim of an uncaring family, and unable to make do for herself, thus turning "to the poor-master, an' [he]

Likewise to be found was a reincarnation of the "counterfeit cranke" ("his face from the eyes downward all smerd with fresh bloud, as though he had new fallen") portrayed in 1566 by Thomas Harman. The latter-day equivalent was pictured by the secretary of the City Board of Charities of Portland, Oregon, in 1890:

> In one instance, a strong, healthy young man was found piteously appealing for aid because of having his arm amputated at the shoulder. His efforts were crowned with success until a hasty investigation revealed the fact that his "lost" arm was carried close to his body and beneath his clothing. In another case, a man hobbled from door to door with crutches, on the plea that both legs had been broken, an ankle crushed, and his spine seriously affected by a fall less than six weeks before. An investigation by a competent physician established the fact that such was not the case; but that there was nothing except laziness to prevent him from doing a good day's work.

In fact, beggary once again seems to have paid well. Harman's crank earned fourteen shillings a day, at a time when an honest laborer counted six pence a good day's earnings. His modern counterpart likewise did well enough. The secretary of the Portland Board of Charities observed that professional tramps were making $3 a day with no trouble at all, and the better ones sometimes netted $10 a day. In New York, even the lowliest of beggars ("the worst kind of drunkard") was reported in 1909 to be taking in anywhere from $14 to $21 a week. The average wage of a common laborer was little more than $10 a week.

Itinerant beggars had been a particular problem in the post-Civil War era. "We were accustomed during the war," said Sinclair Tousey, of the New York Prison Association in 1877,

> to have a song about certain armies marching "three hundred thousand strong"; the same might be said with regard to the tramps of the present day, and the question how to dispose of them, is one of prime importance. The opinion seems to be general, that the tramp will not work, if he can live without it.

The tramp would not work if he could survive by begging. Unlike city beggars, the itinerant postwar beggars went door-to-door knocking, intimidating the frightened householder into a handout. The lone housewife in a remote farm cottage was the favored target. Women in rural Massachusetts who theretofore thought nothing of traveling alone several miles at night to a church function now said they would no longer go more than a quarter mile without an escort. A Massachusetts law of the 1870s attempted to minimize the vagrant problem by permitting each town to give temporary relief as it saw fit. Springfield provided free over-

This matter of equality between the beneficiary of public relief and the worker whose taxes pay the cost of that relief is, of course, a vexing one. It was troublesome in ancient Rome, as Seneca took notice when he observed in *De Beneficiis* that what the gods bestow they bestow on all alike, and that when it rains it waters the fields of good and bad alike. It was troublesome in England and central to the monumental Poor Law Amendment Act of 1834. It is here met again, through the observing eye of the traveler Abdy, sharpened by the insight of the superintendent himself at the poorhouse in Providence in 1833:

> Almost all, who were under his care, had fallen into distress through their own imprudence, and chiefly from habits of intemperance. When misfortune comes unexpectedly and undeservedly on the industrious and prudent, the charitable sympathy of neighbors usually supplies a sufficient fund for its relief: any permanent provision for poverty deadens these feelings, relaxes the efforts of the indigent to recover or retain their station in life, and merges the wish to secure assistance, by conciliating respect, in the expectation of partaking, whatever may happen, of the relief which imprudent generosity holds out to good and bad alike. Such being the result of experience everywhere, he thought the tendency inherent in such institutions, as that under his care, to produce the very evil they profess to remove, ought to be checked.

The superintendent need not have been concerned. His own institution was hardly like most, and those that were typical of the majority offered nothing to claim affection. Two examples will illustrate this point. First, the almshouse at Danvers, Massachusetts, 1843, as described by Dorothea Dix in *A Memorial to the Legislature of Massachusetts*:

> There she [a young women, insane] stood clinging to, or beating upon, the bars of her caged apartment, the contracted size of which afforded space only for increasing accumulations of filth, a foul spectacle; there she stood with naked arms and dishevelled hair. . . . Irritation of body, produced by utter filth and exposure, incited her to the horrid process of tearing off her skin by inches; her face, neck and person were thus disfigured to hideousness; she held up a fragment just rent off her; to my exclamation of horror.

And the Cook County, Illinois, almshouse, as depicted in *Atlantic Monthly*, August 1881:

> The almshouse proper we found in an infinitely worse condition than the insane department. It contains, probably, more rats, roaches, and other small freebooters than any almshouse in the North, except that on Ward's Island, near New York city. The rooms we entered were untidy, crowded, and heated to suffocation. In the

working-women's ward some children were running about among the women. The women themselves had no visible occupation; their hair was rough, their faces were unwashed, their gowns soiled and torn, and their whole appearance was as forlornly dingy as their environment. One does not marvel, though, when he learns that, owing to the difficulty in getting water, they dispense with baths through the winter. The atmosphere and sights of this room were so horrible that one of our party became faint, and had to go out in the open air, while we all cut our stay short from sheer inability to breathe without nausea.

"This system having been established," concluded *Atlantic Monthly* in a study of indoor pauperism, "it rests entirely with the American people to decide how long they will permit the costly disgrace of its existence."

From time to time the American people did express outrage, with the result that government — from town council to state legislature — investigated, took testimony, listened, debated, deliberated, and occasionally made patchwork reforms. One of the most infamous of all almshouses was the state institution at Tewksbury, Massachusetts. The legislature's Joint Standing Committee on Public Charitable Institutions in 1883 held 65 separate hearings between March and July, compiling 3,066 printed pages of testimony. One sample is sufficient. It is the testimony of Mary Eva Bowen, 24, a syphilitic, who bore her first child at the age of 16 in the Tewksbury almshouse.

Q. Did you see any rats?

A. Oh, yes, sir; rats were walking all over the floor.

Q. How were they at night?

A. At night, in the room I was in, which was directly opposite the bathing-room where the two bath-tubs were; in there were some pipes and large holes in the wall where the rats used to come out. At nights they used to close the door because the rats would come out and walk into the room I was in, walk down the steps to the long ward. Then in the long ward there was a bath-room, and the rats would come out there and get on to the beds and annoy the patients.

Q. Was there any case where any of the patients were eaten by rats.

A. There was one woman we had there that had consumption, so they said, so that she was in such a weak condition that she could not raise her hand to her mouth, even, to take her medicine; she could not take her food without helping, and could not raise herself up in bed. And the rats used to eat her feet; and I have seen her feet — one of the nurses showed me her feet when she was alive. They were all eaten, and parts of the toes were gone.

The public hearings confirmed the worst about the notorious Tewksbury almshouse, along with something else that had only been suspected: It was helping many of Boston's lowliest poor go to college, and in particular to Harvard—posthumously. Investigators uncovered a "death book" in which was kept a record of those dying at Tewksbury. Beside certain names there appeared an "H" or a "B," the former being the more common. "H," it was determined, meant Harvard Medical School, and "B," Boston University. Evidence and testimony brought out the fact that the almshouse was doing a brisk business in bodies for dissection. A former Harvard medical student testified to paying $2 toward a dead child. He and four others also jointly paid $10 for the body of an infant, little more than a year old. To public outrage over such a revelation, Governor Benjamin Franklin Butler added his own wry observation: "Ashes to ashes; ashes to the dissecting knife."

A lesser form of corruption was the use of the almshouse as entertainment. In that age before television and movies, there were fewer forms of ready-made diversion across the byways of the land, and the almshouse, with its diversity of human stowage, sane and otherwise, acquired some measure of popularity as a place of amusement. That it was so, we have the word of philanthropist William P. Letchworth, then president of the New York State Board of Charities, addressing the State Convention of Superintendents of the Poor in Buffalo in 1885:

> The visits of young men with their girls, who, while taking a pleasure drive, call at the poorhouse with the same motive that would take them to a menagerie, and who expect their horses to be stabled while the keeper's wife or some busy employee shows the party through the establishment—such visits, so far from being beneficial, are positively harmful.

There was always talk of reform. In 1911 Alexander Johnson, general secretary of the National Conference of Charities and Corrections, talked hopefully about making the almshouse "into a real home for worthy poor people." An inspector for the New York State Board of Charities, Gertrude Hall, in 1912 told the state's Association of County Superintendents of the Poor that the answer to the almshouse lay not in abolishing it but in perfecting it. She suggested:

> Let all those who dwell in a certain community pay an added tax in order to maintain a home to which any one of them can go, if the time comes when he is too sick, or aged, or forsaken to care for

himself. . . . There is nothing shameful about this proposition, any more than life insurance is shameful.

And yet well into the twentieth century state agencies themselves were admitting to descriptions like these: The Connecticut Department of Public Welfare (*Report for 1921-22*), regarding one particular almshouse:

> The house is an old wooden structure of good size, but did not appear to have been kept in very good condition. The water pipes for the bathroom, which was situated on the second floor, froze a few years ago and were cut off, so that this feature of the house is practically useless.

And the South Carolina State Board of Public Welfare (*Fourth Annual Report*, 1923):

> With few exceptions, homes for the poor in South Carolina are unpainted, dilapidated shacks. The food and clothing provided for the inmates are in keeping with their surroundings. Sanitary facilities are primitive and ill kept, and conveniences are almost unheard of. . . . Institutions of this kind are a detriment to the body politic.

Nor had much changed with regard to almshouse population. In 1910 the U.S. Census Bureau found that there were more people admitted during the year than there were inmates at the start, leading it to conclude:

> The paupers in almshouses are an unstable, rapidly shifting, group; as a matter of fact many of them are not paupers at all in the generally accepted sense of the word "pauperism," which usually implies a permanent condition of indigence as contrasted with "poverty," which may be temporary.

As for the continued relegation to the almshouse of the insane, Alexander Johnson, in his book *The Almshouse* (1911), observed:

> While as a general proposition it is quite true that feeble-minded, epileptic and insane persons ought to be in specialized, and preferably in state institutions, there yet are very few almshouses that do not contain some members of these classes. In some places, indeed, they form the majority of the inmates.

Still around also, despite age-old regulations against taking in itinerants, were the tramps and vagrants who came knocking on the poorhouse door with the first howl of the winter wind. In 1833 a committee of the Massachusetts legislature had complained, "Almshouses are their inns, at which they stop for refreshment." In 1925 the U.S. Bureau of Labor Statistics (*The Cost of American Almshouses*, Bulletin No. 386) quoted an unidentified almshouse matron as conceding: "When they come in out of a cold, blowy snow, or when it is way below zero, and ask you for a night's lodging, what are you going to do about it, rules or no rules?"

By the then most recent count of the Bureau of Labor Statistics (November 1923-November 1924) there were at that time 2,183 almshouses in the United States, with a total population placed at 85,889. The net cost of these institutions was $28,740,535, of which $25,662,954 came from public funds and the balance from other sources, principally the sale of produce at poor farms.

There had also been a special census of almshouses by the U.S. Census Bureau in 1923, that being one of a series begun in 1904. Prior to that time, such information as this was collected as part of the regular decennial census. The 1910 special census of almshouses showed about the same population as would be found in 1924 but a greater number of facilities. The bureau reported that in 1910 it counted 84,198 inmates (2,370 of them age 14 and under) residing in 2,419 poorhouses (ranging in size from New York City's Home for the Aged on Blackwells Island, 2,739 inmates, to the Keith County Poor Farm in Ogallala, Nebraska, 1 inmate). The 1904 report accounted for 81,764 inmates at 2,476 institutions.

These few statistics suggest a pattern of declining almshouse population against a sharp increase in the general population. And indeed, such a conclusion is borne out by going further back, using decennial census records:

Almshouse Population — The United States

Year	Number	Per 100,000 Population
1880	66,203	132.0
1890	73,044	116.6
1904	81,764	100.0
1910	84,198	91.5
1923	78,090	71.5

Source: U.S. Census Bureau.

Clearly there was a decline. Was the end of the almshouse era at hand? The answer in retrospect is yes, and yet it was hardly a certainty at the time. In 1925 there were almshouses in all states except New Mexico. In 40 states they were operated by county government; in the rest, by municipal or state government. With its use still relatively widespread, the end of the almshouse would have been difficult to foresee with certainty.

On the other hand, not a great many people cared one way or the other. A substantial number of almshouses were scarcely visible as such. Leasing arrangements existed in all states except seven. Thus a contractor, using some old farmhouse or other suitable structure, might maintain a poorhouse for a public agency. Such a facility was often hardly recognized for its purpose by the public. Except for those in the large cities, the almshouses of the early twentieth century were small facilities, generally of fewer than 100 inmates.

Was the almshouse era ending? It was a matter of one's perspective. Some thought it had already ended — surely a great many, if one accepts an account by the U.S. Bureau of Labor Statistics of a young social worker appointed state inspector of public institutions in a large Eastern state in 1925. He was surprised when he found out that his inspections would include almshouses. He hadn't supposed, he said, "there were any poorhouses any more, except in the movies."

Three years later the almshouse was the subject of a plank in the platform of a candidate proposing "a drastic revision" of things. He made it clear in a speech in Rochester, N.Y., on October 22, 1928: "I think one of the most oppressing things I have to do on occasion in this State is to visit the County Poorhouse. . . . We need a drastic revision of the poor laws, and I propose to recommend it." The candidate — for Governor of New York — was Franklin D. Roosevelt.

5

A PLUNGE INTO THE WAVES
The Federal Government Becomes a Relief Agency

The primacy of federal responsibility for social welfare was more than a century developing—largely in the halls of Congress. Above, from the Illustrated News, *January 1, 1853: the U.S. House of Representatives as it appeared then. President Pierce, in 1854, vetoed a federal subsidy for the indigent on grounds that he could "not find any authority in the Constitution for making the Federal Government the great almoner of public charity throughout the United States." In times to come, in the same Constitution, sufficient authority for federal responsibility was readily found.*

Thus far, relief of the poor in the United States has unfolded as a function of state and local government, and primarily of the latter. Basically, that will remain so until the New Deal, when federal involvement in the welfare of its citizens will establish itself as preeminent. That involvement, however, will show itself to be not so much a new concept of the role of the federal government as an intensification of a role that had been developing for more than a hundred years. To begin, that century or so earlier . . .

It was shortly before nine in the morning—a frigid and blustery morning in January—that the first tongue of flame thrust its way through the roof of a cabinetmaker's shop in Alexandria, Virginia. Another flash followed, feeding on the shop's store of wood and varnish, and soon the building was lit up like a torch. A brisk northwest wind fanned the flames until an adjoining home was likewise ablaze, and then another. Soon an entire block of Royal Street was an inferno. And then another block.

Alexandria firemen, hopelessly outnumbered, put out an urgent call for help. Responding from nearby Washington was a contingent of marines from the U.S. Navy Yard and a fire engine from Capitol Hill. High winds and freezing weather, meanwhile, sided with the conflagration, and by nightfall the most populous and flourishing part of Alexandria lay a smoldering ruin. Forty families faced this night of January 18, 1827, homeless and, in a great many cases, now penniless for want of insurance.

It was for this emergency the federal government first gave relief to the needy, appropriating $20,000 for (quoting the act) "the indigent sufferers" of Alexandria.*

---

*In several cases prior to this, Congress had appropriated funds for relief of needy foreign citizens, but clearly as an aspect of foreign policy. As for domestic relief prior to 1824, there were various acts of Congress that show a predisposition to help the needy but they require no more than a footnote since the recipients were not necessarily indigent. Congress on a number of occasions postponed or suspended duties on goods or merchandise destroyed by fire. The first such was in 1790. Another early form of assistance was relief of survivors of military officers killed in duty, as well as pensions for disabled veterans. The first of these also was in 1790. By an Act for the Relief of Sick and Disabled Seamen of 1798, the government began construction of marine hospitals (the first being in Norfolk in 1800). These are to be distinguished from the State Marine Hospital at San Francisco in that they were not for the public (except during epidemics), and were financed not by public funds but by a tax of 20 cents a month on seamen employed on U.S. vessels. An interesting though different form of assistance was provided by a private act of 1819 by which a township of U.S. land was given to the Connecticut Asylum for the Deaf and Dumb, apparently as a form of subsidy.

Alexandria's was by no means the worst fire in the young nation's history. Boston had some bad ones in 1818 and 1825, the latter destroying an estimated $2 million in property; and Savannah, in 1820, was devastated by what was probably the worst U.S. fire to that time: 463 buildings leveled in eight hours. Indeed, on the day before the Alexandria fire there was a serious one in Cincinnati.

Severity was therefore not the deciding factor. What prevailed on Congress to set a precedent for federal funding of relief was the immediacy of the human tragedy. This disaster could be seen. From the windows on the south side of the Capitol there was a clear view across the wide expanse of the Potomac. The smoke in Alexandria, six miles away, was clearly visible. The extent of the disaster was obvious. The House had been debating a bill imposing a duty on woolens, but the knowledge, and indeed the sight, of what was happening so close at hand, gnawed. It became increasingly difficult to talk about wool. Pennsylvania's Rep. Charles Miner impulsively introduced a joint resolution. It would give, as quickly as possible, $20,000 from the federal treasury to provide shelter, clothing, and other necessities for the fire victims of Alexandria. But not for all of them—for "the indigent sufferers," the bill stipulated.*

The House gave the bill first reading immediately—as much as it could do for the moment—and then, its heart no longer in wool duties, adjourned. Next day, the House passed Miner's resolution 109 to 67 and sent it to the Senate, which, two sessions later, gave its approval 27 to 17. On Wednesday, January 24, 1827, less than a week after the fire, President John Quincy Adams signed relief into federal law for the first time.

It had not been unanimous. Those who supported the measure saw in it a human response to a human need that transcended constitutional

---

*It should be noted that Alexandria, at the time, was a part of the District of Columbia, which was administered by Congress. The uniqueness of the relationship appears to have been of little consequence. Proponents raised it hardly at all; opponents argued that it was of no effect. Said Virginia's Rep. William Cabell Rives: "This is not a question of exclusive legislation, properly so called, over the District of Columbia, but it is a question respecting a grant of the national funds." Similarly, the future President, James Knox Polk, then a Representative from Tennessee, on a bill to supply wood to the poor of Georgetown, as quoted in the Washington *National Intelligencer*, February 2, 1831: "He [Polk] might be told that Congress was the exclusive Legislature for the District. Be it so. But was that any good reason that they should give away all the revenue of the nation to the people of the District of Columbia?" The House, nonetheless, approved by a vote of 108 to 79 the donation of 30 cords of wood, on hand in the vaults of the Capitol, in answer to a plea from the mayor of Georgetown. No action was required of the Senate, since it was the House that had jurisdiction over the District of Columbia and the wood was already on hand and thus did not require an appropriation of funds. Furthermore, if relief of the indigent in the District had been intended as a responsibility of Congress, it would have been undertaken prior to 1827.

doubts. That was clearly the feeling of Rep. Churchill Cambreleng of New York:

> I confess I am, in this instance, actuated by an impulse, such as I should feel on seeing a fellow creature about to perish amidst the waves—I should plunge in to save him regardless of the consequences. . . . it is not a time to stop to examine our Constitutional doubts. I trust that the citadel of the Constitution will never be assaulted; but if it ever should be, God grant, it may never be surrendered to an enemy more formidable or dangerous than charity.

Likewise, North Carolina's Rep. Samuel Carson:

> When I had last night returned from the smoking ruins of Alexandria, and had laid myself down at night upon my bed, I could not but reflect on the situation of many of my fellow beings who had the night before slept in security, and this night had not where to lay their heads—who had that very morning risen in comfortable, perhaps affluent circumstances, and at night found themselves without a dollar in the world. . . . After witnessing a scene of suffering and distress like this, I am unable to refuse my assent to the bill.

Those who opposed the measure argued that constitutional questions transcended the means proposed, since the same end might be achieved through private charity. So said Rep. William Cabell Rives of Virginia:

> Even taking as our guide the most liberal construction [of the Constitution] which has ever been suggested, can it be pretended that the objects of this bill, the relief of the unfortunate inhabitants of Alexandria—for whom I feel as much sympathy, and am willing to evince it, with my own means, as far as any gentleman—is, in any manner connected with the payment of the debts, or providing for the common defence and general welfare of the Union? No, sir, it is purely an act of private charity, which we undertake to perform at the public expense, instead of our own.

And Rep. Andrew Stevenson of Virginia, later that year elected Speaker of the House:

> Nor, Sir, can I admit that the goodness and benevolence of the act is any justification for transcending the powers of the Constitution. I know very well that the power of doing good is often wisely withheld, for fear of carrying with it the power to do evil. The greatest and most abominable of tyrannies and usurpations originate often in professions of great good and benevolence. The liberties of no

country were ever overthrown, that it was not placed to the account of some supposed good.

From the vote of 109 to 67 it is clear the majority was not convinced by arguments to the contrary. Both the immediacy and the enormity of the dreadful human drama played out on so close a stage did the convincing. It was not the time, as Mr. Cambreleng said, to stop and examine constitutional doubts. There is, however, a short epilogue to the story. After the vote, some of those congressmen who opposed the measure, some in fact who opposed it most strongly of all, got together and, from their pockets, took up a collection. It came to a then-very-ample sum of $700, which was duly dispatched to the mayor for distribution to the needy fire victims of Alexandria.*

A little less than half a century later,† a far more disastrous fire compelled Congress once again to consider federal assistance. This time, direct aid was ruled out in favor of indirect assistance.

The Great Chicago Fire of October 8, 1871, was easily the most spectacular fire of the century — a thousand times more devastating than Alexandria's. In spite of, or because of, its spectacular proportions, the Chicago disaster did not borrow directly on the precedent of Alexandria. The federal government sent no outright grant for the rebuilding of Chicago or the relief of its victims. But it did show — some congressional qualms notwithstanding — that federal intercession in disaster relief was not far from becoming an accepted corollary to the "common defence and general welfare" provision of the Constitution, which, not a half-century before, was cited as precluding such intercession.

There was not the need for direct federal aid in Chicago. Its plight — which in 1871 could be flashed instantly by telegraph — instantly became the plight of cities and towns and churches and lodges and businessmen and everyday people all over the country. Help began pouring in even as the flames still flickered: from Cairo, Illinois, 100 barrels of flour and a carload of cooked provisions; from Quincy, Massachusetts, four carloads of flour, potatoes, and shoes; from New York City, a trainload of clothing, bedding, and the like, and $150,000 in contributions; from school children in Washington, D. C., $1,000 they collected among themselves in one day.

Such an outpouring of love and care lifted spirits and helped Chi-

---

*Three future presidents were in Congress at the time and voted on the Alexandria bill: Rep. James Buchanan, yes; Rep. James Knox Polk, no; and Sen. Martin Van Buren, no.

†Meanwhile, President Pierce vetoed legislation that would have provided federal aid for the indigent insane (see Chapter 6).

cagoans want to help themselves. Three days after the fire was over, the burned-out Chicago *Tribune*—using the press of the Aurora *Beacon* and printing with a font of type sent by the Cincinnati *Commercial* on paper donated by the St. Louis *Democrat*—offered the editorial opinion

> that [a federal loan of a hundred million dollars] is not the way to rebuild Chicago. It must be rebuilt by its own people, on their own credit, and with that self-reliant energy that had already erected one of the noblest cities of modern times. [But] there is one way in which the National Government may do a substantial benefit without stepping outside its legitimate functions. The government must have public offices here. . . .

On December 21st, ten weeks after the fire, Congress appropriated $4 million for construction of a building (this one to be "fireproof") housing a post office, custom house, subtreasury, federal courts, and pension and revenue offices. Other indirect help Congress also provided in a package signed into law the following April 5th by President Grant: imports for relief of disaster victims permitted duty-free; and internal revenue taxes (not to be confused with the income tax at this time) suspended for whatever time prior to the disaster they were still owed. This combination Congress had first provided in 1866 for victims of a fire in Portland, Maine. In retrospect, it would seem a meager enough response, and yet there was the question of precedent even here. The legislation took two and a half months to get through Congress and was buffeted by such objection as that of Sen. Zachariah Chandler of Michigan:

> Adopt this as a precedent to be followed in the future, and there will not be a catastrophe anywhere by fire that you will not be compelled to make good. You turn this great Government into a universal insurance company against fire all over the United States, and you cannot help yourselves.

Precedent or not, the federal government continued to offer occasional assistance in times of disaster, and by no means indirectly. In coming years there were these responses:

- 1874—For victims of floods along the Mississippi River, $59,000
- 1875—Grasshopper ravages in the Midwest, $180,000
- 1882—Floods along the Mississippi again, $365,000
- 1884—Floods along the Ohio River, $500,000
- 1890—The Mississippi again, $150,000

Something common to all these responses is that each was relief of a natural disaster. The sufferers were all sufferers by circumstance. But some disasters may be partly man's doing. Ought the government also to come to the rescue when man is at least partly responsible for his own plight?

A NEW DIMENSION TO RELIEF

Although it was some years earlier that gold had been discovered in the Klondike, it was the summer of 1897 that the great gold rush to the north began, its story of easy riches ballyhooed in the press from one end of the country to the other. Some of it was highly romanticized, but even the factual had to seem exciting enough: the arrival of a ship with $750,000 in gold one day, and another with $800,000 a few days later. Miners, prospectors, adventurers, and everyday people caught gold-rush fever and set out for the Klondike. Railroads, steamship lines, and outfitting houses spurred them on, seeing a bonanza of business in the making. Few were the voices of caution—some newspapers in the state of Washington, for example—warning of the risks and advising that ample provisions be taken.

Many prospectors were in too much of a rush to listen. They took what they could carry, counting on supplies to reach them later. But there had been a drought, and the Yukon River was low. Supply ships could not get far enough inland to help. As winter set in upon the prospecting country, 175 miles from the Arctic Circle, thousands of the get-rich-quick were beginning to go-hungry-quick instead. Pockets stuffed (in some cases) and bellies empty in nearly all, they faced two choices: Make the perilous winter journey back to the coast, or stay in the Klondike hoping help might come in time. In the mining capital of Dawson, either was a bleak alternative. By mid-October there was not a pound of bacon or beans or flour to be had—except from someone who had hoarded and would now sell, according to one report, a 50-pound sack of flour for $125.

The federal government, at this point, was well aware of the situation and considered the possibility that a rescue mission might be needed, even though there were many at home whose concern was diminished through a perception of the miners as heedlessly foolhardy individuals. At a cabinet meeting on September 14, 1897, Secretary of War Russell A. Alger laid out before his colleagues a batch of telegrams urging relief. One, from the Tacoma Citizens' Committee, warned that starvation had even then begun. Alger said help would probably be needed, and sent an infantry captain to report.

By early December aid was more than probable. Congress took up a bill appropriating $200,000 for the purchase of provisions. These would be sold to miners who could pay for them and given to those who were now penniless. The bill also included arrangements for transportation: 500 reindeer and their drivers.

The fact that many miners could well afford to pay for supplies—that many, in fact, were downright rich—made it a uniquely troubling sort of relief bill. Clearly concerned was Rep. Joseph W. Bailey of Texas, speaking in the House on December 16th:

> I believe it is a noble trait for men to put their hands into their own pockets and freely give to relieve the distresses of their fellow-men, but I do not believe that we have the right to put our hands into the public Treasury and to take the earnings of men who are poorer than many of those whom we seek to relieve, and give that money to people who are better able to give than those from whom they take.

"But, Mr. Speaker," argued Rep. Joseph G. Cannon, of Illinois, later the Speaker himself,

> there are people in that region now who must have immediate relief. How plain a story shall demolish the objections of our honorable friend from Texas. There are 5,000 people on the upper Yukon, most of them with gold—more gold than we have, more gold than the average citizen has—gold, gold, gold! But people can not eat gold. . . . They would pay a dollar a pound for meat—yes, $2 a pound—but there is no meat there to be bought. Nor can any meat or flour be put there by private enterprise.*

The relief mission was signed into law December 18th by President McKinley but was never carried out. Although supplies were bought and reindeer transported from Norway (arriving late in February 1898) the War Department cancelled the mission on March 1st on grounds that the danger then was past. In the meantime, the Klondike miners had subsisted on supplies taken in and shared by arriving prospectors, as well as with help sent by the Canadian government.

A few years into the new century it was another natural disaster, one on a par with the Chicago fire, that got federal relief again in motion—this one in San Francisco on April 18, 1906.

To victims of the earthquake and ensuing fire, Congress sent $2.5 million. Furthermore, it sent it speedily—so speedily, in fact, that there was clearly no longer any question about the federal government hav-

---

*Meat prices at home ranged from 5¢ a pound for stew beef to 15¢ a pound for Porterhouse steak (Washington *Post*, October 10, 1897).

ing a duty to respond in times of need. An act appropriating $1 million of the total was approved on April 19th, one day after the disaster; and the rest on the 24th.

Over the next decade, natural disasters on a lesser scale continued to result in federal assistance—in a round figure, $3 million worth—mostly for flood relief, and more often than not along the Mississippi.

Up to this time Congress had found in the federal treasury a means of responding to the plight of the nation's citizens caught up in the anguish of fires, floods, famine, and natural disasters in general, as well as disaster compounded by human mistake. Economic tribulation—that with which the vast, modern welfare system seeks chiefly to cope—came next.

It came, like life itself, springing from the soil. To quote the *Farm Journal* of March 1916:

> The great problems in the very beginning of this country were agricultural, and so they have continued. . . . After much delay, there has been formulated by a joint committee of Congress an elaborate bill . . .

The elaborate bill was what became the Federal Farm Loan Act of 1916, signed by President Wilson in July. It established a network of 12 federal land loan banks under the supervision of a Federal Farm Loan Bureau, a concept in part inspired by the machinery created by the Federal Reserve Act in 1913, and committed $9 million in federal funding toward making the concept work. Two years later Congress pledged another $200 million (not necessarily all to be spent) for the purchase of farm loan bonds.

In its first hand-to-hand combat with economic tribulation, the federal government thus appropriated more—perhaps 20 times more—for farm relief within eighteen months than it had for all forms of domestic relief in nearly a century since the fire in Alexandria.

"The great problems in the very beginning of this country were agricultural, and so they have continued," the *Farm Journal* observed. In the second decade of the twentieth century, farm ownership was decreasing. Rural population in general was becoming city and town population. Crop production was lagging and food prices were soaring. Farm debt, likewise, was on the rise. It was not a bright picture. "No thoughtful man," said Alabama's Rep. Henry Steagall in a 1916 speech in Congress, "can look at these figures without alarm."

Some of the alarming figures were these: Between 1890 and 1910, city population increased 100 percent; rural population, meanwhile, decreased from 71 percent of the total in 1880 to 54 percent in 1910. During the same period, owner-operation of farms (as opposed to operation by tenants) declined from 75 percent to 63 percent.

All these statistics were coming to mean something at the store. Food prices, said Steagall, went up a staggering 80 percent between 1896 and 1912, while crop production during roughly the same period increased only about 10 percent. Meanwhile, in 1890, only about 28 percent of U.S. farms had mortgages on them; in 1910 the total was 34 percent. Agricultural credit was becoming increasingly tighter. Many who needed a mortgage, just to get by, could not arrange for one; and those who were able to had the threat of foreclosure forever hanging over their heads—a threat exacerbated by a drought now, or excessive rains then, or by whatever else might come along to wreak havoc with the harvest and leave a farmer broke.

To his colleagues in Congress (lots of them city folks), Oklahoma's Rep. Scott Ferris lamented:

> This trend of American boyhood rushing to the city and abandoning the farm renders it necessary for one farmer to produce enough to support five residents of the city, which is all out of proportion, all wrong, and should be remedied by this Congress, as distinguished from the next. You of the East—of the crowded centers engaged in business other than agriculture—complain of the high cost of living and assert that your living expenses are more than you can bear. Can there be a better panacea for this ill than to improve the conditions of the farm, enable the farmer to secure better credit and enable him to enjoy more of the good things of life, so that the boy who has abandoned the homestead and gone to the city may return and again take up his abode in the rural community?

Predicted Rep. Jouett Shouse of Kansas: The Farm Loan Act will rank with the Federal Reserve Act, and "the two will be considered in history the most important pieces of constructive legislation in 50 years."

The legislation sought to provide relief for the farmer by offering long-term loans of up to 36 years at 6 percent interest (against a nationwide average of 7.5 percent). Loans might be for as little as $100, or as much as $10,000, and would be available through farm loan associations or cooperatives. These would act as agents for a district land bank, which would be capitalized at $750,000, an amount to be subscribed by the federal government if not first subscribed by the public. Only first mortgages would be permitted.

Such a system had been in effect in Europe and worked well by all accounts. The first was the Crédit Foncier in France, established in 1852. After that came the Landschaften in Germany, and still other systems in other countries.

In spite of—in many cases, because of—the European precedent, the concept was not universally esteemed in the United States. It was argued in Congress that the federal government was getting into the banking business. The New York *Times* denounced the legislation in a series of editorials, of which two excerpts serve to characterize opposition there as well as elsewhere in the country:

> There is developing in this country a notion that the people, especially agricultural people, are born with a right of access to unlimited amounts of cheap capital. The cheaper it is the better. The kind of rural credit wanted in this country is consistent with that faith. The farmer wants to be subsidized. . . . He is an individualist in his own case, and yet as naive as a Socialist about the impersonal, anonymous power of the State to practice unbounded benevolence.
>
> *May 8, 1916*

> If Government is to assist anybody with money, it ought to assist everybody, which is plainly absurd. [This] is a bill to make voters rather than to supply mortgages to those who cannot get them.
>
> *July 21, 1916*

It was an election year—1916. Wilson, who signed the Federal Farm Loan Act on July 17th, faced Charles Evans Hughes, late of the U.S. Supreme Court. But the farm loan legislation, controversial though it had been in Congress, turned out to be of no apparent consequence in Wilson's victory. Hughes—in that very close election that he at first thought he won—carried the farm states of Illinois, Indiana, Iowa, Michigan, Minnesota, and Wisconsin; Wilson won the other farm states— and the election.

Furthermore, rural credit never was a partisan issue. Theodore Roosevelt, in 1909, first proposed a study of it based on the agricultural credit system in operation in Germany. Three years later President Taft went a step further, saying in so many words that he favored such legislation on a joint state-federal basis. Reconciling opposing points of view into a workable and generally acceptable public policy took until 1916.

How well the rural credits system might have worked was never really to be judged. During World War I, the government maintained price supports on wheat and hogs. It withdrew them in 1919, with the result that prices dropped. In the summer of 1920 all agricultural prices were in a sharp decline, and the need among farmers was not for long-term mortgages but short-term credit that was quickly available. An amendment to the Farm Loan Act in 1923 attempted to assure this by establishing 12 intermediate-credit banks, but a continued decline in prices left this an insufficient remedy.

Over the next few years there was debate in and out of Congress, as well as during the presidential campaign of 1928. Something more was needed. What? Both the Republican and Democratic parties were in general agreement on the rough outlines of what it would be, and both supported it in their 1928 platforms. The concept emerged in 1929 as the Agricultural Marketing Act, backed with working capital of $500 million from the U.S. Treasury. To make that capital available as loans, or as much as would actually be needed, the act established a Federal Farm Board, which would attempt to get farmers to work together through marketing associations. That, however, was not necessarily to be easy. Most of the 6.5 million farmers in the United States were decidedly independent folk, and fewer than one-third had so far joined cooperative marketing associations, even though these held out the promise of greater efficiency in production as well as the marketing of crops.

The Agricultural Marketing Act—farm relief, as it was known around the land—was signed into law on June 15, 1929, by President Hoover, who had first advocated such a measure nearly a decade earlier.

One day late in October that year of 1929—in another market far from the farm—there would be the beginning of the Great Depression that would doom not only the Federal Farm Board but many another enterprise to failure. Meanwhile . . .

6

TAKING AMELIORATIVE MEASURES
Social and Economic Determinants

The Great Railroad Strike of 1877: from Frank Leslie's Illustrated Newspaper, *August 4, 1877. Although the immediate result was a wave of conspiracy laws, the strike helped to focus attention on the unemployed needy, and also contributed toward a growing reliance on federal authority. The positive results were another instance of fear of disorder — that recurring factor in social legislation from ancient times to the present.*

Lines of the jobless, faces down, many with shacks to call home. Soup kitchens for lunch, and hunger for supper. The Depression.

The numbers out of work were staggering, but it was more than numbers:

> Who can calculate the injuries of another description that flow from it? The demoralization that necessarily results from want of employment, and its attendant dissipation? The heart-rending pangs felt by parents whose prospects of supporting their families are blighted and blasted?

Such was the anguish of a committee in Philadelphia as it made public some gloomy statistics on unemployment there,* not in the Great Depression but in the first great economic crisis in the United States, the depression of 1819–21.

Some of the findings: the combined payrolls of 30 principal trades and industries, which in 1814–15 had averaged $58,340 a week, were down to $12,822. And some more dismal data:

Philadelphia: Employment in Selected Trades

	1814	*1819*
Cotton	1,761	149
Iron-casting	1,093	52
Paper manufacture	950	175
Thread-making	444	20
Coach-making	220	67
Overall (30 trades and industries)	9,188	2,137

Niles' Weekly Register estimated that, in Philadelphia, there were altogether 20,000 out of work; in New York, another 10,000 men, all able-bodied, and a like number of women seeking jobs; in Baltimore, 10,000.

It had been supposed that this sort of thing wouldn't happen in the United States. A visitor from Scotland named James Flint wrote home from Indiana in 1820 (*Letters from America*, Edinburgh, 1822):

---

*Philadelphia *Aurora-General Advertiser*, October 5, 1819.

... on seeing a person whose external appearance would have denoted a beggar in Britain, I concluded that the unfortunate must have been improvident or dissipated, or perhaps possessed of both of these qualities. My conjectures may have on two or three occasions been just, as people of a depressed appearance are very rarely to be seen, but I now see the propriety of divesting myself of such a hasty and ungenerous opinion. Last winter a Cincinnati newspaper advertised a place where old clothes were received for the poor, and another where cast shoes were collected for children who could not, for want of them, attend Sunday schools. The charitable measure of supplying the poor with public meals [soup kitchens], has lately been resorted to at Baltimore.

These are "hard times," said Brooklyn's *Long Island Star*. In Bedford, Pennsylvania, according to one newspaper account, a tavern keeper, "considerably embarrassed in his worldly concerns," went to his bedroom, took out a pistol, and shot himself to death. He left a wife and six children. A Poughkeepsie, New York, man who couldn't find work stole a horse so he would be arrested and thus have a place to stay and food to eat. According to the Detroit *Gazette*, harvest workers in some states in September 1819 were being hired at half the pay of prior years. In Batavia, New York, Samuel M. Hopkins, president of the Genesee County Agricultural Society, lamented in October, 1820:

So totally has money disappeared, that it may be doubted whether there is in this district enough to pay interest, on the amount of interest.... Last year we talked of the difficulties of paying for our lands; this year the question is how to exist.

In Philadelphia, the *Aurora* offered "Friendly Advice to Laboring People": how to fix barley broth, potato soup, cabbage soup, and potatoes and cabbage, in order to make "a little go as far as possible."

The depression of 1819, along with the panic that set it off, was the first great economic crisis in the United States, the first real depression, the first encounter with widespread unemployment wholly rooted in economic origins.

There had been earlier periods of unemployment, in some places severe, but a cause could be found in some perceptible circumstance or condition—embargo or war, in particular—that was inherently external in origin. A depression in 1808–09 was clearly the result of the embargo passed by Congress in December 1807 to prohibit all shipping between U.S. ports and Europe. The embargo was Jefferson's device for keeping the United States out of the Napoleonic Wars, but its immediate effect was stagnation of U.S. commerce. For the next two years there was depression and unemployment in the port cities of the East.

New York was particularly hard hit. By a contemporary account, there were 120 failures among merchants and traders. Some 500 vessels lined the harbor, out of use. Thousands of merchant sailors went wandering about looking for work. "The streets near the water-side," wrote English visitor John Lambert in his *Travels* (London, 1814), "were almost deserted, the grass had begun to grow upon the wharves."

Some of the sailors, and others reeling under the hard times, looked to the city government for assistance. A group of them took out an ad in several New York newspapers calling for a mass meeting in City Hall Park, January 9, 1808, for the purpose of "enquiring of him [the mayor] what they are to do for their subsistence during the Winter." Although Mayor Marinus Willett, great-great-grandson of the city's first mayor, publicly decried such a way of expressing a grievance, the meeting took place and served its purpose. On January 11th the mayor and council announced a threefold plan: (1) indoor relief (maintenance of unemployed merchant sailors at the Navy Yard in Brooklyn at the city's expense); (2) work relief (in particular, the leveling of Inclenberg, or Murray, Hill); and (3) a soup kitchen (at the city almshouse, whereby a family of four might receive weekly rations of four quarts of soup, four pounds of bread, and three pounds of beef or pork).

Of these choices, free rations proved easily the most popular. At the council's meeting one week later it was reported that 2,951 rations had been distributed. As of the same date, 18 seamen had signed up for the Navy Yard but only one had gone. No work relief was undertaken because of inclement weather.

Although these relief measures prefigure those of later depressions, the crisis itself did not. It was clearly the result of the embargo. As the embargo was dismantled, trade improved and the crisis passed. It was no more complicated than that.

The depression of 1819–21, on the other hand, was even then seen as a manifestation of deeper troubles. There was a growing recognition that the economic system sometimes made men idle by producing fewer jobs than there were workmen to fill them, so that it was no longer sufficient to apply the age-old explanation that "he who is idle is an idler at heart." There were too many out of jobs and genuinely seeking work for the old adage to hold up. So observed *Niles' Register*, August 7, 1819:

> the cities have been . . . always overcharged with unproductive persons, as well as infested with idlers; but now, thousands who are best disposed to support themselves decently by labor, are in a state of positive suffering—because they have not any thing to do.

The depression of 1819–21 was a culmination of inflation, uncontrolled speculation, and a contraction of credit. Like later depressions, it was preceded by a boom of prosperity, a manifestation of which, in this case, was the establishing of the New York Stock Exchange in 1817. The onset of depression was accompanied by sharply declining values. Real and personal property in the state of New York is estimated to have dropped from $315 million in 1818 to $256 million in 1820. In Pennsylvania, land that had been going for $150 an acre in 1815 was selling for $35 in 1819. Agricultural workers in Massachusetts earned $1.50 a day in 1818; the next year, 53 cents. Turnpike workers in Pennsylvania saw their wages fall from 75 cents a day to 12 cents in the same period. It is estimated that, at the worst of the depression, a half-million were jobless; and that the crisis, as it spread from city to country, in some way touched the livelihood of one person in three.

There was substantial response from the private sector. Churches took up collections for the needy. Soup kitchens were set up, primarily through private charity. In Philadelphia, the United British Emigrant Society opened an employment office, keeping an open book of "Notices of Laborers Wanted" along with names and addresses of persons to whom to apply.

Nevertheless, underlying all, there was the ever broadening response of government, as so clearly recorded by Thomas Griffith in his *Annals of Baltimore* (Baltimore, 1824). Of events in 1819, Griffith wrote:

> The distresses of the citizens were greatly increased by the failure of the City Bank, and mismanagement of the office of [the Bank of] the U. States, and some other banks, accompanied by the fall in the price of flour and tobacco in foreign markets, affecting the prices of all kinds of property here. . . . A society was organized for the gratuitous distribution of soup to the necessitous, and soon after, another one for the prevention of pauperism generally; but the removal of the limitations of the number of out pensioners of the almshouse, which had been at thirty only, for both city and county, and the appointment of managers of the poor in each ward, empowered, as well as the trustees, to send proper objects to the alms-house, which took place this year, appears to have superseded the use of private charity for adults, in a great measure, and the operations of these societies have been superseded, as well as public collections for charity.

Work relief was a recourse at once practical to the unemployed and practical to those who paid its cost through taxes, and it was finding new favor even though extensive use of work relief would be the better part of a century away. Nonetheless, sounding very much like a report of the WPA in the next century was the annual message of Pennsylvania Governor Joseph Hiester on December 6, 1821:

> . . . when the various improvements for which public money has been appropriated, shall have been completed and paid for, the in-

terest of the state in property of this description [public works], will exceed two million of dollars. . . . Permanent bridges have been erected over our principal rivers and streams, and nearly two thousand miles of turnpike road have been completed, extending in every direction, thereby facilitating the transportation of produce to market, adding to the convenience and comfort of traveling, and promoting the general interest of the state by a more intimate connection of its various parts. When the different roads for which appropriations have been made shall have been finished, Pennsylvania will present an extent of artificial roads not surpassed, perhaps not equaled by any of her sister states.

Meanwhile, in Congress, Pennsylvania Rep. Henry Baldwin, early in 1820, had sought to deal with the depression by getting to one of its presumed causes. Heeding cries from Pennsylvania manufacturing interests, he introduced stiff tariff legislation that, he said, would "cover our country with smiles in less than six months." A frowning Senate said no, and it was not until 1824 that new protectionist legislation got through Congress.

Congress did enact one form of help for victims of the depression: a relief act for purchasers of public lands, signed into law in March 1821 by President Monroe. Debt on public lands, by 1819, had reached $23 million and was increasing with the depression. It was feared that forfeiture would become widespread. The 1821 act allowed for a return to the U.S. government of any land owned as of July 1, 1820, and not yet paid for. It thereby permitted the hard-pressed to keep that for which they did pay and not sacrifice the entire tract through foreclosure.

In these various ways—including the other remedies that existed through publicly administered poor law—did government, local and national, attempt to deal with the effects of the depression of 1819-21. As for the economic causes, those were considered outside the province of government except for the tariff legislation, which Congress postponed until a later date. Indeed, not only did government maintain a hands-off attitude toward the economy, it presumed for some time not even to notice that anything might be wrong. In his annual message in December 1818—half a year after a series of deflationary moves on the part of the Second Bank of the United States that would trigger the financial panic of 1819—President Monroe made no mention whatever of the nation's economy; in December 1819 he conceded a fluctuation of the currency, but suggested that things were getting better; in his Second Inaugural, in March 1821, he did take note of a general depression in prices, but only insofar as necessary to explain a decline in federal revenue.

Public comment, as reflected in newspaper articles, editorials, and letters to the editor, was predominantly laissez-faire, as for example the New York *Advertiser*, June 11, 1819, advising that men who expect relief from the pecuniary pressure of such times as the present, from their legislative proceedings, "reckon without their host." . . . Nothing would be more likely to raise a general insurrection in our country, than a legislative attempt to regulate private affairs.

In 1821 the economy began to recover, but another financial panic was not far in the future.

New York City: February 13, 1837, a bitter cold and windy day. The streets were posted with signs: "Bread, Meat, Rent, and Fuel! Their Prices Must Come Down." The signs told of a rally that afternoon in City Hall Park to protest high prices and increasing unemployment.

Some 5,000 responded, and they remained a peaceful lot until someone jumped up on the platform and called out (or words to the effect), "There's flour in the warehouses. Let's demand it be sold at a fair price, or take it if it isn't." Thereupon, several hundred protestors set out for Eli Hart & Co., 173-75 Washington Street, where they seized barrels of flour and smashed them on the sidewalk. Women among the crowd then scooped up the flour in their aprons. Police arrived too late to stop the destruction, but arrested 53 rioters.

The price of flour had been soaring. In the past year and a half it had gone from $8 a barrel to $16, principally because of a domestic shortage caused by bad weather and a poor harvest. Imports then resolved the crisis of supply but also raised the price substantially.

For reasons beyond the price of wheat, 1837 was another year of financial panic. According to an account in *Niles' Register*, nine-tenths of the factories in the East were shut — an estimate patently high but indicative of how severe the crisis was perceived. In Philadelphia, between one-half and two-thirds of the clerks and salesmen in the city's large commercial houses were out of work. By the beginning of 1838, losses through commercial failures were estimated to have reached $50 million nationwide. One-third of New York City's labor force of 200,000 was wholly or substantially without subsistence. The city's almshouse was full to overflowing, as were private charitable institutions.

What helped significantly to turn the economic tide was Western expansion. The *Weekly American* in a still-small trading village called Chicago in May 1837 reprinted a report that had first appeared in the Boston *Merchantile Advertiser*, April 14, 1837:

> The emigration of the great west is rapidly increasing from different parts of the country. The present stagnation in business and the disastrous effect . . . upon our mechanics and laborers . . . will tend to send many of them from our large towns and cities, where their services [heretofore] have been in constant demand some years.

One who preached the crusade was a young editor, later to be celebrated as the founder of the New York *Tribune* but in 1837 immersed in his first journalistic venture, a paper called *The New Yorker* (no kin to the present magazine). An early and wordy example of his advice appeared October 7, 1837:

> The West doubtless offers the fairest inducement to the emigrant who wishes to rise to competence and independence by patient industry and economy. Thitherward should be directed the steps of most of those who leave the Northern States to seek a more inviting field of labor.

In later years, a more concise Horace Greeley would find six words ("Go west, young man, go west") sufficient for the same advice.

In 1857 there was another panic, triggered by a drastic drop in the price of stock of the Ohio Life and Trust Company—from 102 to 17 in four days. That was followed by a general decline on the stock market over the next two months. In October alone, some 1,400 banks went bankrupt—more banks than there were in the country at the time of the 1837 panic.

Chicago, by winter, had 20,000 jobless. As a token measure of assistance, the city government reduced the pay of street cleaners from 75 cents a day to 50 cents and used the balance to spread relief among hungry families.

New York City had more mass rallies. On one occasion unemployed workmen by the thousands marched the streets with banners: "Bread or Blood," "Hunger Is a Sharp Thorn," "We Want Work." As if to fulfill a prediction of Mayor Fernando Wood that "not a few will resort to violence and force," a mob of the jobless made ready to storm the U.S. Sub-Treasury and Custom House. An urgent call from city officials brought out a contingent of soldiers and marines, who dispersed the mob and prevented a raid on government vaults containing some $20 million.

Nevertheless, the jobless had made their point. The city council, that same day, approved an ordinance that had been lying on the table for weeks to put 2,000 men to work on the improvement of newly planned Central Park, whose 840-acre site had been acquired in 1856. Yet relief, rather than public works employment, remained the mainstay in New York as elsewhere. Record numbers of applicants resulted in record expenditures for publicly funded outdoor relief: $96,000 in 1856, $109,000 in 1857, and $139,000 in 1858. In all, during 1858, the city relieved or supported at public expense (indoor and outdoor) 130,150 persons. Statewide, the total was 261,155, a figure representing 7.4 percent of the population.

"DISTRESS AS WAS NEVER KNOWN"

The week, as told in the headlines:

RAILROAD WAR: STRIKERS IN FULL CONTROL
Washington *Star*, July 21, 1877

REIGN OF THE MOB!
A BLACK SUNDAY FOR PITTSBURGH
Pittsburgh *Post*, July 23, 1877

STRIKES EXTENDING: ALL THE GREAT
TRUNK RAILROADS CRIPPLED
New York *Times*, July 24, 1877

WAR OF THE STRIKERS:
WESTWARD THE COURSE OF COMMUNISM
Richmond *Dispatch*, July 26, 1877

MOB RULE: PEOPLE HAVE HAD ENOUGH OF IT
Cincinnati *Gazette*, July 27, 1877

STRUCK OUT: FIGHT WITH THE COMMUNISTS
AT AN END
Chicago *Tribune*, July 28, 1877

Unparalleled prosperity was followed by another panic, more severe, in 1873. Panic precipitated stagnation in business and industry. By the beginning of 1875 an estimated half-million in the country were out of work. In 1876 and 1877 some 18,000 businesses shut their doors, a majority of the nation's railroads went into bankruptcy, and two-thirds of its iron mills and furnaces blew out their fires.

Discouragement was rampant. Faith in government wavered. Political corruption, said the New York *Sun*, had become a poison extending "to every vein and nerve in the public body." More than half the last election's voters had a particular reason to feel disgruntled: The man to whom they had given a quarter-million vote plurality in the 1876 presidential election was not president. Rutherford B. Hayes was—the choice of a 15-member Electoral Commission. By mid-summer of 1877 the *Sun* saw the distress "such as was never known in the United States before."

The basic economic problem was a surfeit of labor, making labor cheap, and the focus of labor unrest was the railroad. Decades earlier the railroads had boomed; now they were losing money: in part because of the depression, in part because of cutthroat competition, in part because of the rivalry of canals. During the 1873-77 period of economic stagnation, the 11 roads (including the New York Central, Baltimore and Ohio, Erie, Lackawanna, and Philadelphia and Reading) chiefly affected by the great railroad strike of 1877 saw their gross earnings drop 16 percent while indebtedness rose 52 percent. At the time of the strike, four of the railroads were bankrupt, five had stopped paying dividends, and two had continued dividends only by substantially increasing indebtedness.

At the same time, it was not necessarily appropriate to feel sorry for the railroads. Employee relations, in particular, were not their specialty. "A railroad," said the New York *Herald,* July 28, 1877,

> is a great and complicated machine, but it is a blunder in him who manages it if he considers the men who help him to work it only machines also. They are men, human beings, creatures with affections, enjoyments, hopes. . . .

And the Baltimore *American* a week earlier:

> The method pursued by the company in working the men is about the greatest grievance. This method is economical, and in carrying it out the employees say they are treated just as the rolling stock or locomotives. . . .

Hitting railroad employees hardest of all were a series of pay reductions, most recently an across-the-board 10 percent cut, and the loss of overtime for delays. The latter was especially galling. As an example, the run from Baltimore to Martinsburg, West Virginia, about 100 miles, was a full day's work. The trip itself, if all went well, took six hours, but there was at least another hour to fire up the engine at the start and an hour or more to clean it up at the end of the trip. Yet delays along the way were routine. Prior to 1877 the railroad crews were paid for this extra time. Now that was not the case, even if the trip to Martinsburg took 40 or 45 hours. The railroads said there was no choice: Depression economics were such that there was much less freight going westbound than east. Indeed, the trains running west were often empty.

On this western run was struck the spark that ignited the great railroad strike of 1877. July 17th, Martinsburg, West Virginia: Disgruntled trainmen stop a Baltimore and Ohio freight and refuse to let it proceed. Federal troops move in. Nine men are killed. The unrest spreads. Railroaders take up the strike around the country. Freight is burned. Even passenger trains are seized. The railroads screech and grind to a halt.

By now the combatants number 100,000. Major rioting scorches Baltimore, Pittsburgh, Chicago, St. Louis; lesser but no less frightening upheaval singes the country from coast to coast. "Not since the dark and threatening hours of 1861 has the nation been called upon to confront such a grave condition of affairs," observes the New York *Herald*. "Is this rebellion?" asks the Chicago *Tribune*. Anarchy is more like it, anarchy such as the country has never seen. In Pittsburgh, a violent climax to the whole convulsive week: strikers and police in a pitched battle; twenty-six dead; Union Depot in flames.

When it was over the damage nationwide was estimated at not less than $100 million, making it a calamity at least half as costly as the Great Chicago Fire six years earlier. The nation was in shock but chose not to lay all the blame on the railroad men. The New York *Herald*, July 31st, reported that many unions had urged honest working men to stay out of the riots, and suggested the workmen

> have won a debt of gratitude from the community, and no efforts should be neglected to better their condition and to obtain employment for those of them who are idle.

Similarly, the New Orleans *Daily Picayune*, July 27th, reflected on the widespread belief that the newly developing Communist movement had fanned the flames:

> It has already hurt their cause, and is still injuring it. The line of distinction ought to be drawn very sharply and clearly when the mob takes advantage of the strike to attempt the overthrow of society.

There were manifold effects to the week of rioting. State legislatures rapidly enacted conspiracy laws. Labor began turning more and more to politics as an avenue of change. Significant to a perspective of the development of welfare was the impetus for central authority. Local police and state militia were hard pressed to put down the rioting, and in some cases were wholly ineffective. Thus the cry for federal intervention, as echoed in the Chicago *Tribune*, July 27th:

> The inefficiency and weakness of State Governments in struggling against a concerted uprising of the mob classes have been abundantly demonstrated. . . . But everywhere a like feeling of security and hope is found among the people. They have faith in the strength of the National Government. . . .

The cumulative effect of wave after wave of depression and unemployment, now more sharply focused by this cataclysmic week in July

1877, was an increasing sense that government should do something about it all. But what? A very few spoke about nationalization of the railroads and other forms of industry. They were hardly to be heard. Heard but hardly to be taken seriously was the patently demagogic response of Pennsylvania Rep. Hendrick B. Wright, who told railroad strikers in Wilkes-Barre that when Congress convened he would introduce legislation to take $10 million out of the federal treasury and pass it out among the working men of the country.

More reasonable, and indeed foreseeing, was the conclusion of a *Daily Picayune* editorial on July 28th, which voiced what more and more were coming to believe:

> Behind the paramount duty of restoring order and suppressing lawlessness in the great crisis which now agitates a large portion of the country, lies the problem of finding an outlet for the surplus labor, and relieving the cry of the unemployed for bread. The pressure for industrial relief will remain after the present disturbances are quieted. When the civil authority is re-established, as it must be, at whatever cost, the urgent question will be what to do with the hungry thousands who have no occupation, and whose inforced idleness creates a reckless, dangerous element which is a standing threat to society.

The World's Fair year of 1893 was another snared by depression. Some contemporary estimates placed the unemployed at 1 million. Chicago, despite the fair, was no exception. Indeed, when the fair ended the last Thursday in October, it set loose a small army of fairground workers to join the lines of those standing idle. As cold weather set in, Chicago's jobless and homeless began jamming into police stations and the corridors of city hall for nightly lodging. Relief stations and temporary lodging houses also opened around the city. Employment stations offered street cleaning jobs for men and sewing jobs for women, but only to a lucky few. One member of the city's street cleaning committee was Jane Addams, who saw work relief a double-edged tool. It risked permanently lowering wages, she contended. It was better to have men work half a day for 75 cents than a full day for a $1. Failing to convince the committee, she resigned, declaring that the purpose of the program was not cleaning streets but helping the unemployed.

Elsewhere in the nation there was like hardship. In New York during the winter of 1893–94 outdoor relief continued to be restricted to supplies of free coal, but in 1894 a $1 million public works program was instituted to put 2,000 men to work. Other cities also turned to work relief:

- Dayton, $300,000 for sewer construction;
- St. Louis, enlargement of a small lake to provide employment

for 900 at no cost to the city (it held a street car company to a long-standing commitment);
- Chattanooga, $2,500 to employ men to break up stone for the streets;
- Burlington, Iowa, $3,000 for street improvements;
- Helena, Montana, $8,000 on street grading;
- And Detroit (bringing to mind Claudius, A.D. 41-54, putting 30,000 men to work draining the Fucine Lake for an imperial estate) $20,000 for filling in a reservoir no longer in use.

Out of the cold depression winter of 1893-94 also bloomed new hope, symbolized elsewhere in Detroit. There, in the spring of 1894, Mayor Hazen S. Pingree conceived a venture that eventually flowered in cities and towns across the land. Detroit set aside 430 acres of land, most of it donated by public-spirited citizens, and divided it into 945 plots that it turned over to the needy to use as gardens. The poor might grow not only their own food but crops—potatoes, beans, cabbage, and the like—to sell for a small income.

Thus, by the end of the century, recurring depression and widespread unemployment had seemed to become a way of life, and the methods of dealing with their effects, even if persistently ad hoc, had formed a pattern. The economic exigencies of the nineteenth and early twentieth centuries represent a potent force in the transition from old poor law (for the poor) to economic security (for nearly everyone). There were other determinants as well: early Communism; the labor movement; reformers, critics, and visionaries; immigration; and European precedent.

EARLY COMMUNISM

The depression years of 1873-77, and particularly the great railroad strike, gave Americans their first real look at Communism, as two contemporary comments attest. From the New York *Tribune*, July 25, 1877 (during the strike):

> His [the Communist's] work in Paris is known. It is the blackest page in the history of the nineteenth century. His work in the United States we are beginning to know.

And from *International Review*, September 1877 (after the strike), W. M. Grosvenor, a frequent advisor to the government on economic policy, who went further:

> By the light of flames at Pittsburgh, we may see approaching a terrible trial for free institutions in this country. The Communist is here . . . The gaunt Communist has placed his foot on American soil,

and already intelligent men are heard crying for a large standing army. . . .

If a century's perspective makes the latter, in particular, overstated, it must be kept in mind that the week and a half of the railroad strike was a frightening time. Coming little more than a decade after the Civil War, it must have seemed that another such calamity was threatening to convulse the nation. It was widely believed that the Communists, heretofore chiefly seen as the holders of noisy rallies in major U.S. cities, were, if not the instigators of the railroad riots, at least manipulators of them. It could hardly be otherwise. "The homeless beggar, the wandering tramp, the unemployed and needy workman," said the New Orleans *Daily Picayune*, August 4, 1877, a few days after the strike,

> will find their spokesmen and their leaders, we may be sure. Hunger is a sort of fanaticism in itself, and a thousand unscrupulous demagogues are only waiting to preach communism and agrarianism to all too willing ears.

Still easily remembered at the time was the Paris Commune of April–May 1871. The new Atlantic cable made news from Europe almost instantaneous, and such events now took on the immediacy of hometown news. The Commune, bloody and violent beyond anything of the revolutions, was not Communist in its origins, but Marx's praise and vision of it as a foretaste of class warfare, coupled with its very violence (the Communards burned public buildings and put to death the Archbishop of Paris; the government, breaking up the Commune, arrested 38,000 and put to death 20,000), made it fearful to contemplate anything like the Commune becoming reincarnate in the United States. To the point is an excerpt from the 1874 Annual Report of the New York Association for Improving the Condition of the Poor:

> There is a dangerous socialistic element of foreign origin in this City, whose boldly avowed principles are utterly at variance with the letter and spirit of our political, social, and religious institutions, which, uncontrolled, would re-enact the horrible scenes of violence, robbery and carnage in New York, that so recently caused the streets of Paris to run with blood.

It happened that 1871 was also the year that Marx and Engels' *Communist Manifesto*, originally published in Germany in 1848, made its first appearance in English in the United States. As the "Manifesto of the German Communist Party," it found print in New York's *Woodhull & Claflin's Weekly*, December 30, 1871, and there was nothing ambivalent about its message:

> Let the ruling classes tremble at a Communist revolution. The Proletarians have nothing to lose in it save their chains. They will gain a world. Let the Proletarians of all countries unite.

Even before the railroad strike, the American Communist was in evidence. In December 1873, the first winter of the depression, sections of the First International in the United States combined with local trade unions for a meeting (December 11th) at the Cooper Union in New York. An overflow crowd produced resolutions demanding an eight-hour work day, a limit of $30,000 on the wealth of any one individual, and public approval of all bills before becoming law. Still another resolution advised unemployed workers, during "this time of need," to send their debts to city hall for payment from the public treasury.

The meeting was a sequel to one on November 15th organized by German workers in the tenth ward. It was resolved that the city request a loan of $10 million "from the National Government" to help out labor, and that "all penniless, houseless and involuntary idle people [be] the wards of the nation, and should not be suffered to roam through the streets of our towns and cities uncared for and neglected."

A rally at New York's Tompkins Square on January 13, 1874, attended by several thousand persons, was clearly Communist in origin. From a house nearby fluttered a red flag. On the platform waved another red flag, this one in the hand of Justus Schwab, the leader of the rally and a declared Communist. Many of those attending had sticks and clubs. Police broke up the gathering since it had been denied a permit. Thirty-five persons were arrested. Schwab's red flag was confiscated and impounded in the 17th Precinct police house.

In the wake of the railroad strike, American Communists turned more militant. A San Francisco publication entitled *Truth, A Journal for the Poor*, on December 15, 1883, published an article headlined, "Street Fighting: How to Use the Military Forces of Capital When It Is Necessary! Military Tactics for the Lower Classes." Elsewhere, militant socialist publications advised: "Get ready for another 1877. Buy a musket for a repetition of 1877." "Buy dynamite for a second 1877." "Organize companies and drill to be ready for a recurrence of the riots of 1877."

Advice to militants also could be tempered, when that better seemed to serve the cause. Speaking of the indiscriminate use of dynamite, *Truth* on January 26, 1884, cautioned:

> Its effect would be directly reactionary. Either it would induce repressive laws abrogating the rights we now have which permit us to spread our doctrines, or it would wring from the fears of the bourgeoisie such ameliorative measures as might postpone for centuries the final struggle for complete emancipation.

Ameliorative measures? Were the dynamite revolutionaries, speaking among themselves, unwittingly counseling society? A year later, writing in *Johns Hopkins University Studies*, the distinguished economist Richard T. Ely, whose students included Woodrow Wilson, offered a reply for society:

> The two words used by *Truth*, "ameliorative measures," indicate the correct method of dealing with social problems. We must listen to complaints of those who feel that they are oppressed, and not suppose that the demands of even socialists are unjust, simply because they are made by socialists. Who can object to them when they complain because they are not allowed to rest one day out of seven; because child-labor is tolerated; because families are scattered in workshops, and family life in any true sense of the word becomes an impossibility?

Even more to the point was *The Nation*, May 9, 1878:

> The American Communists, for instance, are not strong enough, or ever likely to be strong enough, to embody one of their ideas in an act; but they are, or probably will be, strong enough to make people afraid of riots, and to stimulate that kind of legislation called "labor legislation," which seems to grow naturally out of the deep-seated public sympathy with poverty. . . .

THE LABOR MOVEMENT

Had there been a labor movement early in the nineteenth century, it would have found the climate of crisis a fertile one. The nation's first real depression, that of 1819–21 (touching the livelihood of one in every three and leaving a half-million jobless), has already been examined in some detail. Suffice it to add here the appraisal of one who was there. From his memoirs, a conversation of John Quincy Adams, then secretary of state, with Secretary of War Calhoun, on May 22, 1820:

> We conversed on politics past, present, and future. Calhoun's anticipations are gloomy. He says there has been within these two years an immense revolution of fortunes in every part of the Union; enormous numbers of persons utterly ruined; multitudes in deep distress; and a general mass of disaffection to the Government, not concentrated in any particular direction, but ready to seize upon any event and looking out anywhere for a leader.

Despite so gloomy a state of things, the only cry ascribable to labor was on the part of individual workers, occasionally banded together for rallies, calling for work relief from local government. Against that, one may look ahead to the close of the century.

In December 1893 Chicago was locked in the nation's worst depression to date. City unemployment, with the World's Fair closed, was hovering around 40 percent, or about 180,000 workers. Men lined up in the early morning blackness for soup kitchens that didn't open until 10 A.M.

In City Hall, jobless men slept in the corridors, some covered with blankets of old newspapers. In City Hall, likewise, convened the annual meeting of the American Federation of Labor (AFL), among other things to deal with the effects of depression and to elect, to a twelfth straight term as president, Samuel Gompers. Now, at century's end, labor was speaking more and more with one voice, usually Gompers', as at the opening session of the AFL on December 11, 1893:

> [Organized labor] voices the hopes of the future and calls to account those responsible for the present. Last night I walked through the corridors of the City Hall and saw hundreds of men lying on the stone flooring, on the iron steps, and some asleep standing up — all men in enforced idleness. Those responsible for these conditions should take warning. They are sleeping in false security. The men responsible for these things, who send out their protests, in which we join, against the bomb in Barcelona, against the bomb in Paris, and against the assassin's bullet in Chicago, must understand they must concede to the solution of the problem that organized labor presents or they will be confronted with the guerilla warfare to which I have alluded.

The demands of the AFL, then seven years old and a quarter-million strong, were translatable to specific action on the part of government: massive federal aid for road construction. The AFL took the position that, while private charity is an applaudable option,

> it is the duty of the city, state and national governments to give immediate and adequate relief; that a system of society which denies to the willing man the opportunity to work, then treats him as an outcast, arrests him as a vagrant and punishes him as a felon, is hereby condemned as inhuman and destructive of the liberties of the human race; that the right of work is the right of life; that to deny the one is to destroy the other; that when the private employer can not or will not give work, the municipality, state or nation must.

Clearly, labor at century's end was not what it had been in the depression of 1819–21. It now had muscles to flex and was preparing to throw its weight into the determining of national policy in the twentieth century. The AFL initially stayed out of partisan politics. Indeed, its constitution declared that party politics "whether they be Democratic, Republican, Socialistic, populistic . . . should have no place in the conventions of the American Federation of Labor." It was a restriction that lasted only until after the turn of the century. In 1906 the AFL executive council laid down a policy calling for the defeat of antilabor candidates, and AFL speakers went on the stump in a number of elections. In 1908 the AFL went further: Its journal, *American Federationist*, acted virtually as a campaign organ for Bryan, while some 1,100 locals contributed funds for campaign literature and speaking tours by Gompers and others. In 1912 the AFL abandoned all pretense of official neutrality and endorsed Wilson, albeit as the lesser of evils. Lukewarm at first, labor grew fonder as Wilson, once president, named mineworker William B. Wilson his secretary of labor, and fonder still as President Wilson signed into law the Clayton Anti-Trust Act (1914), which Gompers hailed as labor's Magna Charta.

Organized labor clearly came to have an impact on legislation in the new century. Beyond work relief as a means of dealing with unemployment, labor could take credit for a hand in bringing about:

- *the eight-hour day* (in effect, by the beginning of the twentieth century, though with widely varying provisions, in 21 states and the District of Columbia)
- *workman's compensation* (the first law in the United States was New York's, in 1910, which was promptly declared unconstitutional, but the idea spread, and by 1921 all but six states and the District of Columbia had compensation statutes)
- *minimum wage* (Massachusetts had the first general law setting a minimum wage, in 1912, followed by eight other states the next year)
- *six-day week* (Massachusetts and New York, in 1913, required that factories and mercantile establishments give one day of rest in seven)
- *the Clayton Anti-Trust Act* (in 1914, which exempted labor unions from prosecution for conspiracy in restraint of trade, restricted use of injunctions against unions, and legalized peaceful strikes, picketing, and boycotts)
- *federal child labor laws* (the first congressional act, in 1916, was overturned in the courts, but revived in legislation of the 1930s)

Furthermore, during this same period there were laws: protecting labor from conditions endangering health, regulating and improving physical conditions of employment, and prohibiting or limiting night work for women and children.

This labor legislation, as a whole, and workmen's compensation in particular, helped to create the climate of change that culminated in the far-reaching social legislation of the 1930s. Organized labor, with its vast army of organized voters, obliged government to expand its role in society.

At the same time, labor legislation had the effect of diminishing the need for charity, both public and private, by making provision for the laborer (injured, sick, or unemployed) who might otherwise have become a charity recipient, and indeed by protecting him from job-related injury or death that, in earlier times, might have relegated his dependents to the charity rolls.

REFORMERS, CRITICS, AND VISIONARIES

Notable to the nineteenth century was a proliferation of reformers, critics, and visionaries, whose voices or writings called the public to a heightened awareness of society's treatment of the poor. Some criticized the status quo. Some proposed new ways of doing things. Some turned public opinion by directing public scrutiny to conditions theretofore known to few beyond the impoverished themselves. Some had profound impact on the course of publc welfare; others, little or none.

Not everyone, of course, notices the same evil, or, noticing it, regards it in the same way. Hence there is no one remedy in common to all reformers. There was diversity then; and so here, as reflected in a cross-section of thought by the known and little-known, beginning just before the turn of the nineteenth century with THOMAS PAINE, who surely deserves mention for a program akin to social security that he proposed in 1792 in Part Two of *The Rights of Man*. It had these five essentials:

- *Aid to Dependent Children* (A state grant, which Paine suggested at £4 a year, for children under 14, as an alternative to traditional poor relief. "By adopting this method," said Paine, "not only the poverty of the parents will be relieved, but ignorance will be banished from the rising generation, and the number of poor will hereafter become less. . . .")
- *Old Age Assistance* (At the age of 60, when "his labour ought to be over," a worker would begin receiving a state pension. A lesser pension should be available at 50. "This support," said Paine, "is not of the nature of a charity but of a right.")
- *Public Works Employment* (The state would provide employment at all times for the poor who could not find work.)
- *Birth, Marriage, and Funeral Assistance* (A state grant would be given to each needy couple at the time of marriage and again on the

birth of a child. A funeral allowance would be available to survivors of a person who traveled in connection with his work and died a distance from home.)
- *Subsidized Education* (The state would pay a certain amount to each needy school child, for up to six years, to assure his proper education.)

This broad program Paine proposed to have financed by a progressive income tax ranging from 1.25 to 46.2 percent. He proposed it for England, although it would have been as applicable to America as English poor law, which it was intended to supplant. Presented as it was during the ascendancy of laissez faire, nothing could have been expected to come of so visionary a scheme. Indeed, to be consistent, Paine himself should have argued against it. One year earlier, in an *Answer to Four Questions* (1791), Paine denounced such bureaucracy as would have been essential to his social security program:

> I am very decided in the opinion that the sum of necessary government is much less than is generally thought, and that we are not yet rid of the habit of excessive government.

While offering no such plan of his own, one of Paine's contemporaries was an outspoken critic of the poor law; and given his own reputation for thrift and industry, **BENJAMIN FRANKLIN** must have sounded convincing as he castigated the system for cultivating laziness and dependency, as he did in "On the Price of Corn, and Management of the Poor" (1766):

> I am for doing good to the poor, but I differ in opinion about the means. I think the best way of doing good to the poor is, not making them easy in poverty, but leading or driving them out of it. In my youth, I travelled much, and I observed in different countries, that the more public provisions were made for the poor, the less they provided for themselves, and of course became poorer.

Dublin-born **MATTHEW CAREY** (1760–1839) was a Philadelphia publisher (the Pennsylvania *Herald*), bookseller, and writer on matters political, social, and economic. His writings circulated widely. Carey observed that there were those who were hardly lazy and yet who lived in a virtual state of poverty despite the fact they worked from sunrise to sunset. This was so, he said, because the pay of some occupations in Philadelphia in the 1830s was not enough on which to live. A common seamstress, for example, could not earn more than nine cents a week making shirts; if aged or of little skill, no more than six to eight cents. Yet eight to ten cents was necessary for the bare necessities. A canal laborer with regular employment from spring to fall and occasional work during the winter might earn $130 a year, and his wife might bring in another $13 or so for the year. Yet their combined income of $143 was less than the $145 Carey estimated to be necessary to feed, clothe, and house a family of two adults and two children.

Still others were poor, observed Carey, because they were too ill or infirm to work, and in many cases their infirmities were a direct result of their occupations. Carey was perhaps the first American to call attention to occupational health. In his *Plea for the Poor* (Philadelphia, 1836), he quoted portions of Charles Turner Thackrah's *Effects of the Principal Arts, Trades and Professions, and of Civic States and Habits of Living, on Health and Longevity*, which had been published in London in 1830 and established Thackrah as the pioneer of industrial medicine in England. Some of Thackrah's observations, as quoted by Carey:

- Plumbers are exposed to the volatilized oxide of lead, which rises during the process of casting. . . . It is apparent that the occupation undermines the constitution.
- Potters suffer from the lead used in glazing. Immersing their hands in a strong solution of this mineral, they are often attacked by colic; and if kept in this department, they at length become paralytic.
- The process of picking flax is generally the most injurious to health. A large proportion of the men in this employ die young. Very few can bear it for thirty years; and not one instance could be found of any individual who had been forty years in this or any of the dusty rooms.

"Away then," argued Carey, "with the miserable clamour about the idleness of the poor."

There were those who believed the best hope of the poor lay in the American free enterprise system—if as free for labor as for industry—and one who said so convincingly was a man who had known poverty and risen high with hard work. Here he was March 6, 1860, making a speech in New Haven:

When one starts poor, as most do in the race of life, free society is such that he knows he can better his condition; he knows that there is no fixed condition of labor, for his whole life. I am not ashamed to confess that twenty-five years ago I was a hired laborer, mauling rails, at work on a flatboat—just what might happen to any poor man's son.

Cheers and "tremendous applause," according to the New Haven *Daily Palladium*, greeted the remarks of ABRAHAM LINCOLN.

HORACE GREELEY's New York *Tribune* in 1864 called the slum a place where "garbage steams its poison in the sun" and "the daily food of pestilence awaits its coming." Such simple descriptions of poverty were often the most eloquent encouragement to reform. A longer sample:

> In a dingy attic in the fourth story at 8 Vandewater street lies the body of Mary Carpenter, a deserted wife whose death was hastened by starvation. It will be buried to-day, and a single carriage, containing her four small children, will follow her to the grave. Word was sent to the Oak street police station a few days since that a dying woman would like to be taken to a hospital. Capt. Petty found what he says was the most affecting scene he has ever witnessed in twenty years' experience as an officer. The panels had been kicked from the door, which hung by one hinge. The narrow window was without sash or blinds. Over the uncarpeted floor were scattered fragments of utensils and broken furniture. There was not a whole article in the room. A heap of straw in one corner supplied the place of a bed. A lounge, without legs or back, supported the form of a woman, whose sunken eyes, hollow cheeks, and trembling fingers told as plainly as her words that she had been a long time without food. She attempted in vain to comfort her little ones, who were sobbing around her. Her husband, a longshoreman, deserted her a week ago, when she was ill. The small wages that the eldest daughter, aged 13, was able to earn in a factory, were taken from her every week, and spent in drink. He only came home when intoxicated, and then to beat his wife and break the furniture. Mrs. Campbell [sic] died on Saturday in Bellevue Hospital. The children begged so hard to have their mother buried out of the Potter's Field, that Capt. Petty ordered an undertaker to make a respectable interment, and will bear the expense himself.
>
> New York *Sun*, July 30, 1877

Another whose descriptions shamed and shocked authorities into action was DOROTHEA DIX (1802–87). When she substituted as a Sunday school teacher at a Massachusetts house of correction, she got a firsthand look at treatment of the insane (most of them poor). She spent the following two years visiting almshouses and jails throughout the state, and in 1843 wrote her *Memorial to the Legislature of Massachusetts*, which contained many another example to match the description of the young girl caged in a cell at the Danvers almshouse (see Chapter 4).

Dorothea Dix visited 27 states, covering 60,000 miles, as she toured and wrote about other such facilities. One result of her work was a new asylum for the insane established by the New Jersey legislature in Trenton in 1845. Another result: a bill passed by Congress in 1854 that would have granted 10 million acres of public lands to the states to finance care of the indigent insane. President Pierce vetoed it, arguing that Congress then ought to do as much for all the indigent, and, "I can not find any authority in the Constitution for making the Federal Government the great almoner of public charity throughout the United States."

> This association of poverty with progress is the great enigma of our times.
>
> *Progress and Poverty,* 1879

It is some measure of his popularity in his own time that HENRY GEORGE (1939-97), running for mayor of New York in 1886, polled more votes than the future president, Theodore Roosevelt (68,110 for Liberal-Labor candidate George, 60,435 for Republican Roosevelt), although neither came close to the winner (Democrat Abram S. Hewitt, 90,552).

Henry George was at the peak of his fame: a frequent lecturer in the United States and Britain, and the author of the remarkably popular *Progress and Poverty*, which was privately printed in 1879 and commercially published in 1880, thence to go on to sales of some 2 million copies in the United States and translations into several foreign languages.

Progress and Poverty was a product of the depression of 1877. It was this work that chiefly advanced his "single tax" plan: that taxation should be of land alone. Land, he contended, had inevitably become scarcer with economic progress, and this meant that the landowner (who might stay idle) benefited at the expense of both labor and capital (who had to be productive). Tax only the land, said George, and there would be sufficient revenue for government to redress the balance of resources between rich and poor. His theory won George many friends and readers, even if no practical results.

One of the best-known reformers of her day was JANE ADDAMS (1860-1935). Inspired by her first-hand look at a London settlement house, she returned home to open up her own: Hull House, a once elegant, red-brick mansion in a Chicago suburb that in 1889 became a neighborhood center for impoverished immigrants. Writing about Hull House four years after its founding, Jane Addams suggested that not all the poor need, or indeed want, monetary charity, and that a helping hand sometimes serves the purpose better than a hand-out.* "As one of their

---

*Evocative, this is, of Edward Denison in Victorian England. Son of a member of the House of Lords and nephew of the Speaker of the House of Commons, Denison went into the factory slums of London to live, there to observe first-hand how public relief was changing the lot of the poor. He wrote (*Work Among the London Poor*, 1884): "Things are so bad down here, and giving money away only makes them worse. I am beginning seriously to believe that all bodily aid to the poor is a mistake. . . . Build school-houses, pay teachers, give prizes, frame workmen's clubs, help them to help themselves, lend them your brains."

numbers has said," she wrote (*Philanthropy and Social Progress*, 1893),

> they require only that their aspirations be recognized and stimulated, and the means of attaining them put at their disposal. Hull House makes a constant effort to secure these means for its neighbors, but to call that effort philanthropy is to use the word unfairly and to underestimate the duties of good citizenship.

An immigrant from Denmark at age 21, JACOB RIIS (1848–1914) turned newspaper reporter and covered the police beat for the *Tribune* and the *Sun* in New York. He is better remembered as an author whose beat was the slum, a calling that led Police Commissioner Theodore Roosevelt to refer to him as the most helpful man in New York.

Riis had already caught the attention of the reading public when, in June 1888 he appealed to *Tribune* readers for flowers to be distributed to those poor who might spend their lives without ever seeing a field of daisies. So many flowers were left at the *Tribune* office that Riis needed all the police reporters on the staff, plus volunteers from the Police Department, to see to their distribution among the poor.

In 1889 Riis wrote a 19-page article for *Scribner's Magazine* that captured the public imagination, and a year later expanded it into a book, *How the Other Half Lives*, that became his best-known work. It was the right thing at the right time. Coming just as immigration was reaching its peak—and suspicion and resentment of newcomers likewise—*How the Other Half Lives* made human beings out of this diverse lot of strange-speaking, strange-looking new Americans. An excerpt from the original version as published in the December 1889 *Scribner's*:

> It is in hot weather, when life in-doors is wellnigh unbearable with cooking, sleeping, and working all crowded into the small room together—for especially in these East-side tenements much of the work that keeps the family is done at home—that the tenement expands, reckless of all restraint. Then a strange and picturesque life moves upon the flat roofs. In the day and early evening mothers air their babies there, the boys fly their kites from the house-tops, undismayed by police regulations, and the young men and girls court and pass the growler. In the stifling July nights, when the big barracks are like fiery furnaces, their very walls giving out absorbed heat, men and women lie in restless, sweltering rows, panting for air and sleep. Then every truck in the street, every crowded fire-escape, becomes a bedroom, infinitely preferable to any the house affords. A cooling shower on such a night is hailed as a heaven-sent blessing in a hundred thousand homes.

IMMIGRATION

News item from *Niles' Register*, January 19, 1839:

> The following persons arrived here [New York] by the British barque Chieftan, on Monday, from Liverpool, and were taken in a body to the almshouse, viz: . . . Hugh Lacky, 23 years old, has been five years in the poor house . . . William Mackay, 15 years old, was four years in the poor house . . . Mary Hay, 23 years old, in the poor house one year; Catharine Steele, aged 14, was three years in the poor house. The majority of them appeared in the uniform of the poor house, in which some of them had spent the greatest part of their lives.

Still wearing the uniform of the Edinburgh poorhouse, these rather pitiful creatures, just off the boat from Liverpool, were paupers who had been shipped off to the United States for no other reason than to let others bear the burden of their upkeep.

This particular contingent—there were 11 in all, ranging in age from 13 to 58—did not remain in the United States. The mayor of New York investigated, found that no bond had been posted, and ordered the paupers returned to Liverpool. State law (federal restrictions on immigration would not come until 1882) required the payment of head money or of a bond covering maintenance of an immigrant not likely to be self-supporting.

Immigration of Europe's poor began in the earliest days of the colonies. For a time after the revolution, there was a relatively small inflow of newcomers, but the tide increased after 1815 with the resumption of peace both in Europe and in America. Indeed, by 1820 the influx of foreign poor was at the top of the list of causes of pauperism, in the opinion of the Society for the Prevention of Pauperism in the City of New York.

Concern about the influx of immigrants grew during the depression of 1837, even though the westward migration was picking up dramatically; immigration was increasing just as dramatically. The Irish potato famine of the 1840s left 1 million dead of starvation and disease there, and half again that many seeking a new home, most of them in the United States. Total immigration to the United States in 1851 was 379,466. Of those, nearly a quarter-million were Irish. In 1845, floods ravaged the Danube, Elbe, Main, Moselle, and Rhine valleys in Germany, laying waste to crops and inundating the land with poverty; German emigration sped up accordingly.

Many immigrants, notably those fleeing economic disaster, were not the hard-core poor of Europe. They had known a decent life and were thus new to poverty. They supposed a new land and a new start would offer the best opportunity of a return to earlier circumstances. Some immigrants fell ill and died on the voyage over—the victims of notoriously adverse steerage class conditions—in some years, as many as one in six. Dependents thus became charity cases on arrival. The same was true of families with fathers who became too sick to work. The healthy ones, meanwhile, often fell prey to the unscrupulous, who bilked them of whatever little money they had, or set them to work at pitifully small wages. Others arrived healthy, settled down easily, and prospered in the land of opportunity. Then they wrote home and encouraged still others to come:

> I hope brother William and family will come all together, for they can get spinning here. . . . It is a very pleasant country as ever I saw. Clear days for weeks together, not a cloud to be seen. I hope brother James and wife will come.
>
> Thomas Lister, weaver,
Philadelphia, April 26, 1830,
to relatives back in foggy England

What the Thomas Listers thought was clearly a factor in immigration, and was clearly recognized at the time. *Chambers' Journal* of London, as quoted in *Littell's Living Age*, Boston, put it into so many words: "a motive [for coming] has been the great success of some of the earlier settlers."

There was encouragement on the other side of the Atlantic as well. In Great Britain, trade unions sometimes got up funds to send unemployed members to the United States. Another sort of stimulus was that typified by the Marquis of Lansdowne in the years immediately following the famine. He spent £17,059 on free passage to the United States for those men, women, and children on his estate in Ireland who were in the poorhouse or on outdoor relief and were thus chargeable to him as landlord. He concluded it was cheaper to pay their passage than to continue paying what they added to his share of the poor rate. Through Lansdowne's patronage alone, 4,616 of Ireland's poor came to the United States.

Not all those encouraged to emigrate were necessarily honorable and industrious. German newspaper accounts cited at the 1876 Conference of Charities told of justice in Lüneburg in 1865:

> Within the last few months, our chief justice has pardoned three of the greatest criminals in the kingdom, on condition they emigrate to the United States. . . . The culprit Camman, who was condemned to death for highway robbery and murder, has had his punishment commuted to emigration to America.

Not all who were honorable were necessarily industrious or accomplished. Speaking at the 1886 Conference of Charities, F. B. Sanborn, former chairman of the Massachusetts Board of State Charities, offered the obvious: "The impulse to emigrate from one's native country does not ordinarily inspire first those who are comfortable, fully occupied, firmly established, or reputably engaged. . . ."

Honorable, if not successful, were the countless others who, like the Edinburgh paupers still wearing their poorhouse coats, were encouraged to emigrate or, indeed, sent on their way by foreign governments, especially England. It must have seemed, from contemporary reports, that there was an organized effort on the part of European governments to rid their countries of as many as possible of their dependent citizens.

Whatever their reasons for coming, and whatever their circumstances, they came: 20 million of them in the course of the nineteenth century. That a substantial number of newcomers were the dependent needy was recognized even before the heaviest tide of immigration (four out of five nineteenth-century immigrants came after 1860). In 1850, according to the U.S. Census Bureau, a total of $3 million was expended on paupers in the United States. Of the 134,972 persons assisted, 51 percent were foreign-born. In New York, the ratio was 2 to 1; in Massachusetts, 3 to 2; in Wisconsin, 3 to 1.

In 1855 the Philadelphia Society for Relief of the Poor reported that it took in 1,266 persons, of whom 79 percent were immigrants. That same year New York's publicly funded Bellevue Hospital found immigrants totaling 85 percent of its admissions. In 1880 the New York State Board of Charities reported there were 56,058 in the state's almshouse — 61 percent foreign-born.

With such a vast influx of population there was inevitable friction. Impoverished foreigners were often perceived as having brought trouble on themselves and inconvenience to the community by emigrating in the first place. Catholics constituted a large proportion of newcomers — a fact inherently disconcerting to a basically Protestant population and remindful of old-world animosities. A good many newcomers were also confirmed tipplers, as against a relatively more abstemious native population, and for many an immigrant the first real acquaintance in the United States, after the relief officer, was the saloon keeper.

Reaction to immigration was pronounced in New England, where, at mid-century, it coincided with a revival of puritanism. A "momentous, profound and difficult" problem, said the Massachusetts Sanitary Commission of the increasing incidence of foreign-born pauperism in an 1850 report to the state legislature. Immigration, especially of paupers, should be discouraged, said the commission: "Every man in whose veins courses any Puritan blood, as he looks back upon the events of the past, or forward to the hopes of the future, is appalled and astounded."

A moderate assertion, compared to the *Chicago Medical Gazette*,

March 5, 1880, on the disproportionate use of public medical relief by foreigners:

> We are, alas! overrun with a degraded foreign population . . . who have no higher aim than to extort from the world about them the best possible living under the circumstances. Instead of hesitating to accept a charity, they not only expect it but scheme and plot to get it. It would be a revelation to some of our parlor philanthropists could they realize to what an extent this is the case.

If the relief officer was often the first acquaintance, and the saloon keeper the second, the third was likely to be the ward boss, and so we find the immigrant coming to power politically—a power, given his vast numbers, to be reckoned with. From *The Nation*, October 18, 1866:

> They [the immigrants] form, on the contrary, large, compact communities of their own, perfectly impervious to American influences, in which no Americans are ever seen except on business errands, in which American opinions are never heard, American papers never read, and in which as little is known of the movements of American society as in Germany or Ireland—in which the prejudices, passions, habits, interest, and vices of the Old World retain all their sway—communities, in short, as distinctive, as essentially foreign, as the population of Dublin or Hamburg, and kept constantly recruited by fresh arrivals. The political significance of this may be inferred from the fact that out of the 129,000 voters in New York City, 77,000 or nearly two-thirds, are foreigners, and nearly all drawn from the most ignorant class of European society. This means, of course, that the government has been transferred to their hands without any restraint or condition except such as their consciences may impose.

It may thus be seen that nineteenth-century immigration, besides contributing to the poor problem by adding vast numbers of poor, also contributed toward a changed political climate: one where there was first-hand knowledge of developing European socialism and the embryonic welfare states taking shape in Germany and England. The ranks of the immigrants were fertile to the reaping of votes for social change.

EUROPEAN PRECEDENT

> The Reichstag Opened
>
> BERLIN, Nov. 17—The Emperor's speech emphatically points out that the social evils are not to be remedied by repression alone, but rather by concurrent promotion of the welfare of the working classes.

The Emperor says he will look back on all his successes with greater satisfaction if he can bequeath to the fatherland new and lasting guarantees for continuous peace at home, and to the necessitous a more secure and generous measure of that assistance to which they have a claim.

New York Tribune
November 18, 1881

Thus was proclaimed the modern era of social security. The speech of Emperor William I was not read by the emperor, however; he was ill, and, on the advice of his physician, he remained home and left the reading of the speech that opened the Reichstag to his Chancellor. But Bismarck, it was, who likely wrote the speech in the first place; and Bismarck it was whose policy it set forth.

"Social evils are not to be remedied by repression alone, but rather by concurrent promotion of the welfare of the working classes," proclaimed the Iron Chancellor. Repression had been tried. The preceding decades had seen the rise of German industrialization, and the rise of socialism in Germany.

These first socialists were mostly followers of Ferdinand Lassalle, who held (as opposed to followers of Marx) that working class conditions could be bettered within the existing system, and that the state could even be a partner in the movement for social progress. One sign of their growing power was the granting of universal suffrage in the Reichstag elections of 1867. Even so, the socialist movement was no threat to the existing order of things. At the conclusion of the Franco-Prussian War of 1871–72, it was reckoned that there were about 125,000 socialist votes in Germany. "We can kill them with a stick," declared liberal Reichstag member Eduard Lasker.

By 1874 the socialist vote had increased to 350,000, and in another three years to a half-million. Now the government was uneasy. A stick would no longer do. Moreover, in 1875 there had been a Socialist Congress at Gotha, which brought together the followers of Lassalle and Marx, produced demands for sweeping new working class rights, and gave evidence that Marxist (revolutionary) socialism was now in the ascendancy.

Two attempts on the life of the emperor in 1878, both ascribed to the socialists, gave grounds for doing something. The result was the antisocialist laws, under which Germany abolished the Socialist Party and prohibited all meetings and publications, thus, in effect, driving its leaders from the country. But the movement itself went underground. Not only did it survive, it thrived.

The drastic remedy of repression did not work, as Bismarck himself allowed in the 1881 speech to the Reichstag. Thus, a new policy was needed. As a common saying of the day had it, "Bismarck will cure socialism by a hair of the dog that bit him." Or, as Bismarck himself expressed it, "by concurrent promotion of the welfare of the working classes."

Germans had known a poor law much like England's,* but that was obviously no longer the answer. In April 1881, seven months before the Reichstag speech, Bismarck proposed: "The end I have in view is to relieve the towns of a large part of their poor law charges by the establishment of an institution having state support and extending to the entire empire."

But there were still the same nagging questions: Might there be a man willing who simply could not find work? Might poverty sometimes be the result of sickness or accident that is job-related? What about those economic forces under little or no control of the individual? In a conversation recorded by his secretary, Moritz Busch, on June 26, 1881, Bismarck explained his thinking: *Die Staat muss die Sache in die Hand nehmen, nicht als Almosen, sondern als Recht* . . .

> The state must take the matter in hand, not as alms-giving, but as the right that men have to be taken care of when, with the best will imaginable, they become unfit for work. Why should the regular soldier disabled by war, or the official, have a right to be pensioned in his old age, and not the soldier of labor? This thing will make its own way; it has a future. When I die, possibly our policy will come to grief. But state socialism [as opposed to party socialism] will have its day; and he who shall take it up again will assuredly be the man at the wheel.

There we have the Bismarck of "Christian paternalism," who believed the state had a moral responsibility to take care of its own. Looking more deeply, we find another Bismarck — the unquestioned master of the art of statecraft — heading off the challenge, taking the socialist in, patting him on the head, and asking him what all the fuss is about.

In so doing, Bismarck sought to lure the socialist away from his partisan loyalties, but there was more to it than that. There was the effect on the population as a whole. This the wily Bismarck confided to Busch in another conversation about the same time:

> Anybody who has before him the prospect of a pension, be it ever so small, in old age or infirmity is much happier and more content

---

*The Prussian *Landrecht* of 1794 decreed: "It is the duty of the state to provide for the sustenance and support of those of its citizens who cannot . . . procure subsistence themselves. [But those who choose not to labor] shall be kept to useful work by compulsion. . . ."

with his lot, much more tractable and easy to manage, than he whose future is absolutely uncertain.

What evolved was the cornerstone legislation of modern social security:

- *Sickness Insurance Act* (June 15, 1883): Insurance paid two-thirds by employee and one-third by employer. Within ten years, it covered 8 million workers. Benefits included free medical attendance and medicine from the beginning of an illness; free admission to a hospital in some cases; sick pay at one-half of regular wages; sick relief to women for four weeks after childbirth; and burial expenses.
- *Accident Insurance Act* (July 6, 1884): Paid entirely by employer. Gradually extended to nearly all types of jobs. Applied to bodily injury or death on the job. Compensation consisted of cost of treatment plus a fixed allowance during incapacity in case of accident, or survivor's allowance in case of death. In case of total disability, compensation amounted to two-thirds of an average year's earnings.
- *Invalidity and Old Age Insurance Act* (June 22, 1889): Generally compulsory, beginning at age 16, with all wageearners below management level. Employee, employer, and state contributed. Employer made his contribution in the form of a stamp pasted weekly in employee receipt book, which remained in employee's possession when changing jobs. Old age pensions began at age 70, provided income was not above a specified level. Invalidity pensions were applicable to non-job-related incapacity, since an on-the-job accident would have created eligibility under accident insurance.

As remarkable as they were, these German insurance laws of the 1880s still reflected the conception that change should be no more sweeping than necessary. The 1883 sickness insurance law, for example, expressly used existing agencies—guild benefit societies, miners' societies, communal organizations—to help with the administration of it. At the same time workers of Germany made the most of the new laws. By 1892 nearly 1 billion marks (more than $235 million) had been paid out under the three forms of social insurance.

It was natural that other countries should take notice. At the time Invalidity and Old Age Insurance went into effect, *The Times* of London (June 19, 1889) decided the results would be worth watching:

England has tried most of the political experiments of the last 500 years. She has been the laboratory of nations. When a foreign statesman has the courage to try a novelty on this colossal scale we can look on with wonder . . . but ready to believe and willing to hope. . . .

The United States was looking on also, albeit with detached curiosity for the most part. Nevertheless, a special report of the U.S. commissioner of labor in 1893 was devoted entirely to an analysis of Germany's new social insurance law. Its essential conclusion was akin to that in London:

That Germany with such means at her disposal should be willing to try a social experiment on a scale so vast, ought at least to excite the gratitude of all other people, for if she fails the lesson will be invaluable, and if success follows, the example may prove so useful that other nations will find many of the obstacles removed by this bold and skilful pioneering.

We turn ahead: Birmingham, England, June 10, 1911. It is two weeks before the coronation of George V, but an event nearly as exciting is at hand. There are 3,000 people jammed into the Birmingham Town Hall to hear a speech. They are the lucky ones with tickets. Another 67,000 or so tried to get tickets and could not. The speech is about a controversial national insurance law for England. The speaker says he is an ambulance driver. "I have just joined the Red Cross," he tells them, "I am in the ambulance corps. I am engaged to drive a wagon through the twistings and turnings and ruts of the Parliamentary road."

He admits that some people think the wagon is overloaded, while others say it is half-empty, and still others accuse him of driving in too much of a hurry. "I am rather in a hurry," declares Chancellor of the Exchequer David Lloyd George, who did most of the work constructing the wagon, "for I can hear the moanings of the wounded, and I want to carry relief to them in the alleys, the homes where they lie stricken. . . . " He speaks for nearly two hours. He folds his speech and sits down amid 3,000 cheers that might have been 67,000 more.

This was an England governed by an overwhelmingly Liberal majority that had been swept into office in 1906 in a startling reversal of power. And even though social legislation had not been a major issue in the campaign, it became a principal concern of the new Liberal administration, and in particular of Lloyd George, the Bismarck of England and the architect of its social insurance.

It was likewise the concern of the administration's young Board of Trade president, Winston Churchill, who had bolted the Conservative Party in 1904. With a convert's fervor, he laid out the administration's position in a speech to the Scottish Liberal Association in Dundee, October 9, 1908:

I do not agree with those who say that every man must look after himself, and that the intervention of the State in such matters as I have referred to will be fatal to his self-reliance, his foresight, and his thrift. . . . when I am told that the institution of old-age pensions will prevent the working classes from making provision for their old age, I say that cannot be, for they have never been able to make such provision. . . . where there is no hope be sure there will be no thrift.

The climate of change dramatized by Churchill's defection to the liberal cause produced England's basic social insurance legislation: the Old Age Pension Act of 1908 and the National Insurance Act of 1911.

The Old Age Pension Act was the kind of law that had been talked about since the German legislation of 1889. It was enacted in England in part for the same reason Bismarck had proposed it: to head off socialism. Unlike Germany's program, Britain's was noncontributory, which meant its pension benefits would accrue immediately. Those benefits were weekly payments of up to 7s.6d. for married couples with incomes of less than £31 a year, beginning at age 70. It was not to be a dole: Pensions would be denied to those "who failed to work habitually according to their ability and need" and those who had "failed to save money regularly." Even so, there were dire warnings of a state pension system disheartening the thrifty and encouraging the idle.

The National Insurance Act — the subject of Lloyd George's ambulance driver speech — was nevertheless more controversial. Once proposed in Parliament, it was an immediate object of suspicion. The press helped stir up opposition. The insurance industry mounted a bitter attack. Even some unionists argued it would represent a confiscation of working-class wages. The controversy notwithstanding, it became law, and gave Britain the distinction of having the first compulsory unemployment insurance act. In its original form, it covered about 2 million out of a work force of 15 million. Employee, employer, and state contributed equal amounts. Benefits began after the first week of unemployment. The act also included health insurance, modeled on the German program.

Both health and unemployment insurance were contributory in contrast to the old age pensions, reflecting lessons learned. The pensions were costing more than anticipated (£8 million instead of £6 million the first year), so that noncontributory health and unemployment insurance almost certainly would not have passed Parliament. Furthermore, contributory insurance got around the age-old dilemma of deciding who was deserving of assistance and who was not. Everyone was deserving, provided he had paid in. Similarly, it was not considered charity in that its beneficiaries "earned" their benefits. Churchill talked about rights earned as opposed to rights bestowed.

Once again, the United States was watching, this time less with detached curiosity than with outright disparagement. "England's folly," said a New York *Times* article (August 4, 1908) of the pension act: ". . . we have the spectacle of the most conservative of civilized nations pledged to carry out a Socialistic measure in its most irresponsible, unstable and theoretical form."

"A socialistic demand for a general divide up of whatever there is," moaned the San Francisco *Chronicle* (July 22, 1908), ". . . degrading to human nature and wholly indefensible."

"The project is emphatically a leap in the dark," declared the Chicago *Tribune* in an editorial (July 26, 1908), *but*

> worthy of the prolonged and prayerful consideration of those Americans who are frightened even by the most urgently needed remedial measures and are quick to cry radicalism or socialism when the profoundly conservative and patient American people, after years of abuse of privilege, are finally forced to protest and act.

7
NOVUS ORDO BEGINS
The Coming of the New Deal

The Great Depression changed attitudes about public relief by making destitution more visible and by often disclosing the down-and-out to be friends and neighbors. From this economic crucible flowed the social legislation that substantially changed a way of life. And yet, looking back, one can see that change was coming even before the exigencies that made a veritable "revolution" possible.

A snug and pleasant street is Mount Vernon Avenue in Marion, Ohio. One strolls along, secure, though it's a gray morning, this Friday in October, and one's collar is turned up high upon the neck.

The wind whips Old Glory atop a flagpole down the street, and that catches the eye, and thus the house that's there. It's a sturdy house, but welcoming, with a big front porch like umpteen thousand others across the land. And yet not quite. Something's different. Where's the grass that any respectable front yard ought to have? Crushed limestone instead.

One pauses a moment, and hears, off in the distance, the sound of band music and softly tramping feet, getting a little louder with each step. A parade, and it's coming this way. One waits a bit, and there it is: the drum majors first, all brightly uniformed; and then the trumpets and the trombones, and the tubas and the thumping big bass drums. And then the marchers. Marchers. There must be hundreds of them, maybe thousands. But what's this? They're all women. Some are waving flags, and some are cheering, their spirits hardly dampened by the chill, dreary weather this first day of October 1920.

Up to the home with the big front porch they trek, their vanguard spilling into a front yard that, in the wet, would be a quagmire save its limestone lawn. This yard's not new to feet. From a resting place under some apple trees in back darts a swarm of men, pads and pencils in hand. "Here he is." A cheer goes up among the women as the front door opens onto the big front porch and a big, grandfatherly man — white-thatched, trim and neat in striped serge jacket and white flannel trousers — steps out, beaming confidently, raising his hands in thanks, nodding, waiting patiently.

It turns out this is "Social Justice Day." And this is the "Front Porch," center stage of Campaign 1920. These thousands of women from far and wide throughout the East and Middle West have come to hear a speech by U.S. Senator Warren G. Harding, the odds-on favorite to be the next president of the United States.

On this pleasant street in the middle of America — in this quintessence of the snug and sturdy — one might have expected to hear a snug and sturdy speech. Yet when it was done, when the campaign oration of this damp and windy morning was over and a normal quiet had returned to a normal street, a reporter for the New York *Tribune* could be found jotting down on his pad, "There was no doubt in the mind of any present that Senator Harding has gone far in advance of all party platforms." And everybody's favorite mystery novelist, Mary Roberts Rinehart, could be heard giving her opinion to a correspondent for the

New York *Times*: ". . . the most advanced liberalism. There is nothing equivocal about the promises made by Senator Harding."

What Harding did on October 1, 1920, in advance of any party platform, was to foretell the New Deal more than a decade ahead of its time. To the thousands of women assembled at the Front Porch, Harding proposed that the federal government assume a new and far-reaching responsibility for the welfare of *all* Americans, not just the poor. He called for creation of a federal Department of Public Welfare that would have jurisdiction over social services, child welfare, women's rights, public health, veterans' benefits, and education.

So stunning a proposal, especially for a relatively conservative Republican, would raise eyebrows, as Harding was well aware. "I have no doubt," he observed,

> that there will be some who will find in this proposal cause for calling me an extremist; but when we have a task to do, which has been dictated by our conscience and approved by our wisdom, let us straightway find the way to do it.

Cause for calling him an extremist was hardly characteristic of Harding's campaign. For the most part, he spoke in platitudes, talking at great length and saying little. His travel was mostly to and from the Front Porch. Opponent James M. Cox and his running mate, Franklin D. Roosevelt, burned up the railroad tracks from one end of the country to the other and moved hardly at all in the standings. War, Wilson, strikes, inflation, the League of Nations: these were the issues, and issues that favored the Republican standard-bearers, Harding and Coolidge. Harding's basic strategy, therefore, was to say nothing that might counteract the expected shift: Stay home, on the Front Porch, and let the campaign come to him. And come they did. The 5,000 who pilgrimaged to Marion on October 1, 1920, "Social Justice Day"—to the accompaniment of a campaign band the last mile of the way—nowhere near set a record. On October 18th, "First Voters Day," more than 25,000 college students, women, and foreign-born citizens, all about to vote for the first time, made the trek to the Harding home.

The campaign was the most expensive to date for either party, a public relations extravaganza unparalleled in U.S. politics to that time. Yet, at heart, was Harding's appeal for a "return to normalcy," by which he meant, he said, not a return to the "old order" but to a "regular, steady order of things . . . without excess."

How, then, to explain a social justice plan "in advance of any platform"? Harding was a seat-of-the-pants politician, and a good one, not unlike Franklin D. Roosevelt. Late in September, his campaign, once such a sure thing, had been losing ground, largely over his party's division on the League of Nations issue. An audience of thousands of women — voting for president for the first time under the Nineteenth Amendment that had just taken effect — was a made-to-order opportunity. Harding had been running an "image" rather than an "issues" campaign. The image proffered was that of the common man, in contrast to the imperious Wilson, whom Republicans sought to make into a vicarious opponent, in record if not in person. A grandfatherly Harding demonstrating concern for the welfare of his fellow man would affirm that image and, at the same time, let him outflank the liberal opposition. A proposal that might have been extreme for some other Republican in some other time and place in this case endeared him to a zealous cadre of missionaries who carried the message of social equality back to other women (voters now) around the country.

Campaign strategy aside, Harding could make a good case for his federal Department of Public Welfare. The United States, at this time, he pointed out:

- spent twice as many federal dollars on hog cholera as on child welfare;
- recorded an infant mortality rate almost as high as the number of U.S. casualities in World War I (a quarter-million a year);
- ranked fourth highest among 16 major countries in maternity death rate.

The statistics cited make it evident that Harding's first concern was health — not only of the poor but of everyone. His new department would have public health as its principal function; it would stimulate, through research as well as through education, a more active role on the part of local government.

Child welfare would be another goal. There were already some federal programs in this area, but they would be significantly expanded.

Another function would be women's rights. Said Harding: there must be "increasing enlightenment in industry and business which will tend to break down distinctions of sex in matters of remuneration, and establish equal pay for equal work."

The farmer was another intended beneficiary of increased government attention. He was in particularly desperate straits in the postwar period.

These broad thoughts Harding outlined during the campaign. Subsequently, he refined his proposal to provide for a Department of Public Welfare that included, specifically, a Division of Education, a Division of Public Health, a Division of Social Service, and a Division of Veterans' Service Administration. To be a little more specific, according to a Harding spokesman, as quoted in the New York *Times*, May 8, 1921:

- The department would see to "the essential things that are necessary to make the best American citizens from the physical standpoint."
- It would provide the federal machinery for assuring "the proper education of teachers."
- It would make provision for a competent social service director who would "say what is necessary and also what is right."

What was once a campaign proposal of candidate Harding now had turned into a legislative goal of President Harding. But even before the plan was introduced as a bill in the Senate, opposition began building. The New York *Times*, in an editorial on January 3, 1921, sounded a common objection: "For the next few years, at least, Federal activities should not be extended. . . . Retrenchment is imperative. Let the several States attend to 'public welfare' in their own way." The American Federation of Labor also made known its opposition on grounds that the new department would absorb agencies that were in the Department of Labor. When a bill was introduced and hearings began before the Senate Committee on Education and Labor in May 1921, Samuel Gompers was more blunt in a telegram to the committee: "The enemies of organized labor would like to ruin the labor department by dismembering it under the guise of creating a department of welfare." For like reason there was opposition from many in education — those who wanted to see a federal Department of Education established instead. Skeptics joined the fray. Although Harding had argued cost-saving, there were those in Congress who contended the new department would increase spending.

When the hearings concluded on May 21st, opinion was so divided there was clearly not enough support for passage. Nothing more was heard of Harding's plan to centralize, in Washington, responsibility for the welfare of the nation's citizens.

Since Harding's proposal did not directly influence the sweeping social legislation of the 1930s, it has been forgotten in the dusty attic of history. Yet it is significant in retrospect. It presaged essential elements of the New Deal, and showed that attitudes toward welfare and social service legislation were changing where change counted.

It was the parade heard down the street.

SOCIAL TRENDS AND "SOCIALISM"

It is a paradox that some of the most far-reaching social proposals of the twentieth century have come under Republican administrations (as another example, Nixon's Family Assistance Plan [see Chapter 9], a more radical piece of legislation than anything enacted in the name of the Great Society). Under a successor to Harding there was the Report of the President's Research Committee on Social Trends in 1933. Among its recommendations:

- "A solvent unemployment fund would do much to mitigate the distress which many now suffer before finding new openings."
- "An extension of old-age pensions to care for victims of progress may bulk large in future discussions."
- "It is conceivable that without any surrender of our belief in the merits of private property, individual enterprise and self-help, the American people will press toward a larger measure of public control to promote the common welfare."
- "The six-hour day and the five-day week are methods of distributing the loss of jobs in a less inequitable fashion."
- "Unless there is a speeding up of social invention or a slowing down of mechanical inventions, grave maladjustments are certain to result."

Just how advanced were those proposals, at the time, may be judged by the fact that "compulsory unemployment compensation," "old-age pensions," and the "six-hour day and five-day week" were all part of the Socialist Party platform of 1932. And yet here they were being presented in the name of Herbert Hoover. The presidential committee had been appointed by Hoover in September 1929, one month before the stock market crash, because, said Hoover, the country needed more action in social welfare. It was typical of Hoover's careful, scientific approach to everything, however, that what action there was proceeded at the pace of a research scientist in the laboratory.

That is not to say that the extent of the crisis was misunderstood. The committee's report acknowledged that "impressive" social action was needed or "there can be no assurance that these alternatives . . . violent revolution and dark periods of repression . . . can be averted." But so far as the Hoover presidency was concerned, the report was after the fact. It was made public on New Year's Day 1933, two months after the election, and was quickly interred in the dead file, nevermore to be anything but a footnote to history. By a twist of fate, however, the Washington *Post* took an editorial look at it first, and, irony of ironies, denounced as "socialism" this product of an administration just trounced by the voters for its seemingly stodgy conservatism.

How many of the committee's recommendations Hoover would have pressed for had he been reelected it is not possible to say, but it is reasonable to conjecture. Hoover, in his memoirs, wrote that he wanted legislation on "old-age pensions, insurance against irregular employment, better housing, and care of children." Some new program of social legislation certainly would have followed reelection. The sense of direction was already there in Harding's time. How vastly greater the pressure as the calendar turned to 1933. Something new was coming; but it had been *pledged* by another.

THE CRUCIBLE YEARS

The situation was unprecedented. Heretofore, when a man was nominated for president, he waited for his party's delegation to visit him (it had sometimes taken weeks) and then declared his acceptance. Franklin Delano Roosevelt wouldn't wait. He would take charge. He would dispel any notion that his physical condition might hinder his quest for votes. He would show himself an aggressive campaigner, an aggressive leader, ready to grapple with the nation's problems. So FDR went to Chicago, to the Democratic National Convention in the summer of 1932, to the people who had nominated him over Al Smith, to tell them he would accept. Furthermore, observed the Chicago *Tribune*, he went "in an airplane, symbol of the new age, touching the imagination of the people."

The plane was an American Airways tri-motor, for which arrangements were made hurriedly the night before when news of the convention's fourth-ballot decision reached the Executive Mansion in Albany. With Governor Roosevelt, Eleanor, and a few of the family and staff aboard, the silver plane lifted off at 7:30 the morning of Saturday, July 2, and headed due west on a course that would take the craft through squalls and bumpy air. FDR, who had flown often as assistant secretary of the navy, seemed not to notice, though he did chew gum nearly the whole time. Throughout the flight, he was preoccupied with the speech he would give later that day, and he worked on it almost constantly. From time to time he would look out at the clouds, deep in thought. Then, his words chosen, he would dictate over the din of the engines to his personal secretary, "Missy" Le Hand, who, between tips and dips of the aircraft, turned his words into a rough draft. At 4:30, two hours late, the plane slipped through low-hanging clouds to land at Chicago Municipal Airport.

At 6 P.M., neatly dressed in a blue suit, a red rose in his lapel, FDR made his way to the podium at Chicago Stadium to address the Democratic National Convention. It was his: 20,000 delegates' and spectators' voices going hoarse, 40,000 hands getting sore, and over it all the organ blaring away "Happy Days Are Here Again." FDR stood patiently, waiting for the demonstration to subside, beaming, teeth-clenched, head thrust high, waving again and again, and still again.

He read his speech in a loud voice. The crowd seemed more interested than anything else in what he had to say about Prohibition, and he told them what they wanted to hear: The Eighteenth Amendment was doomed. Tumultuous applause.

He went on, now picking up the theme of his "forgotten man" speech of the past spring—the speech in which he denounced Al Smith as a demagogue. "Men and women, forgotten in the political philosophy of the government of recent years," he intoned, "look to us here for guidance and for more equitable opportunity to share in the distribution of national wealth." Primary responsibility for relieving distress arising out of the Depression, he went on, lay with local government, but the federal had "a continuing responsibility for the broader public welfare."

His speech was not a long one. A little past 6:30, FDR was winding up, and had every reason to expect there would be another ovation like the one earlier. Yet, smart politician and orator that he was, he knew the value of a punch line—something to sum up the whole speech in a couple of words, something also to suggest, perhaps, that a new age flew in with the first airplane used in national politics. "I pledge you," he told them, "I pledge myself to a new deal for the American people."

The Republicans met two weeks earlier, in mid-June, also in Chicago, also in the cavernous Chicago Stadium.

Unlike the Democrats, the Republicans had no choice to make about a standard-bearer; there was an incumbent to renominate.

Like the Democrats, the Republicans made use of modern technology. At either end of the vast hall was a motion picture screen, on which flicked a short film of the president urging a balanced budget. The talkie was produced for the occasion by California delegate Louis B. Mayer, the second "M" of MGM. Like the Democrats, the Republicans also sang "Happy Days Are Here Again."*

There was singing in Washington about the same time, songs like "Tipperary" and "Hail, Hail the Gang's All Here." The singers were some 20,000 members of the "Bonus Expeditionary Force," camped in Washington to press their case for a veterans' bonus they had long been promised. The bonus was actually approved by Congress in 1924, in the form of a 20-year endowment that would become payable in 1945. Now, three

---

*"Happy Days Are Here Again" was a popular song written in 1929. It was featured in the movie, *Chasing Rainbows*, and made the top of the hit parade in February and March 1930. It subsequently became the "official tune" of Republican Governor "Sunny Jim" Rolph of California. After it was used by the Republicans at their 1932 national convention, Roosevelt let it be known that the song would be a good tune for the Democrats. On July 10, 1932, Cook County (Illinois) Commissioner Charles H. Weber was reported in the New York *Times* to have announced a personal campaign to make a singer out of every Democrat provided the singing he did was "Happy Days Are Here Again." The song went on to become the national anthem of the New Deal.

years into the Great Depression and down-and-out, they wanted cash on the barrel-head.

Their moment of triumph came on June 15th, when the House of Representatives, after impassioned debate — Rep. Edward E. Eslick, in mid-sentence, slumping dead on the floor of the House — passed the veterans' bonus bill by a vote of 211-176. The bill provided for $2.4 billion in bonuses, a sum equal to more than half the entire federal budget, to be paid immediately by cranking up the press and printing a like amount of new dollar bills.

The marchers' moment of defeat came two nights later when the Senate, working through the dinner hour, readied the bill for a vote a little past 8 o'clock. On hand, outside, were 10,000 veterans, swarming the steps of the Capitol, standing patiently in the great plaza, sprawling on the grass under the great elms of the Capitol grounds. Inside, in the Senate galleries, were a few hundred of the men, as many as could fit, their frayed and faded olive drab a stark contrast to the stately surroundings. The vote was no, and it wasn't even close. The news was relayed outside. A bugle called the men to attention. As they listened to the result, they bared their heads, and then, spontaneously, sang "America."

Elsewhere there was song, of sorts. Composer Richard Rodgers once remarked that a song is the voice of its times. Number One on the *Variety* hit parade the summer of the bonus marchers was "A Shanty in Old Shanty Town."

A typical shantytown was three acres of ash heaps and junk in Youngstown, Ohio, hard by the now still mills that once manufactured prosperity. Here the unemployed passed their days, except for the hours out begging money for food. It was fashionable to eat at home. Eating "out" meant the city garbage dump.

Dwellings were diverse in architecture: some mere caves, covered with pieces of tin; others veritable little houses built of packing crates, with windows and doors filched from lumber yards. This town had a resident population of 150 to 200, and was called as were hundreds of others around the country, "Hooverville." Pittsburgh's was under the wing of Father James R. Cox, the hunger march leader, who supplied each shanty with a placard reading, "God Bless Our Home."

Elsewhere, just as in Youngstown, there were other manifestations of the Great Depression. One was becoming all too common around the country:

FATHER OF TEN DROWNS SELF;
JOBLESS, JUMPS FROM BRIDGE

He had worked in a steel mill for 27 years, and now he was unemployed. His gas and electricity had been shut off; the house would go next. As he stood on Spring Common Bridge, watching others go to work, he took off his coat, folded it neatly, set it by the railing, and jumped into the swirling Mohoning River.

In Pittsburgh, a sickly lad of eight helped to get free medicine for the needy. He went to a newspaper office with an ad putting up for sale his dog, "Teddy Bear," hoping thereby to get money for medicine. The newspaper found a pharmacist who was willing to supply not only the boy but other poor people with medicine at no charge. "Teddy Bear" stayed with his master.

Sears Roebuck had some good news for its 38,000 employees: a wage cut of 5 to 10 percent. Other employees in other companies were getting wage cuts of 100 percent.

Some of those laid off criss-crossed the country in search of work, usually in vain. A man and his wife from Fairview, Illinois, walked into a police station after weeks on the road, asking directions to the local relief office in Yakima, Washington. The couple had a letter promising a job, and had walked all the way with a heavy suitcase. A sympathetic police sergeant shook his head in pity. They had gone in the wrong direction and were in Rockville, Maryland. The sergeant offered them a free dinner and a night's lodging in the jail.

In Pittsburgh, a steel worker whose wages were $30 a week in 1929 was getting $15 in 1932, if he still had a job.

The city of Philadelphia in June 1931 borrowed $3 million as an unemployment fund. It was gone by December, and the city itself turned panhandler, seeking to raise additional funds through contributions. The city's relief committee took in nearly $10.5 million in cash and pledges; but by early spring of 1932 there was no realistic hope of that fund lasting beyond May. The benefits it paid out averaged $4.38 per week per family, which was barely subsistence-level.

Prior to borrowing the $3 million in June 1931, the city closed its relief stations for a three-week period. The result was rising tempers and increasingly loud demands for food, creating alarm among relief workers. By late winter 1932, Philadelphia had 1,800 police trained for riot suppression and the use of tear gas.

A letter to the editor of the New York *Times*, June 7, 1932, urged government to get across the message that the greatest obstacle to recovery was fear itself.

A REFERENDUM ON CHANGE

The depression "really isn't anything more serious than a case of the hives." In such a way did Hoover's secretary of the interior, Ray Lyman Wilbur, M.D., diagnose the nation's ills in June 1932. A month earlier, Dr. Wilbur told the National Conference on Social Work, meeting in Philadelphia, that the depression was likely to be beneficial rather than unduly harmful to the American child—a conclusion that startled delegates.

Over such appearances of complacency did Hoovervilles get their name and Hoover his lasting, and undeserved, reputation as someone who cared more about big business than about the little fellow. In reality, there was the Hoover of war relief, perhaps the world's preeminent authority on large-scale alleviation of human suffering. There was the Hoover who inaugurated a relief drive in October 1931 by calling it (and they are his own words, since he wrote his own speeches) "an opportunity to lighten the burden of the heavy-laden, and to cast sunshine into the habitation of despair." There was also the Hoover who insisted that direct federal relief was not in the U.S. tradition; the Hoover who, in the closing days of the 1928 campaign, had told a cheering crowd at Madison Square Garden that American life in the years after the World War had been "challenged with a peacetime choice between the American system of rugged individualism and a European philosophy of diametrically opposed doctrines of paternalism and state socialism," and the American way had prevailed. It was Hoover by a landslide that time.

Two years later, the nation had plunged into depression. Hoover maintained the body economic would still heal itself, but he began to take significant measures—more than had ever been taken by a predecessor in the White House—to meet economic crisis through government action: a $423 million increase in public works, a cut in taxes, unprecedented pressure on the business community, the Hawley-Smoot Tariff Act to protect jobs.

In 1931, with the wheels of industry still slowing down, he sped up public works spending still further (to $780 million for the year), but continued to draw the line against any direct or indirect federal dole. "Our people," he said in December 1931, "are providing against distress from unemployment in true American fashion by a magnificent response to public appeal and by action of the local governments."

Early in 1932 Hoover proposed three measures further increasing government's response: additional capitalization of the Federal Land Banks to aid agriculture; home loan banks, of a like nature, to save homes; and the Reconstruction Finance Corporation (RFC).

The last was Hoover's most significant economic measure. It has been so regarded in retrospect, and was so regarded in prospect. Said the Washington *Post* reporting it the day it was signed into law: "America's greatest peacetime economic effort." The measure cleared Congress a little after 3 o'clock the afternoon of Friday, January 22, 1932. It was delivered to the White House at 6:03 P.M., and signed into law by Hoover at 6:11 P.M.

The RFC, with initial capitalization of $500 million, and authorization for up to $2 billion, was empowered to make loans to banks and other financial institutions, as well as to railroads, industry, and agricultural credit corporations. By August 1932 it had issued loans totaling more than $1 billion. Projects financed by the RFC its first year covered a broad spectrum: a toll bridge in Sabula, Iowa; a slum-clearance apartment complex in the Bronx; electrification of the Pennsylvania Railroad between New York and Washington. RFC and other federally funded self-liquidating projects embarked upon during the Hoover Administration also included: the San Francisco-Oakland Bay Bridge; the Los Angeles water supply system; New York's Jones Beach; authorization, in 1932 alone, for $653 million in construction of post offices and treasury facilities across the country.

Meanwhile, pressure continued to build for federal assistance. An unemployment relief bill (Costigan-LaFollette), appropriating $375 million, passed the House but lost in the Senate in February 1932. Early in July, after considerable wrangling, another bill (Wagner-Garner), providing for $2.1 billion in unemployment relief, passed both houses and went to the president. Hoover had already threatened a veto on grounds that the bill distributed funds to the states on the basis of population rather than need (states with lesser need would be equally welcome "to dip into the Federal Treasury") and in general that the bill had become tainted with "pork barrel characteristics" on its circuitous way through Congress. The use of federal funds was not the issue (although Pennsylvania Senator David Reed, voting against it, lamented that "we are lifting the lid of Pandora's box and we'll never be able to close it").

Hoover, accepting the bill in principle, asked Congress to take another crack at it, and to revise those features of the Wagner-Garner bill that he found objectionable. Congress did just that, and in the closing hours of the last day of the session passed a new bill providing for $2.12 billion in unemployment relief. Hoover, next day, pronounced the bill cured of its "pork barrel infection," and said he would sign it into law. The result was $300 million immediately available to the states for relief of the most exigent need; $1.5 billion in loans to states and other public agencies for long-range relief; and $322 million in federal public works. Of the total appropriation, $1.8 billion represented increased capitalization of the RFC.

The congressional session of 1932 thus concluded with the most impressive record, to date, of government response to economic emergency.

Such measures notwithstanding, there was gloom and uncertainty. "Are We Going to Have a Revolution?" asked a headline in *Harper's*, August 1932. And there were others like it:

"Will Revolution Come?"
> *Atlantic Monthly*, August 1932

"Relief and Revolution"
> *The Forum*, August 1932

"Does America Need a Dictator?"
> *Current History*, September 1932

In the midst of the nation's worst economic crisis, there was speculation as to whether or not the existing order had perhaps run its course, and whether some different form of government might be necessary to restore stability to the land. No one was actually suggesting a change of government, other than the Communists. But many wondered: Could it happen here? Could matters get so much worse that the existing order no longer seemed worth preserving?

There was no revolution because the system, though it creaked and groaned like a ship riding out a storm, showed it could take it. The system, economic as well as political, proved itself seaworthy in a violent gale.

And yet, a "revolution" was preached: "the right kind of revolution, the only kind of revolution this nation can stand for — a revolution at the ballot box."

That was Roosevelt in Indianapolis on October 20, 1932, telling the nation what it was he wanted on election day. Well before then, virtually every political observer in the country predicted he would get it, and when it was over and the votes were counted, a "revolution" it was, a turn-around of sweeping proportions. The 444-87 landslide that had been Hoover's victory four years earlier had now become a 472-59 defeat. Thus did Herbert Hoover, 19 years in continuous public employment, join the ranks of the nation's 10 million jobless. "Democracy," he wrote later in his memoirs, "is not a polite employer."

Was the election of 1932 a referendum on social policy? The candidates themselves thought so. Many might have said Prohibition, but Socialist candidate Norman Thomas, two days before the November 8th election, disagreed. "Too many people are hungry for that," said Thomas.

"This is a contest between two philosophies of government," argued Hoover at Madison Square Garden on October 31st.

Roosevelt, in Indianapolis on October 20th, had put it on the line: I want "a revolution at the ballot box."

At the same time, there was a tradition of voting out the party in power during hard times, a venerable rite of autumn in U.S. politics.

Van Buren, a winner over Harrison in 1836, lost to Harrison in 1840. In between came the panic of 1837. Buchanan, a clearcut winner in 1856, chose not to run for reelection in 1860; slavery and the alarms of civil war were the major factors, but the panic of 1857 cannot be discounted. In 1876 the Democrat Tilden was the winner in popular vote, ostensibly turning out the Republican Party, which held office during the panic of 1873. The reverse in fact occurred in 1896, with the election of McKinley and the eviction of the Democrats who had presided over the panic of 1893. And in November 1930, American voters observed the first anniversary of the stock market crash by electing a Democratic Congress.

Essentially, the election of 1932 was a referendum on change — on doing something, anything, about the Depression. Norman Thomas, back from a cross-country swing shortly before the election, said he had found lots of Roosevelt votes but fewer Roosevelt rooters. Journalist William Allen White, two weeks before the election, saw the electorate of 1932 voting not for or against a man, but rather "putting into the ballot box their resentment at the untoward events that have torn them from the moorings of the last three years."

ACROSS THE THRESHOLD

The situation is "desperate." Unless there is "heroic and instant action . . . chaos and revolution [will] run their course." Thus, in an extraordinary front-page editorial, did the old-line Republican Akron *Beacon Journal* on March 3, 1933, plead for the federal government to intercede in the banking crisis.

Fortune magazine, the previous September, found that the nation had suffered through three years of "muddled purpose" and concluded that "across the threshold lies a new federal policy."

Baltimore *Sun* correspondent J. Frederick Essary, writing in *Literary Digest*, July 1933, said what many had decided: If the New Deal fails, the nation won't be any worse off than it was when FDR took office, so the country might as well give it a try.

The chief agency for giving it a try was the 73rd Congress, which convened March 9, 1933, and continued in session until the early morning hours of June 16, a span, as it happens, of exactly 100 days — a span made legendary by the compilation of a record of legislation unparalleled in its impact. During those 100 days, Congress granted every major request of the new president. It gave him powers greater than any chief executive had ever possessed. It appropriated more money ($5.27 billion) than had ever been spent in one year, except for the war budgets of 1918-20. It mandated an increase in taxes ($550 million) that alone was roughly as much as the entire federal budget three decades earlier.

Notable, of course, among the many bills that became law during this first session of the 73rd Congress were those relating to economic recovery and social welfare, and in particular: the Civilian Conservation Corps, the Federal Emergency Relief Administration, the Public Works Administration, the Civil Works Administration, the Home Owners' Loan Act (providing $2 billion for refinancing mortgages on small homes), similar legislation for refinancing farm mortgages, and legislation establishing a joint federal-state employment system.

Roosevelt's first relief measure probably was also the most universally applauded: the Civilian Conservation Corps (CCC), which was signed into law 11 days into the new president's term. Its goal: provide 250,000 jobs by mid-summer, and at the same time carry out useful work conserving natural resources. In late March, jobless men across the country began lining up at army posts and induction centers, ready to fight the war of recovery. Their ranks included college graduates and high school drop-outs, professional men and unskilled laborers. They would serve six months, at $30 per month. By late 1933 there were some 300,000 in the ranks, getting paid $9 million per month and sending $6.5 million back home to help needy fathers, mothers, sisters, and brothers, who in turn might help a needy economy. The CCC ended in 1942 with the nation going off to war.

The second New Deal program was the $500 million Federal Emergency Relief Administration (FERA). Part of its funding came from the RFC—those funds that, under Hoover, the RFC had been authorized to loan to the states for local relief. Now those funds would go to the states as grants. Another distinction from the old system was that the White House, through FERA and its administrator, Harry L. Hopkins, would have jurisdiction over the distribution of relief funds rather than the autonomous and bipartisan RFC. Hopkins, formerly New York State relief administrator, took office at FERA in May 1933, observing that there were then 16 million persons on relief nationwide—"an unconscionable number." "It will not be my business to perpetuate in the United States a policy which will keep any such number on the relief rolls," declared Hopkins. The dole would have to go, and work relief takes its place.

The thrust of New Deal recovery policy was public works spending. Title II of the National Industrial Recovery Act, which became law in mid-June 1933, appropriated $3.3 billion for public works, making it the largest single outlay in peacetime to that date. By the end of October, more than $2 billion had been allocated. Projects included: the Civilian Conservation Corps, $301 million; naval construction, $238 million [one might recall Themistocles and the Athenian fleet]; river and harbor work, $99 million [or the Emperor Claudius]; Grand Coulee Dam, $63 million; the Tennessee Valley Authority, $50 million; New York City's Triborough Bridge, $44 million, and Lincoln Tunnel, $38 million; Boulder

Dam (first named, and later renamed Hoover Dam), $38 million; and low-cost housing in various cities, $37 million.

The program was under the jurisdiction of the Public Works Administration (PWA), likewise created by the National Industrial Recovery Act, and headed by Secretary of the Interior Harold L. Ickes. Like the Hoover public works program, this one was somewhat slow in starting; by the end of 1933, comparatively little of its appropriation had been spent.

Meanwhile, the administration's fourth major relief effort was in preparation, this one the Civil Works Administration (CWA). To be recalled here is Hopkins' advice that the dole had to go. This is where the CWA came in. Whereas FERA was seeing to federal funding of locally administered relief, and PWA was administering large-scale public works, CWA would concentrate on short-term work relief: that which was praised here for requiring a recipient to earn his relief check, and criticized there as being nothing but "make work."

With $600 million in funds, the CWA set out to employ 4 million unemployed workers by the winter of 1933-34. So announced Roosevelt on November 8, 1933, when the act became law. Those participating would work a 30-hour week for an average salary of $12.50. Their tasks would include constructing playgrounds, clearing creek beds, reclaiming public lands, building feeder roads, and carrying out construction projects that were not part of the PWA. Certain professional persons— actors, musicians, and the like—would work at their own trades. Thus, said Roosevelt, in his first annual message to Congress on January 3, 1934, such assistance to the needy would "not be mere relief, but the opportunity for useful and remunerative work." Nor would the program be permanent; a response to the economic downturn in the fall of 1933, it would continue only into the spring of 1934.

At its peak, January 1934, the CWA had more than 4 million men at work, but even so, it made no dent in overall unemployment. The jobless total in January 1934, by estimate of the American Federation of Labor, was 13.3 million; in January 1933 it had been 13.1 million.

Of the New Deal programs thus far undertaken, the CWA was the most conspicuous. In order not to be a mere dole, it turned to projects of vast variety in pursuing its goal of usefulness: from giving concerts and plays to exterminating troublesome starlings on Washington streets. In New York City, in January 1934, more than 1,000 out-of-work actors lined up to apply for 150 CWA acting jobs. Those selected produced free plays—from Shakespeare's *Midsummer Night's Dream* to George Kelly's *The Show-Off*—in school auditoriums, hospitals, and museums. In Philadelphia, in March 1934, concerts of "high caliber" that won "prolonged applause" (quoting a New York *Times* review) were presented by the Civic Symphony Orchestra, an ensemble of 85 jobless musicians given two months of CWA employment. Not to be left out, the Society of American Magicians sent a delegation to Washington to see about CWA jobs for the down-and-out among its members. The delegation was headed by Theo Hardeen, brother of the late Houdini; it found that pulling a rabbit out of a hat was easier than pulling down a job.

Overall, the CWA paid wages running from 30 cents an hour for unskilled labor to $1.20 for skilled. The average pay was $14 per week. Such wages were good, sometimes too good. In Toledo, metal manufacturers were paying 35 to 40 cents an hour to regular employees under wage restrictions imposed by the National Recovery Administration (NRA). Some men quit and got on line for CWA jobs at 50 cents an hour. Beyond trouble over wage scales, the CWA suffered from charges of graft and corruption.

Roosevelt, early in 1934, announced plans to disband the CWA. The program had served its purpose of putting men to work over the winter, he said; by spring, workers leaving CWA employment should have a good chance of finding seasonal outdoor work.

Later in the year FDR announced that a far more comprehensive program was in the works, one that would help not only the jobless but all Americans. On November 9, 1934, he revealed that the program was being developed at weekly staff meetings, and that, when the work was completed, the result would be legislation for the "permanent stabilization of American life."

8
NOVUS ORDO CONTINUES
The Age of Social Security

Novus Ordo Seclorum: *"A New Order of the Ages." The Great Seal of the United States, on the reverse of which appears that inscription, became a part of the one-dollar bill to proclaim the Age of Social Security (and the New Deal).* Annuit Coeptis *means "He [God] Has Favored Our Undertakings." The date on the unfinished pyramid is 1776.*

Novus Ordo Seclorum

So reads the inscription on the Great Seal of the United States: "A New Order of the Ages."

The seal was adopted by the Continental Congress in 1782, and thereafter was used primarily to authenticate official documents, the inscription remaining barely known to the public. Both the seal and the inscription began to gain currency, literally, on August 15, 1935, when, by direction of FDR and Treasury Secretary Henry Morgenthau, Jr., the Great Seal became a part of the one-dollar bill.

Although the Treasury Department's announcement ascribed the reason for the change to a different procedure for printing the signatures on the bill, something more was suspected—particularly since the signatures are on the front and the Great Seal appears on the back.

Could "A New Order of the Ages" be a commemoration of the New Deal? There were those who thought so—the Milwaukee *Journal*, for one, as it editorialized about "New Deal dollars" a few days later, before the new money was even off the press.

Redesigning the currency is a long-since-forgotten matter, but what precipitated it is part of a way of life. The day before the Treasury Department's announcement was the day FDR signed the Social Security Act.

Social security remains every bit as important as it seemed to be when, in the week it became law, *Newsweek* headlined it: "History's Most Ambitious Welfare Plan." It was the social security bill on which administration staff members were meeting weekly late in 1934 and into 1935, backed up by 14 advisory groups of interested citizens. It was the social security bill that dominated the 1935 session of Congress. Yet it was a session otherwise not insignificant, by virtue of:

- Establishment of the National Labor Relations Board (succeeding the labor board that went out with the National Industrial Recovery Act when it was declared unconstitutional)
- A "soak the rich" revenue act increasing income and inheritance taxes, thereby raising $250 million (which was enough to keep the federal government going for 11 days)
- A work-relief act with an appropriation of nearly $5 billion

Social security, however, was clearly the number-one bill of the session, in part because it was so many matters in one: old age assistance, old age pensions, unemployment compensation, aid to dependent children, public assistance to the disabled, and federal subsidization of public health.

That so much was embarked upon; that so much more authority was concentrated in Washington; that the scope of the federal government's responsibility was extended to so much wider a portion of the population, and indeed now, potentially all of it — that all this was so makes it worth observing that the outcome of the bill in Congress was never really in doubt. The only question was the final form, a matter of details. Washington *Post* correspondent John W. Maloney, a few days after the bill cleared Congress, remarked: "Considering its abrupt departure from American tradition, the measure has met with amazingly little opposition in Congress."

That is not to say there was no disagreement. Preliminaries aside, debate in the House of Representatives took nine days. Yet, when the vote was taken, something was clear: With an outcome so lopsided as 372 to 33, government responsibility for social security was the majority opinion of the land. Even those who were against it were opposed more in degree than in substance. Was it not too much to attempt at one time?, ran this argument. To the point, Republican Albert J. Engel of Michigan, on the floor of the House, April 12, 1935, a week before passage there:

> When an individual is sick, the doctor leaves a bottle of medicine and says, "Take a teaspoonful every two hours and you will get well." The patient gets well, but every once and a while some fool comes along and swallows the whole bottle and dies. Some of these social reforms are all right, and I am in favor of them. If we take a spoonful at a time, we might get well; but I am wondering what will happen if we swallow the whole bottle.

Why support should be so broad, we have seen: the vicissitudes of industrial society, the labor movement, the precedents of social legislation in Europe, immigration, the works of reformers and social critics, the federal government's ever-broadening conception of its role in society, and, inevitably, the failure of the old poor law to suffice amid the complexities of modern industrial society.

Long before the 74th Congress established social security, it was ventured that some Congress, sometime, would do so: "A mighty wave of demands for the passage of some such law will roll in from every section of the country, and the issue will have to be met."

In so many words did Rep. Victor L. Berger, on August 7, 1911, speak on the first old age pension bill to come before the House of Representatives—his own. Berger, a native of Austria who represented northern Milwaukee, was the first Socialist elected to Congress. His bill would have provided a pension of $4 per week from the federal treasury to virtually everyone over age 60. With an estimated cost of $347 million — an amount equal to the entire defense budget, including military pensions — it was not seriously considered by anyone except Berger. Yet waves there were. They washed the shores of state after state, resulting in a considerable number of state statutes that set a precedent for the Social Security Act.

The first continuing old age pension law was that of the Territory of Alaska in 1915 (for which the vote in the territorial Senate was unanimous). It provided for a monthly pension of $12.50 for the aged indigent. Arizona, the same year, passed a law providing old age assistance and aid to dependent children (and abolishing almshouses as well), but it was ruled unconstitutional on technical grounds. As of 1935, the year of the Social Security Act, 28 states and two territories had adopted old age assistance laws. Similar laws were in effect in 42 countries, including all the major nations of the world save the United States and China.

The old age assistance provided by the various states, however, was often meager, particularly during the lean years of the Depression. A typical benefit provided by the New York Relief Bureau was $2 per week. Old age assistance ranged from a high of $26.08 monthly in Massachusetts to 69 cents a month in North Dakota.

Wisconsin adopted the nation's first compulsory unemployment insurance law in 1932, and in 1935 was joined by New York, then by Washington, Utah, and New Hampshire. In 36 states, the District of Columbia, and two territories there was also some form of assistance available to widows and dependent children as of 1935.

In large measure these laws were products of the Depression, which had brought widespread need to a head and, at the same time, changed attitudes about public assistance. The Depression made destitution much more visible than it had ever been before, and oftentimes disclosed the impoverished to be friends and neighbors *known* to have been hardworking and self-supporting. Gone, by 1935, was the once general belief that destitution was axiomatically the product of indolence. The Depression, furthermore, dramatized the insecurity of the masses in the Machine Age and the inadequacy of the old poor law in dealing with unemployment and poverty on a broad scale. Side by side, there was the now established rule of looking to the federal government for solutions, and this was especially true of state and local governments facing bankruptcy.

There was thus a readiness, across the land, to join Roosevelt in saying it was the "plain duty . . . of the Nation"—the federal government—to see fully to the welfare of its people.

This meant the pendulum had gone full swing since President Pierce had interpreted the Constitution in 1854 in considering the bill, lobbied by Dorothea Dix for federal subsidy of help for the indigent insane (see

Chapter 6). Argued Pierce's veto: "I can not find any authority in the Constitution for making the Federal Government the great almoner of public charity throughout the United States." In the same Constitution, by 1935, sufficient authority for federal action had been readily found.

Meanwhile contributing to the acceptance of social security were those radical reformers whose conception of change made the administration proposal desirable even for the lukewarm. It was clearly preferable to many another plan that was quickly catching on. Notable were:

- The *Townsend Plan*, brainchild of California physician Dr. Francis Townsend. It would have meant a $200-a-month pension to everyone over age 60, provided the money be spent within the next 30 days (to stimulate the economy). It would have been financed by a highly inflationary federal tax exactable on every single business transaction in the country.
- Louisiana Sen. Huey Long's *Share the Wealth* scheme, which promised every American family a guaranteed, minimum annual income of $2,500. Long claimed 25,000 "Share the Wealth" clubs around the country by early in 1935.
- Novelist Upton Sinclair's *EPIC* (End Poverty in California) campaign, which proposed that the government pay $50 a month to every aged person.
- The *Lundeen Plan*, promoted by Minnesota Rep. Ernest Lundeen, which promised $10 a week to every unemployed worker. The estimated annual cost was $10 billion, which would have been raised by an increase in the income tax.

The Townsend proposal, in particular, caught on and got serious attention in Washington and in state legislatures around the country. Supporters formed Townsend Clubs that, in 1935, were estimated to have a total membership of anywhere from 3 million to 10 million. The Lundeen plan went so far as to get the approval of the House Labor Committee in March 1935, but it was set aside with the vote on social security.

There were those who thought social security went too far; and those who argued it was insufficient. For the great majority in Congress, the administration bill appeared to be a reasonable, workable compromise, and surely to be preferred over some more radical measure that Congress might have found itself pressured into accepting if it failed to act on social security.

Also significant to passage of the Social Security Act was the aggressive leadership of FDR, who repeatedly summoned the nation to duty, as in a message to Congress on June 8th, two months before the signing of the Social Security Act:

156 / WITH CHARITY FOR ALL

> Among our objectives, I place the security of men, women and children of the Nation first. . . . It is our plain duty to provide for that security upon which the welfare of the Nation depends.

Congress debated it, but without much dispute, and by a wide margin, gave the President what he asked.

"SOME MEASURE OF PROTECTION"

As the foundation of a modern, national, public welfare system, the Social Security Act of 1935 was considerably more than what is called "social security" today. It was:

- *Contributory Old-Age Pensions ("social security")*: These were initially fixed at $10 to $85 per month depending on salary and length of employment. The cost was to be met by a payroll tax of 1 percent (rising to 3 percent by 1949) paid each by employee and employer. The tax was to go into effect January 1, 1937. Benefits would begin in 1942.
- *Old-Age Assistance*: This was a temporary program to take care of the elderly needy who were already retired and thus could not participate in "social security." In a sense, it was a temporary dole. Combined federal-state assistance averaged $30 a month.
- *Unemployment Compensation*: This was scheduled to begin in 1936 as a payroll tax of 1 percent (rising to 3 percent in 1938) on employers. The tax financed unemployment compensation benefits, the amount in each case to be fixed by the state according to its contribution.
- *Public Assistance to the Blind*: This was offered in the form of federal grants to the states, on a fifty-fifty basis, the federal government paying up to $15 monthly per person.
- *Aid to Dependent Children*: The federal government promised up to $6 monthly per needy child on a one-third matching basis. Crippled children as well as the financially needy were eligible.
- *Health Services and Vocational Training*: This was in the form of grants to the states on a fifty-fifty basis for state health services to mothers and children, and for vocational training of the disabled.
- *Public Health*: An initial appropriation of $8 million to the states to enable them to provide more adequate health services.

By no means would everyone be a beneficiary. "We can never insure 100 percent of the population against 100 percent of the hazards and vicissitudes of life," said FDR, signing the measure into law.

But we have tried to frame a law which will give some measure of protection to the average citizen and to his family against the loss of a job and against poverty-ridden old age. . . . If the Senate and the House of Representatives in this long and arduous session had done nothing more than pass this bill, the session would be regarded as historic for all time.

The historic nature of the occasion was not lost on observers at the time. Extraordinary public attention was focused on the signing of the law in mid-August 1935. *Newsweek* magazine told the story in a picture of a frail old man walking, underneath which was the caption: "Roosevelt Starts Paving the End of the Road." The editorial conclusion of the Baltimore *Evening Sun* was typical of countless editorials across the land: The Social Security Act was "recognition that unemployment and dependence in old age are for many the inescapable consequences of our economic system." Where there was criticism, it was generally of degree rather than substance. " . . . not well worked out," offered the San Francisco *Chronicle*. Others advised Depression-weary Americans not to expect the millennium. Said the St. Louis *Post-Dispatch*: " . . . too high hopes should not be roused by the act. It is not a Depression cure."

Such doubts notwithstanding, it was obvious the Social Security Act would directly affect the lives of countless Americans at the outset, including those benefiting from unemployment compensation, aid to dependent children, and other provisions. To determine exactly how many would participate in old age pensions, the government sent out a questionnaire (Form SS-4) to every one of the nation's 3 million employers, asking how many employees each had. Then to each of 26 million employees it sent Form SS-5 asking name, address, employer, place of business, date and place of birth, names of parents, sex, and color. In return, the government promised each qualifying applicant something brand-new to the American scene: a social security number.*

Deductions for social security began with the first paychecks of 1937. Three years later (Congress had meanwhile advanced the beginning of payments from 1942 to 1940), the first benefit checks started going out to the nation's mailboxes, as headlined the Boston *Evening Transcript*, February 1, 1940:

---

*The name to appear on the first social security card was picked at a public drawing. It was John D. Sweeney, Jr. When the press tracked down Sweeney for an interview on how it felt to be secure about old age, they found him at the Princeton Club in New York, discovered he lived in a 15-room home in affluent Westchester County, that he was a Republican who had voted for Landon, and, furthermore, that he had a long wait for his first social security check. He was 23, the son of a wealthy manufacturer. Sweeney said he was nonetheless in favor of social security.

POSTMAN'S RING SIGNALS
FIRST OLD AGE BENEFITS

The first checks went to 3,700 persons across the country, those first processed out of 23,029 claims initially filed. But, said the Social Security Board, new recipients were being added to the rolls at the rate of 800 per day, and by the end of the year, it was estimated, 912,000 retirees would be receiving old age benefits and 47 million workers would be paying into the program. The average payment to a retired couple was $42 a month.

UNDOING THE DOLE

Whatever their differences, Roosevelt and Hoover had been alike in denouncing the dole. FDR repeated his position in his annual message, January 4, 1935:

> The lessons of history, confirmed by the evidence immediately before me show conclusively that continued dependence upon relief induces a spiritual and moral disintegration fundamentally destructive to the national fiber. To dole out relief in this way is to administer a narcotic, a subtle destroyer of the human spirit. . . . The Federal Government must and shall quit this business of relief.

FDR described the dole as "the giving of cash, of market baskets, of a few hours of weekly work cutting grass." It was not the answer.

What *was* the answer, Roosevelt was soon to announce: a vast new program that would put the sturdy unemployed to work on useful projects, and leave those incapable of work to the care of state and local government, working with federal assistance furnished under the Social Security Act.

The vast new program was the Works Progress Administration (WPA), renamed in 1939 the Work Projects Administration. In theory it would put men to work so they could demonstrate their employability, as well as, in its overall impact, prime the economic pump.

The funding of the WPA at the outset was the Emergency Relief Appropriation Act of 1935, which was given final approval by Congress on April 5, 1935, the same day social security cleared the House Ways and Means Committee. At $4.88 billion (including $880 million in existing balances) it was then the largest single appropriation in U.S. history, a fact that did not escape even FDR's loyal New Deal Congress. The administration bill, introduced January 14th, tied Congress up in knots for 74 days, backing up the whole of that session's New Deal program behind it. A major objection, over and above the unprecedented cost, was the fact that it would represent a blank check for the administration. Those who were concerned about the vast cost were assured by RFC Chairman Jesse H. Jones that there was "no occasion for alarm about a few billions of additional debt."

One month after the act became law, FDR named Harry Hopkins WPA administrator and gave him orders to get the country off the dole and into work programs or private employment. As for work projects in the public sector, they included highways, rural rehabilitation, water conservation, reclamation, rural electrification, reforestation, flood control, the Civilian Conservation Corps, sanitation, housing, loans and grants for nonfederal projects, and assistance to professional persons (educators, writers, musicians, and the like).

In its six years of existence (it ended with the country going off to war), the WPA at any particular time had some 2 million at work on its diverse projects. But, at $11.4 billion over six years, its cost was great; and there was always about it an aura of waste and inefficiency: in part because administrative competence varied greatly (in New York City there were 100 warehouses full of work material but no inventory of what was in which, even though relief administrators used 21 tons of paper a year and employed 16 clerks who did nothing but make duplicate copies of forms that had been lost); in part because there was a determined effort, almost an obsession, with making all projects be or seem to be legitimate work, at the same time keeping organized labor happy by holding down relief wages and keeping private industry happy by not competing; in part because the WPA was particularly subject to political abuse.

The politicizing of relief came to be a matter of little question; "Common knowledge," wrote New York *Times* columnist Arthur Krock in July 1936. In Kentucky, in 1938, political preference questionnaires were found to have been mimeographed on the back of WPA stationery.

The nature of work relief is such that a certain amount of useless, or at least insignificant, labor is inevitable. The larger the work program the more the inutility.

The largest program was New York's. In April 1935, the city's Board of Aldermen began digging into the many projects administered by the Emergency Relief Bureau, and what it found made headlines around the country. Uncovered, and well publicized, were:

- Two real estate surveys (total cost of $2,239,648 in relief funds) not only duplicating each other but duplicating information already on file in the city's Department of Taxes and Assessment;
- A survey ($290,140) of population trends in the Mediterranean and Euphrates regions for the years 2000 to 1150 B.C. (to keep busy a university classics department);
- A "social recreation, dancing and singing" project administered by a recreation director who claimed a college "bachelor of oratory" degree ($365,014);

- A program to develop leadership ability in boys and girls in safety patrols, recess activities, and inter-class competition ($566,258).

Such revelations made headlines:

'BUNK' IN NEW YORK RELIEF DENOUNCED
Denver *Post*

NEW YORK RELIEF MONEY
SPENT FOR BALLET LESSONS
St. Louis *Post Dispatch*

Such headlines made Washington hot under the collar. A furious Harry Hopkins ripped into critics of work relief: "Those are good projects, all of them. People who don't understand foreign languages sometimes laugh when they hear them. Dumb people make fun of things they can't understand."

The hearings of the New York City Board of Aldermen also made history by giving the country a new word. From the public testimony (the witness is an instructor of arts and crafts employed by the city's Emergency Relief Bureau):

Counsel: Boon doggles?

Chairman: What is that?

Counsel: I would like to find out. We do not any of us know. We should know but we do not know what boon doggles is. We would like to know.

Witness: I spend a good deal of my time explaining it. Boondoggling is construction of gadgets out of waste material.

Counsel: Did these students or pupils come in with a heavy demand for the boon doggles course?

Witness: No.

Counsel: They are all on relief, these people that come to be taught boon doggles?

Witness: Absolutely.

A lot of people were convinced the massive work-relief programs of 1935 and succeeding years, though perceived to be necessary, were loaded with make-work. Now there was evidence, and, what's more, a word for it:

BOON DOGGLES MADE

New York *Times*, April 4, 1935

BOON-DOGGLING FOUND IN N.Y.

Milwaukee *Journal*, April 4, 1935

EVER DOGGLE A BOON?
JOBLESS IN N.Y. LEARN IT

San Francisco *Chronicle*, April 4, 1935

In no time, people were talking about boondoggles, for and against. *Forum* editor Henry Goddard Leach, in June 1935, lamented that all the headlines about boondoggling were giving public relief projects a black eye. Some waste is probably inevitable in public ventures, said Leach; there were probably scandals during the building of the pyramids.*

OTHER NEW DEAL PROGRAMS

There are three other programs of the New Deal that bear a look before proceeding. Two of them (food stamps and public housing) are mainstays of today's welfare society; a third (resettlement) was an experiment of limited application, but is interesting nonetheless.

Food Stamps

The Agricultural Adjustment Act of 1935 opened up federal distribution of food to the needy, although its principal objective was to provide an outlet for surplus commodities accumulated by the federal government through price supports. Such surplus food was distributed from government outlets to persons on relief. From the direct distribution of food it was only a short step to food stamps, which would accomplish

---

*As for the origin of the word "boondoggle": *Scouting* magazine antedated the notoriety with an article on "The Rise of the Boondoggle" in February 1930, authenticating the word's handicraft origin. A boondoggle, said *Scouting*, is a lanyard made of brightly colored leather strips of original and interesting design. One such boondoggle was presented by American scouts to Chief Scout Lord Robert Baden-Powell at the World Jamboree in England in August 1929, thus popularizing boondoggle-making. *Punch*, that month, observed that if you ask a scout what a boondoggle is, he moves his gum slowly from one cheek to the other before answering. The word is said to have been coined sometime before this by scout leader Robert H. Link, of Rochester, New York.

the same purpose and have the additional advantage of utilizing regular channels of trade.

The first U.S. food stamp program was instituted on May 1, 1939, under the auspices of the Federal Surplus Commodity Corporation. It was begun on a trial basis in six cities and gradually extended nationwide. In August 1939, Secretary of Agriculture Henry Wallace reported that where it was tried it was popular. People on relief, he said, preferred getting their groceries at the store rather than through government outlets; furthermore, they were getting more to eat, and a better balanced diet as well.

There were actually two kinds of food stamps at this time, orange and blue. The orange stamp was purchased (at least $1 worth but not more than $1.50 worth per family member per week) and for each $1 worth purchased, 50 cents worth of blue stamps were given free. The orange could be used for any food at the grocery store; the blue were for those commodities on the surplus list. In the fall of 1939 the list included butter, eggs, raisins, apples, pork lard, dried prunes, onions, dry beans, fresh pears, wheat flour, corn meal, and snap beans.

In time, the food stamp program was extended to the needy beyond those on relief: to recipients of old age assistance, aid for dependent children, and aid for the blind. In New York City alone, during 1942, some $30 million in stamps was distributed.

By this time, however, there were no longer surpluses for which to find an outlet. Now there were wartime shortages instead. At the end of 1942 the Department of Agriculture announced that the food stamp program would end on March 31, 1943. When it did, $245 million in surplus food had been distributed to more than 20 million of the needy.

The food stamp program was resumed on a limited basis under Kennedy in 1961 and was made permanent under Johnson in 1964.

Housing

Government responsibility for housing of the needy is essentially a twentieth-century development, although housing regulation, which is related, goes back to ancient times. Babylonia, for example, punished contractors whose buildings collapsed. In colonial America there were building regulations as early as 1647 (New Amsterdam).

Regulation of housing in times past, had it been uniformly enforced, would have benefited the poor by upgrading the minimum standards of safety and health. Had that been so, there would not be this description of city housing, contained in an 1887 report of the New York Sanitary Aid Society:

> To get into pestilential human rookeries you have to penetrate courts and alleys reeking with poisonous and malodorous gases, arising from accumulations of sewage and refuse scattered in all directions, and often flowing beneath your feet. You have to ascend rotten staircases, which threaten to give way beneath every step, and which in some places have already broken down, leaving gaps that imperil the limbs and lives of the unwary. You have to grope your way along dark and filthy passages swarming with vermin. Then, if you are not driven back by the intolerable stench, you may gain admittance to the dens in which thousands of human beings herd together. Walls and ceilings are black with the accretions of filth, which have gathered upon them through long years of neglect. It is exuding through cracks in the boards overhead; it is running down the walls; it is everywhere.

New York's tenement houses had begun going up in the 1830s. The first real inspection was conducted in 1864 by the Council of Hygiene and Public Health in response to concern about the rising death rate. In 1810 it had been 1 in 46; now it was 1 in 35. The rise in the death rate, of course, was not limited to the slums. Horace Greeley observed that "garbage steams its poison in the sun." Some of the poison reached other parts of the city, carrying disease and death with it. Charles Edward Russell, writing in *Everybody's Magazine,* January 1907, warned that "we cannot sow slums without reaping epidemics."

The first comprehensive code governing housing, in 1867, controlled such conditions as distance between buildings, height of rooms, size of windows, requirements for ventilators and transoms, and the ratio of water closets to tenants.

Although enforcement was doubtless minimal, regulation had at least some effect in improving the housing of the poor. As to government actually helping the poor to obtain housing, either through subsidies or publicly financed construction, hardly any thought had been given at this time. An exception was Josiah Phillips Quincy—son of the Boston mayor met in Chapter 4. Appearing before the Massachusetts Legislative Committee on Railways in 1871, he appealed for state assistance with housing for the poor, in this case housing outside the city yet close enough for commutation by train. Said Quincy:

> My request is that you consider the expediency of aiding the working class to obtain homes in the country. . . . The greater part of their moral degradation arises from the utter impossibility of observing in their miserable dwellings, the common decencies of life. . . . If, Mr. Chairman, you wish, as I know you do, to see the laboring population healthy, sober, self-supporting, honest, chaste, religious,

you must enable them to acquire homes, where health is not an exception, where decency is not an impossibility, where squalor and discomfort do not necessarily drive the husband and father to the rum-shop.

In a sense government had been providing housing, if one considers the almshouse public housing. The almshouse took in relatively few, however, and was hardly the answer in any event. What of the masses and their need for a decent place to live?

A Committee on the Expediency of Providing Better Tenements for the Poor examined housing conditions in Boston in 1846. It found them deplorable and called for "the investment of considerable sums in buildings expressly designed for this class of tenants," but as a private venture.

It was in Massachusetts, coincidentally, that the move for publicly financed housing took root. In 1913 the legislature's Homestead Commission reported to the Massachusetts House of Representatives that no nation had private enterprise that was "equal to the task of properly housing the inhabitants." The commission called on government to begin subsidizing housing for the needy, as was already being done in other countries. A year later the American Federation of Labor adopted a resolution proposing federal loans for construction of municipal as well as private housing. In 1915 Massachusetts voters approved a constitutional amendment giving the state the authority to build and sell low-cost homes. As a result, the state in 1917 built a number of suburban homes and sold them to city workers on long-term loans. California subsequently made loans to veterans who wanted to buy homes, while New York chose tax exemptions for the purpose of encouraging construction of low-cost housing.

As in other matters affecting public welfare, the Depression broke down precedent at the federal level. Except for some housing built during World War I, the federal government now entered the housing picture for the first time. In 1932 Congress established the Federal Home Loan Bank System to help save home owners from default on mortgages. In 1933 there came the Home Owners' Loan Corporation (HOLC), which provided additional assistance to home owners on the verge of default as well as to financial institutions holding mortgages on which payment could no longer be made. Between 1933 and 1936, the HOLC made loans of more than $3 billion.

The year 1934 was significant for the National Housing Act, which established the Federal Housing Authority (FHA). The act provided for government guarantee of new mortgages of up to $16,000 each, at 5 percent interest. This, it was hoped, would thaw out frozen capital and create a $15 billion boom in construction—an industry depressed to 27 percent of its 1929 level. FHA loans opened up home ownership to many of marginal income by requiring less in the way of a down payment and allowing more time for repayment.

The Housing Act of 1937, the last major New Deal housing measure, put the federal government to work in slum clearance. Patterned on British laws of the same nature, this act provided $700 million, administered through the Department of the Interior, for knocking down city slums and building low-cost housing for the "ill-housed, ill-clothed" 15 percent at the bottom of the economic ladder.

Resettlement

In ancient Athens, Pericles reduced the ranks of those on public assistance by sending them to colonies: Cherso, Naxos, Andros, Thrace, Italy. Under Roosevelt, they went to Alaska, specifically to the Matanuska Valley. Altogether, nearly 1,000 persons from relief rolls in Michigan, Minnesota, and Wisconsin settled there under the auspices of the Federal Resettlement Administration.

The Alaska colonists began arriving in May 1935. Their first homes in the fertile wilderness were tents, although the government promised houses, schools, shops, and other semblances of civilization by winter. It was an elusive promise. The government, for example, had assured the colony that all necessary building materials would be supplied, but one day, when 24 carpenters arrived to start constructing permanent housing, there were only four hammers. Provisions were late getting there. When it was time for school to start, work had not yet begun on the schoolhouse, but a carload of school desks had already been delivered. Letters of complaint poured back to the United States, some of them followed by colonists.

The whole project suffered from hasty planning and recurrent waste. It was at first under the jurisdiction of the California Emergency Relief Administration, and then became the responsibility of the Alaska Rural Rehabilitation Corporation. Somewhere in between, Washington sent the colony a check for $600,000. It was addressed to California. Authorities there had no idea what it was for and sent it back to Washington.

Despite the harvest of confusion that was the colony's first crop, most Matanuskans stayed, and in time things worked out. Each immigrant Alaskan took title to a 40-acre farm, with all the necessities, and no few luxuries as well, provided by the government on munificent terms: up to 40 years to pay, at interest of 3 to 5 percent.

Supplies did arrive, and houses went up. During their first winter and spring, Matanuskan pioneers cleared the land, and in June 1936 they planted nearly 1,200 acres with hay, grain, potatoes, and vegetables, and began the breeding and raising of horses, cows, swine, chickens, and sheep sent by the government.

The Matanuska colony became a permanent settlement and, by 1948, had nearly 3,000 residents and 8,500 acres of cleared land (from 175 at the start). Those who survived the hardships of climate and bureaucracy decided it was worthwhile after all, confirming the impression of an early visitor, Will Rogers, who, days before he and Wiley Post crashed to their death at Point Barrow, told the new Matanuskans with a hearty smile, "Mighty nice place you got here."

APPRAISING THE NEW DEAL

New Deal social programs never lacked for critics. "Frenzied finance and wet nursing," complained Georgia Governor Eugene Talmadge in 1935: "If they had told us what they planned they wouldn't have carried a bailiwick in the nation."

"Economic blunders, if not in some instances economic crimes," deplored Virginia Senator Carter Glass, a former secretary of the treasury, in 1937.

Al Smith, who had long since regretted helping Roosevelt up the political ladder, declared that the Socialist platform of 1932 and the record of the New Deal were virtually indistinguishable: "The young brain trusters caught the Socialists in swimming and they ran away with their clothes."

The New Deal spoke for itself, FDR countered on many an occasion, as in 1935:

> We are on our way back; not just by pure chance, not by a mere turn of a wheel in a cycle; we are coming back soundly because we planned it that way and don't let anybody tell you differently.

A majority of Americans didn't. The 1936 election, if it is considered a referendum on the New Deal, demonstrated overwhelming approval. The vote was the most lopsided ever: Roosevelt, 523 electoral votes; Landon, 8. It is true that Alf Landon's "country boy" campaign was inept, and that some other Republican might have given FDR a closer race. It is true that votes were undoubtedly bought with relief funds, but they likely had the effect of helping local candidates and of entrenching Democratic power in the cities and counties more than of helping the national ticket. It is true that FDR had been running for reelection since his first day in office, all along playing a shrewd political game: taking, as columnist Mark Sullivan observed, a step to the left, usually a long one, and then a step to the right, usually a short one. But FDR won simply because a vast majority of Americans thought they had gotten a new deal.

The Depression, however, was not yet over in 1936. Nor was it over in 1940, when Roosevelt won an unprecedented third term. It was not over until the United States was at war. Unemployment the year before the country's entry into World War II was almost identical to what it had been the year before Roosevelt was first elected: 8.1 million (15 percent of the labor force) in 1940; 8.0 million (16 percent) in 1931. The peak of unemployment, 12.8 million, came in 1933.

To a significant extent, government reduced unemployment by making government bigger. Despite a 1932 campaign promise to decrease the number of federal employees by 25 percent, Roosevelt increased federal employment by more than 100 percent during the Depression years: from 605,000 in 1932 to 1.4 million in 1941, accounting for 800,000 workers, or roughly 10 percent of the nation's jobless at the time of his election.

Also up substantially was the federal budget. In Hoover's last year it totaled $4.7 billion; in 1941, $13.3 billion, an increase of 185 percent. National debt rose nearly as sharply, from $19.5 billion to $49.0 billion (150 percent) during the same period.

War, not domestic policy, brought unemployment under control, down to 670,000 in 1944. Domestic policy had taken the nation a long way toward recovery, but it did not achieve it.

On the other hand, the New Deal's significance in social welfare was profound. It was what FDR had called for during the 1932 campaign. By the Social Security Act of 1935 and related legislation, even though social security did not embrace anywhere near all of the population, government declared it was assuming responsibility for all Americans, rich or poor, and that was the revolution.

9

NOVUS ORDO BROADENS
The Present Era

> **LBJ Visions A New Age For Nation**
>
> **Michigan U. Class Told of Aim for A 'Great Society'**
>
> By Carroll Kilpatrick
> Staff Reporter
>
> ANN ARBOR, Mich., May 22 — President Johnson here today outlined a program for the future by projecting the vision of a "great society."
>
> It was a major attempt to characterize a Johnson program for the future by explaining his hopes for the quality of national growth.
>
> Mr. Johnson spoke at the University of Michigan commencement exercises after receiving an honorary Doctor of Civil Law degree.
>
> In his address, before ?˙
> 'n Michigan S˙
> ˙t promi˙

Washington Post, *May 23, 1964, page 1. "In your time," Johnson proclaimed, "we have the opportunity to move . . . upward to the Great Society. The Great Society rests on abundance and liberty for all."*

Former President Harry Truman stood a little uneasily, leaning heavily on his cane. His voice faltered now and then. To an observer, he looked all of his 81 years—more than just a mite older than when he used to "give 'em hell"—though his grin was as broad and unmistakable as ever.

"We're gonna do it boys," said Truman, quoting himself, as he spoke of one of his great ambitions as president. He was talking to a visitor in the Harry S. Truman Library in Independence, Missouri.

"Well, Mr. Truman," said the visitor, of the reason for being there that day, "it is twenty years ago that you started this."

"Yes," replied the former President, "I remember that I mentioned it in my State of the Union Message."

Even within his own administration there was some doubt he could do it, Truman recalled, but he told them, "We're gonna do it boys, we're gonna do it. *We* may not make it, but someday . . . "

"Someday" was this day, Friday, July 30, 1965. The visitor was Lyndon Johnson, Truman's successor twice removed. What Truman was gonna do and what Johnson did do, there in the Truman Library, was sign into law a bill of more sweeping social significance than anything since social security: medicare.

When Truman proposed medicare in 1945, not only for the elderly but for all ages, the time was not right. In 1965, it was. And now that a bill had cleared Congress and was ready for signing, Johnson had flown to Independence to put his signature on it in Truman's presence. There, in the company of the vice-president, 12 senators, 19 representatives, 1 cabinet member, 1 governor, and other guests, Johnson (using 72 pens for distribution to the faithful)* signed the 133-page bill into law and then paid tribute to its progenitor: "It all started with the man from Independence," said Johnson, "so it is fitting we have come back to his home to complete what he began."

Medical care and full employment were central to Truman's postwar domestic plan. Truman had been president for five months, and the war had been over for three weeks, when, on September 6, 1945, he outlined domestic goals that included a full-employment law, expanded unemploy-

---

*The 72 pens Johnson used to sign the medicare bill cost the federal treasury $79.92, or $1.11 each. Three weeks later, to sign antipoverty legislation, Johnson switched to a pen costing 17 cents.

ment benefits, an increase in the minimum wage, and an extensive housing program. On November 19th of the same year he made his medicare proposal.

Truman's unemployment compensation proposal was for an extension of the program to states not yet covered and for a nationwide standard of $25 per week for up to 26 weeks. That, however, figured out to 63 cents an hour for a 40-hour week, which would mean more money for being idle than for working, since the minimum wage was 40 cents an hour. The House Ways and Means Committee shelved the bill.

The full-employment proposal would have pledged the federal government to seeing to a job for any adult willing and able to work. It, too, was set aside. Instead, Congress passed the Employment Act of 1946, which established the Council of Economic Advisers to recommend ways of maintaining maximum employment and to help steer the nation clear of future depressions. Subsequent to that, Truman proposed his medical care program and civil rights legislation, both of which Congress deferred to another day.

Truman's domestic program — his Fair Deal — was clearly secondary in impact to his record in foreign affairs. Relatively few of Truman's domestic proposals were enacted; and those that were enacted largely constituted an extension of existing programs. An increasingly hostile Congress (including defectors within his own party) and the Korean War both kept new social legislation to a minimum. Nevertheless, there were these programs enacted:

- Housing legislation, in 1946, providing $600 million in federal assistance, primarily to help returning veterans buy homes; and the Housing Act of 1949, which facilitated slum clearance
- An increase in the minimum wage to 75 cents an hour
- The Social Security Act of 1950, which extended benefits to an additional 10 million persons
- Legislation making permanent the National School Lunch Program. The federal government had begun subsidizing school lunches, on a year-to-year basis, in 1935, under the old Federal Surplus Commodity Corporation. In making the program permanent in 1946, Congress appropriated $75 million to provide nutritious lunches for 8 million pupils in 46,000 public and nonprofit private schools

President Dwight D. Eisenhower was more preoccupied with the Cold War than with domestic matters. Indeed, the Cold War, with its heightened concern about communism, increased suspicion of anything smacking of socialism, and hence of any radical departure in social legislation. Furthermore, high expenditures for defense inhibited increases in domestic spending.

There were, however, amendments to the Social Security Act in 1954 and 1956, notably the latter year, when disability insurance was added to take care of those workers who became premature retirees by virtue of disablement or illness. The Eisenhower Administration also produced HEW, the Department of Health, Education and Welfare, that monster-sized member of the cabinet that had been hatching since Harding's 1920 campaign. It was finally born in April 1953 as an embodiment of such diverse agencies as the Social Security Administration, Public Health Service, Office of Education, Food and Drug Administration, Children's Bureau, Office of Vocational Rehabilitation, and Bureau of Federal Credit Unions. As secretary, Republican Eisenhower named Democrat Oveta Culp Hobby, the second woman to become a cabinet officer.

The administration of President John F. Kennedy marked a return to social activism—the New Frontier. Although such legislation faced an obstacle in the same coalition of Republicans and southern Democrats that had countered much of Truman's Fair Deal, the Kennedy administration saw passage of some significant social legislation. Notable were these:

- Legislation, in 1961, expanding Aid to Dependent Children (ADC) into Aid to Families with Dependent Children (AFDC), which would permit aid to families with an unemployed father rather than only to families with a deceased or absent father, thus seeking to counter the tendency for fathers in such families to desert as a means of generating public assistance
- The Manpower Development and Training Act, of 1962, to help retrain the unemployed
- The Area Redevelopment Act, of 1961, providing loans to depressed areas for the purpose of encouraging new businesses
- The Accelerated Public Works Act, of 1962, establishing grants-in-aid for public works in depressed areas

Kennedy also revived Truman's proposal for medicare, also without success. Unlike Truman, he sought only medical care of the aged as a start.

DECLARING WAR ON POVERTY

Less than two months after the assassination of John F. Kennedy, it fell upon the former vice-president to declare what kind of administration his would be, even for the one year remaining of the term. Thus, early in January 1964 did Lyndon B. Johnson give the Congress "Information of the State of the Union," that which the Constitution required even on such short notice.

Such information took the new president six weeks and 24 different speech writers and rewriters (Mrs. Johnson included) to prepare. The speech came to 3,059 words. Kennedy's State of the Union messages had run 6,000 words; Truman's, in 1946, 25,000.

Speaking in his slow, ambling Texas drawl as he addressed Congress on January 8, 1964, Johnson made it a long speech after all. On the text in front of him were notations to "Pause," "Look Left," "Look Right." He knew how to stir an audience, and this one, in particular. He was still one of them: the many-termed congressman, the strong-armed majority leader of the Senate. He paused frequently, looked left frequently, looked right frequently, making the most of every expressive turn of phrase; and 79 times—once every 39 words—his old colleagues rewarded him with applause.

Johnson set his administration to continuing Kennedy's legislative program, but in particular he would press for cuts in government spending, a reduction in atomic weaponry, broad new civil rights legislation, and

> This Administration today, here and now, declares unconditional war on poverty in America, and I urge this Congress and all Americans to join with me in that effort. It will not be a short or easy struggle, no single weapon or strategy will suffice, but we shall not rest until that war is won.

What victory over poverty would be like was explained a few months later. Speaking in Ann Arbor, May 22, 1964, at the University of Michigan commencement exercises, Johnson revealed a vision that could be summed up in two words. They were headlined next day by the Washington *Post* at the top of page 1:

> MICHIGAN U. CLASS
> TOLD OF AIM FOR
> A 'GREAT SOCIETY'

"In your time," Johnson proclaimed to the graduates and their families and friends, "we have the opportunity to move not only toward the rich society and the powerful society, but upward to the Great Society. The Great Society rests on abundance and liberty for all."

The first major step in securing abundance for all, Johnson had already proposed in March: a $1 billion package of antipoverty measures to begin the War on Poverty. The Economic Opportunity Act of 1964, with an appropriation eventually set at $947.5 million, provided for:

- a Job Corps, through which young men and women might receive remedial education and medical care as well as job training at residential centers
- a Neighborhood Youth Corps, to keep young people from dropping out of high school by giving them part-time work while living at home
- VISTA (Volunteers in Service to America), a domestic Peace Corps, providing service in poverty areas as well as to the community generally
- the Community Action Program, locally administered by federally approved community agencies, with "maximum feasible participation" on the part of the community, making use of federal funding to carry out a wide variety of projects
- a Work-Study Program to provide needy college students with part-time jobs
- loans to farmers and small businessmen

The Economic Opportunity Act cleared the Senate by a two-to-one margin in July 1964 but ran into stiff opposition in the House. The leadership made a head count and found there weren't enough votes to bring the bill to a vote. What saved it was some strenuous arm-twisting. House Speaker John McCormack called Democrats into his office, one by one, to inquire of each his interest in federally funded projects back home in his district. Presidential aides roamed the Capitol and the House Office Buildings, making it look, said one Democrat, like Engine House No. 5 when the four-alarm bell sounds. Johnson himself got on the phone and called reluctant legislators; some, he invited to the White House to pose with him for election year photographs.

The result was that the War on Poverty bill, when it came to a vote early in August, passed by a comfortable margin. On the 20th, on the steps overlooking the White House rose garden, Johnson made it the law of the land. Squinting into the intense sun of a bright summer morning, he beheld a "new day of opportunity" for the nation's needy and declared that "the days of the dole in our country are numbered."

Kennedy had already begun drafting a policy on poverty, although it was not as broad as the Economic Opportunity Act. It was a start for Johnson. What stirred up support for the far-reaching War on Poverty was virtual war itself: the convulsive summer of 1964.

It began in Harlem on July 18th, five days before the Senate's vote on the antipoverty bill. A black boy was shot by a white police officer. The boy, who had reportedly menaced the officer with a knife, died. Four days of violence followed. One rioter was killed, 121 persons were injured and 185 were arrested. Mobs smashed store windows, looted, and hurled debris at police. As the long, hot summer continued, the rioting continued: in Brooklyn's mostly black Bedford-Stuyvesant; in Rochester, New York; Jersey City, Paterson, and Elizabeth, New Jersey; the Chicago suburb of Dixmoor, and, at summer's end, Philadelphia. At the time Johnson was squinting into the sun to sign the Economic Opportunity Act on August 20, the smoke of racial violence was darkening the sky across the land.

Johnson's election to a term of his own in November 1964 — by a landslide victory, with a two-to-one Democratic Congress at his side — generated a new and larger Great Society program for Congress to work on, one providing for even more extensive machinery of government and assuming a still greater role in the lives of the nation's citizens.

Fresh from his huge victory at the polls, LBJ was riding tall in 1965. Like a ranch foreman at roundup time, he kept his congressional ranch hands in their saddles, and, when necessary, also used cajolery, flattery, calls to patriotism and party loyalty, reminders of favors past and hints of favors future, or plain old arm-twisting to get what he wanted out of the 89th Congress. What he got, by the time the first session ended in October 1965, included:

- Medicare, administered through social security, to persons over 65, covering the cost of hospital and nursing home care as well as home nursing services. A supplementary plan (optional at $3 a month) was made available to cover medical costs and doctors' bills. Eligible beneficiaries at the start were estimated at 19 million.
- Medicaid, for persons on public assistance, and, at state option, for the medically indigent generally. Medicaid was included in the medicare act.
- A $1.1 billion program of aid to the depressed 11-state Appalachia region, most of the money going for new highways that would mean temporary construction jobs and bring in new industry for permanent jobs.
- A $7.8 billion housing program providing for public housing, urban renewal, and college campus housing, plus a new cabinet department, Housing and Urban Development, to administer this and existing programs.
- A $1.8 billion extension of the War on Poverty.
- A $3.2 billion program of public works grants to create jobs in depressed areas.
- A $1.3 billion program of aid to all but the wealthiest school districts in the nation.
- Voting rights, medical research, highway beautification, and farm and immigration legislation.

- Public funding of legal aid for the poor through the Office of Economic Opportunity.

All in all, Congress in 1965 appropriated $119.3 billion (an amount to that time exceeded only during World War II) and filled 33,250 pages of the *Congressional Record*, itself a congressional record.

But problems were brewing. The War on Poverty was beginning to get some bad press. At Camp Breckinridge, Kentucky, in August 1965, some 400 trainees at a Job Corps center brawled over the food they were served, making headlines. At Fort Custer, Michigan, early in November, Job Corps trainees fought with local youths and the police after a dance at a local junior high school, making more headlines. The Job Corps, in its first ten months, was reported to have spent $96 million on 12,371 youths at 59 training centers, making more headlines. At $7,760 per youth, the same amount of money could have sent the same number to college for four years.

Elsewhere, there was good news. Project Head Start, launched in July 1965, was off to a start worthy of its name. It was initially intended as a summer-only program but was made year-round by popular demand.

In their scope and diversity, these programs represented an unprecedented involvement of the federal government in the lives of its people. "The nation is witnessing a social revolution," observed Washington columnist Michael O'Neill of the New York *Daily News*. O'Neill was talking basically of the Community Action Program (CAP). Never before had the federal government worked directly with the community (and often that "community" was no more than a neighborhood) in the implementation of federal programs. It had always worked through the state capital, which in turn worked with the municipality. But the Economic Opportunity Act of 1964 had mandated "maximum feasible participation" on the part of the local community.

All too often the result was maximum feasible confusion. Once a community action program got started, those who were not among the original participants often demanded a role, and, in city after city, the more aggressive and more militant frequently pushed aside those who were already taking part. In some cases the Office of Economic Opportunity (OEO) sponsored elections so that "poverty representatives" might be chosen for CAP boards of directors. The OEO even paid the expenses of campaigning in many cases. The average voter turnout was 2 to 5 percent of those poor who were eligible to vote.

Despite the diversity of these various programs, there was a serious question as to how well they were reaching their intended beneficiaries, the hard-core poor. In mid-August 1965, Los Angeles *Times* staff writer Paul Weeks, examining the antipoverty program now that it had been in operation for a year, wrote that one could see the light burning late into the night at the Office of Economic Opportunity in Washington, and yet walk a few blocks away, amid the stark slums of the nation's capital, and seek in vain a single poor person who had even heard of the War on Poverty.

Weeks' story was on page 2. It might have made page 1 except for another story. In the Watts district of Los Angeles people were running through the streets yelling, "Burn, baby, burn." And Watts was burning. Towers of thick smoke stretched upward. Sirens cut through the streets, drowning out rifle shots and the moans of the hurt and dying. Looters chanced the jagged remnants of broken store windows to steal television sets or grab, at random, armloads of shoes that wouldn't even fit. Small children took ice cream. "They've gone crazy," said a black businessman; "you can't talk to them. Even Negroes can't talk to them." What talked was the National Guard (California's 40th Armored Division and its 15,000 troops). What talked were 800 heavily armed, steel-helmeted lawmen. Roadblocks and machine guns talked. The madness stopped, and then the rioters could see what they had done—to their neighborhood, their homes, their stores—like the insane who sometimes mutilate their own bodies: 32 dead, 874 injured, and 737 structures damaged or destroyed.

The worst day of the Watts riot was August 14th. A continent away next morning, some 3,000 of New York City's elderly, members of the Golden Ring Council of Senior Citizens, clambered aboard buses for a pilgrimage up the Hudson River. At their destination they stood in a soft, summer breeze, under the maples and pines of Hyde Park, to help commemorate the signing of the Social Security Act on another August 14th, exactly 30 years past.

On August 20, 1965, as Watts' embers were turning to ash, the Senate approved a $1.65 billion extension of the War on Poverty. But would it be enough? A week later President Johnson warned that "the clock is ticking, time is moving," and Watts could happen again.

A BOX DIVIDED

In 1966 the loyal 89th Congress continued to give the president most of what he wanted, including:

- another $1 billion for the War on Poverty
- a $1.3 billion Demonstration Cities program for renewal of blighted neighborhoods
- an increase in the minimum wage from $1.25 to $1.40 (effective in 1967) and to $1.60 (1968), and, for the first time, extension of the minimum wage to agricultural workers

- rent supplements for low-income families as an alternative to direct subsidization of housing, the supplement representing the difference between 25 percent of an eligible family's income and the amount to be paid for rent

Meanwhile, medicare had gone into effect (it was in January 1966 Johnson gave Truman his medicare card) and by the end of the year, medicaid as well. The Department of Health, Education and Welfare in November gave approval to the first five medicaid systems among the states: those in Maine, Michigan, New Mexico, New York, and Vermont. In New York City, medicaid was slow in attracting interest. The city expected 1 million to apply, but after two months counted only 18,500 indigent poor who had done so, over and above the 575,000 welfare clients who were automatically registered. The city undertook a campaign to attract medicaid clients, at first through radio and television announcements and later through a door-to-door canvass.

The War on Poverty itself was not going smoothly. To a large extent, it was inevitable. So much money was available that there was bound to be squabbling over it: over what programs to carry out, over who made the decisions, over who got how much, over the authority of locally elected government as against the authority of antipoverty agencies. In Newark, for example, the United Community Corporation, the antipoverty agency serving the city, had an 87-member board of directors, only two of whom were city officials.

Since money is power, federal funds by the millions were cleaving the local power structure in Newark and around the country. Elected mayors and councils were being rivaled by nonelected boards and agencies purporting to be carrying out the mandate of maximum feasible participation by the poor. Oftentimes, antipoverty officials drew salaries far in excess of what elected public officials were paid. A New Jersey CAP director divulged his salary as more than $100,000 per year, plus expenses. But the difficulties went beyond this. As more federal money became available and more programs were devised, CAP agencies demanded even more authority.

In Syracuse, New York, in January 1966, there was a two-day "People's Convention for Total Participation of the Poor," sponsored by the Syracuse People's War Council Against Poverty. The convention adopted a resolution calling for outright control of the War on Poverty by the poor. When the Citizens' Crusade Against Poverty, principally funded by the United Auto Workers and chaired by Walter Reuther, assembled in Washington to defend community action programs against their critics, radicals among the delegates so booed OEO Director Sargent Shriver that he had to leave the hall.

In the mid-term election of 1966, Republicans gained 47 seats in the House, narrowing the Democrats' majority to 248 to 187. That majority, however, included southern Democrats who could not be counted on to vote for Great Society legislation, and Johnson was riding a little lower in the saddle.

Riots again swept the country in the summers of 1966 and 1967. Helping to fuel the violence was an influx of unemployed blacks from the South, many of them formerly agricultural workers. When the law was changed in 1966 to extend the minimum wage to agriculture, farmers began laying off men and turned more and more to mechanization.

The riots of 1967 were perhaps the most frightening of all, taking on the ugliness of guerrilla warfare throughout the land. Newark's Springfield Avenue looked like a scene out of World War II. Detroit alone counted 27 dead and damage at more than $200 million. Johnson sent in federal troops only after repeated requests from Governor George Romney, and then only after going on television to observe that Romney, a potential rival for the presidency in 1968, had been unable to bring the situation under control. Newspapers denounced the president for playing politics with people's lives.

Congress now was cooling to ever-larger War on Poverty appropriations. What many thought, Rep. George H. Mahon, chairman of the House Appropriations Committee, said in so many words: "The more we have appropriated for these programs, the more violence we have." Congress, nevertheless, appropriated $1.8 billion for the War on Poverty in 1967 — an increase, but less than the administration had asked.

Helping to build public uncertainty were well-publicized examples of waste, mismanagement, and inequity in the poverty program. In Kansas City, enrollees in a summer youth program for the poor included a young man who drove around in an expensive new Thunderbird. In Detroit, a jobless auto worker, who had been taking home $104 a week when he worked, found he could make $160 a week tax-free in a job-training program. In Johnston, Rhode Island, 73 parents of children in a poverty program owned, among them, 58 homes and 113 cars. A congressional survey disclosed that there was one supergrade ($15,000 +) official for every 18 employees in the Office of Economic Opportunity; in the Department of Agriculture it was one for every 500, and in the Department of Defense one for every 1,000.

For varied reasons, but particularly the Vietnam War and the riots, there was a rising sense of alarm sweeping the land. In August 1967, Senate Foreign Relations Chairman J. William Fulbright declared: "The Great Society is a sick society."

The war in Vietnam had become the most divisive issue in memory. Johnson, in the election campaign of 1964, posed as the peace candidate, declaring he wouldn't send American boys to fight a war "that Asian boys ought to fight," even as he was mapping then-secret plans for bombing North Vietnam. Three years later there were more than 1 million American boys in the Vietnam theater of operations. There had been 16,000 when Johnson took office. In August 1967, when the Johnson administration had been at war for one month longer than all of World War II, the president was still insisting the nation could fight the war in Asia and the one at home — the war on poverty — at the same time. But the cost was steep. Federal spending had already gone up by 50 percent during the Johnson years, and now the president was asking for an income tax surcharge of 10 percent. Fulbright, declaring a "sick society," argued that both wars were going badly. But the problem, he said, was not so much a matter of financial feasibility as the "psychological incompatibility" of trying to do both at the same time.

Lyndon Johnson, in mid-1965, had been as powerful a man as ever occupied the White House. Now, two years later, his war in Vietnam quagmired and his war on poverty floundering, he was a president in deep political trouble. His rating in the polls was at an all-time low of 32 percent. He seemed no longer to have the nation's trust. He was being further and further demoted from president to mere politician by each successive appearance on the nightly news. The war the "Asian boys" were supposed to fight: Would it go on forever, taking the lives of countless American boys? And the war on poverty: Was it holding out more promise than it could deliver, further sagging the hopes of an increasingly disillusioned age? Even the bubbly Hubert Humphrey, that eternal optimist, wondered. Speaking of Model Cities in the summer of 1967, the vice-president said it was like having a hundred kids to a party where there was only one box of Crackerjacks. "By the time we divide up the box," observed Humphrey, "each kid will get just one Crackerjack, and you know that's not going to be anywhere near enough."

In January 1968 the Office of Economic Opportunity began a cutback in the antipoverty program, the result of Congress appropriating less money for the fiscal year and, moreover, transferring some funds to other agencies. A further sign of the shift away from massive government spending was an announcement in May, by the Department of Labor, of a pledge by private industry to create at least 100,000 new jobs for the unemployed, the government paying the cost of training.

Meanwhile, Johnson on March 31st announced, to an astonished nation, that he would not seek another term as president. He would not be a candidate in the 1968 election. That concluded his presidency, for all practical purposes, leaving a nation divided by its incompatible wars and unfulfilled of the vast hopes that had been raised — perhaps less a Great Society than what had to seem, to many, a grated one.

SHOOTING FOR THE MOON

What is welfare? Clearly, now, it is a diversity of programs by which government — the federal as prime mover, working with local and state government — seeks to provide for the general welfare of its people, and in particular those, for some reason either personal or economic, unable to provide sufficiently for themselves. It is "social security" in its broadest sense: old age insurance, survivors' insurance, and disability insurance; aid to families with dependent children; public assistance to the aged, blind, and disabled; food stamps and school lunches; public housing and rent subsidies; medicare and medicaid; and considerably more, as will be seen.

Yet, what is "welfare"? One might ask that at random and find it answered by a conception of welfare as public assistance to a family qualifying for Aid to Families with Dependent Children.

It was certainly so in 1969, when pent-up unhappiness with the operation of AFDC came to an official head. AFDC was the big troublespot in public assistance. Between 1963 and 1969, when there was general prosperity and relatively less unemployment, AFDC, instead of decreasing or even remaining constant, actually doubled in volume. Furthermore, during the 1960s it increased by 273 percent in cost. In New York State, between 1953 and 1967, the number of children supported by AFDC increased by more than 400 percent. In 1967, AFDC was ten times what it had been in 1945. Nationwide, it was increasing fastest among blacks. In 1948, blacks accounted for 29 percent of all AFDC families; in 1961, for 44 percent. During that same period, however, blacks accounted for 60 percent of the overall increase in AFDC caseload.

In 1940, when the program was still known as Aid to Dependent Children, 42 percent of the fathers of beneficiaries were dead. In 1963, two years after it had become AFDC, it was 6 percent. The rest of the fathers were unemployed or disabled, or, more than likely, had abandoned their families.

The ADC/AFDC program had its origins in state widows' laws that existed before the Social Security Act of 1935. These laws, which had been passed in 36 states, provided small pensions to widows with children, who otherwise might have had no means of subsistence. The provision of the Social Security Act creating ADC thus consolidated existing practice more than it broke new ground, and it got little notice. It was certainly never imagined that this innocent little child would become the *enfant terrible* of the whole welfare system.

In his *Public Interest* (Winter 1968) article, "The Crisis in Public Welfare," which contributed significantly to the reform mood of the times, Daniel P. Moynihan, the future U.S. senator, suggested that the framers of ADC likely saw the typical recipient as a God-fearing, hard-working, West Virginia mother whose husband had died in a mining disaster; in fact, by 1968, the typical AFDC family was very large, very urban, most likely black or of some other minority, whose dependence on public support was showing signs of being an inherited trait.

There was an attempt to reform AFDC in 1967 by requiring the mother (or father) to accept work, or at least job training, thus substituting "workfare" for welfare. It had little success. Job training was expensive, and employment was uncertain. It began to seem more efficient just to send the eligible their monthly checks. That left the problem of the "notch," the point at which public benefits and the welfare client's earned income crossed. When the client earned beyond the level of the notch, he or she faced a loss of public benefits. That loss might far outbalance the additional income earned, particularly where food stamps, medicaid, and housing assistance were being furnished in addition to AFDC. Thus it was common for a client to avoid additional income, or even sacrifice a job entirely, in order to stay on AFDC.

That was one of the difficulties with AFDC when the Nixon administration took office in 1969. Another difficulty was the imbalance of payments among the states. Benefits varied widely, from $9.70 a month in Mississippi to $65.30 in New Jersey. The nationwide average was $42.90.

The welfare system generally (AFDC in particular) was a failure. Yet, for the most part, political leaders looked the other way. If they took notice, it was usually in the negative, huffing and puffing over the fraud and abuse, and now and then suggesting some further patchwork reform that had likely been tried, and had failed, a number of times before. The first president really to take the bull of reform by the horns was Nixon, who, in the summer of 1969, declared what was generally known but rarely conceded by government: The welfare system, said Nixon, is a "colossal failure."

The summer of 1969 was otherwise notable for the most important news story of the year, and perhaps of the century: man on the moon. That was July 20th. Four days later the Apollo II crew returned to earth and splashed down in the Pacific, where they were met aboard the carrier *Hornet* by the president of the United States.

The Apollo crew remained aboard the *Hornet*. The president resumed an around-the-world tour that took him to eight countries in nine days. Returning to Washington on August 3rd, a buoyant Richard Nixon had scheduled only a week in the capital before flying off to San Clemente in California for a week's vacation. It would turn out to be a busy week: Senate passage of the controversial Safeguard antiballistic missile system, House approval of a far-reaching new tax law, unveiling of a $10 billion mass transit proposal, and announcement of a major, domestic policy statement Nixon would make to the nation on television Friday night, August 8th.

The subject would be welfare. Only that much was being announced, but it was quickly guessed by Washington observers that it would be something major. A Friday night in August was not a forum for the routine. Furthermore, all three major television networks were preempting regular scheduling to carry the president's message live at 10 P.M.

Few things in Washington remain under wraps for long, and this would be no exception. Friday morning's Washington *Post* had the essence of the speech under a lead-story headline:

NIXON'S RELIEF PLAN
SETS BASIC INCOME

The president's proposal, said the *Post*, would provide for a "revolutionary family security program."

With most of the nation's television watchers watching him (or doing something other than looking at television), Nixon revealed in detail his plan for a massive overhaul of the nation's welfare system, as well as a proposal for federal revenue-sharing with states and cities, beginning with $1 billion the first full year of operation. Revenue sharing had been talked about during the Johnson years. Now it was a concrete proposal, from president to Congress: Do it.

The greater part of Nixon's address, however, was on welfare reform, and the *Post*'s hint of "revolutionary" was not far off the mark. In a sense this, too, was shooting for the moon. What Nixon proposed was a federally funded floor under all families with children—a guaranteed minimum subsistence. It would not be a guaranteed annual *income*, in the sense that it would be available only to families with children rather than to the population as a whole. Nor would it be given out no-strings-attached. The recipient (excluding a disabled adult or a mother of preschool children) would be required to accept a "suitable" job if one were available, or job training as an alternative.

Called the Family Assistance Plan (FAP), the new program would supersede AFDC entirely. It would be a wholly federal program and thus insure a minimum standard of subsistence nationwide, although states could exceed this standard if they wished. There would be no "man in the house" rule barring assistance when there was an able-bodied father in the home. Whether the head of the household might be father or mother, whether unemployed or underemployed or disabled, the family would be eligible for assistance. That was the point: It would be "family" assistance. Thus would the family stay together and the father not be forced to "disappear" so as to make his wife and children eligible for public assistance.

Equally as important was FAP's incentive to working. There would be a sliding ratio of benefits to earned income more realistic than the "notch" of existing programs, which discouraged rather than encouraged a recipient's working. The basic benefit for a family of four would be $1,600 per year, against which the recipient could earn $720 with no loss of benefits. From that point on, the more earned, the less in benefits, until, at $3,920, the recipient was on his or her own.

Besides the Family Assistance Plan, Nixon's welfare reform proposal included a $3 billion-a-year package of manpower training programs and a $1 billion-a-year continuation of the War on Poverty that included an extensive reorganization of the Office of Economic Opportunity and its subsidiary agencies, making OEO in essence a laboratory for experimenting with innovative programs, which, if proven, would then be permanently assigned to HEW, the Department of Labor, or some other department or agency.

Said Nixon to the nation: The present system is "a colossal failure . . . an antiquated, wheezing, overloaded machine [that] breaks up homes . . . often penalizes work . . . robs recipients of their dignity." And further, in the spirit of the times:

> Abolishing poverty, putting an end to dependency—like reaching the moon a generation ago—may seem to be impossible. But in the spirit of Apollo, we can lift our sights and marshal our best efforts.

THAT ELUSIVE GOAL: WORK INCENTIVE

On the same day the Nixon plan made the papers, a Hartford mother of four did likewise, as if to affirm the expediency of reform. Walking home from cashing her $172 biweekly welfare check, she had been robbed by a gang of teenagers. A kindly public had responded by sending her gifts of food and money; a diligent police department by investigating the crime. The police did not find the offenders, but they found something else. Now, on August 9th, the papers were reporting that the woman faced prosecution for welfare fraud: The police discovered she also had a full-time job paying $85 a week. Indignant, the woman responded:

> There are people that do a lot of worse things than go out and work to make money. If a person thinks enough of herself to go out and work, this ought to be appreciated.

Under Nixon's plan it would be appreciated, although the size of her welfare check would be measured according to how much she earned and therefore how much she needed in the way of public assistance. As it was, however, her working while receiving public support constituted fraud and was punishable by a fine of up to $200 and/or six months in jail.

A work-incentive formula was essential to the Nixon plan, not only to make it a viable prospect when it got to Congress but to have Nixon's name attached to it in the first place. Work incentive — that elusive goal since Elizabethan times! FAP held promise of making more people self-supporting by encouraging personal initiative through its sliding scale of benefits, as opposed to the existing system and its penalty for initiative. Under that system, observed Moynihan, a principal in the development of FAP as Nixon's Urban Affairs Advisor,

> you earn an extra dollar and you're out of public housing, earn an extra dollar and you're out of Medicaid . . . out of food stamps . . . really an insane kind of arrangement.

FAP also had the virtue of being a single, unified welfare plan to replace the conglomeration that had developed over the years. In its simplification it had the potential of perhaps actually reducing costs in the long run, even if it substantially increased them at the outset by embracing a greater number of beneficiaries (13 million more on the relief rolls at an additional $4 billion). The plan also would tend to diminish the degree of interference with which government was increasingly asserting itself in the lives of its people.

To Nixon, the great pragmatist, these were all virtues that made the Family Assistance Plan a worthy tool with which to fix the wheezing old machine. At the same time, the political benefits could be appreciated. It seemed to some observers that Nixon might be taking over the constituencies of his two opponents in the 1968 election (the liberal Hubert Humphrey and the conservative George Wallace) and that these, added to his own "Silent Majority," would represent very nearly the whole electorate.

Once the Family Assistance Plan was outlined in the nationwide television address of August 8, 1969, reaction was quick and generally favorable from those who weren't struck speechless that such a proposal had come from a Republican president. Indeed, reported the press, some of those most dumbfounded were veterans of the Johnson administration who "stared enviously" at what had been regarded as too radical for them to have proposed.

House Republican Leader Gerald Ford gave it a hearty welcome: "For the first time it would always pay an American to work instead of going on welfare. This is the true spirit of America." His Senate counterpart, wily old Everett McKinley Dirksen, minority leader, hedged. "I'm going to look a long ways down the road," he said.

Among Democrats there was support mixed with some clearly partisan "but's." Sen. Walter F. Mondale, the future vice-president, thought that "some parts are good, some are bad," but maintained that elimination of food stamps for those on FAP was "outrageous." Senate Majority Leader Mike Mansfield ventured that it had "some interesting suggestions and proposals."

An unlikely ally Nixon found in George Wiley, head of the National Welfare Rights Organization, who declared the Nixon plan "a victory for welfare rights," even if the dollar amount of aid was "totally inadequate." The same criticism would follow FAP through Congress among Democrats, while Republicans would echo Ford's praises.

The FAP proposal was given high priority when the second session of the 91st Congress opened in January 1970. But there was trouble at the start: a United Press International story disclosing a "secret survey" of the House Ways and Means Committee, into whose jurisdiction the bill had gone. The survey, a nonpartisan analysis prepared by the committee staff, produced findings that were, to quote the story, potentially "devastating." According to the staff report, there were flaws in the proposed legislation. For example: "A case could be made that subsidizing the working poor may actually encourage desertion, rather than discourage it." The report also raised the possibility that two brothers rooming together at college, and thus constituting a family with minimal earned income, could receive welfare; and that some families might go out on a buying spree—new color television sets for example—in order to reduce their cash assets and thus qualify for FAP (although this was true under existing law as well).

Meanwhile, the plan itself had undergone some changes. As originally proposed by Nixon in August 1969, food stamps were eliminated for those on FAP. A week later, a few administration officials were predicting that would change, and by autumn food stamps were officially back in. What was originally a nationwide minimum of $65 monthly for the blind, aged, and disabled increased to $90, and by the time the bill had cleared the Ways and Means Committee it was $110.

When the bill came to a vote in the House on April 16, 1970, there was clearly the prevailing opinion, supported by such diverse interests as the AFL-CIO and the National Association of Manufacturers, that the existing system had to be changed, and the Family Assistance Plan passed by the surprisingly wide margin of 243 to 155. Next day there came predictions that the Senate would follow suit.

It would not be the case, as became obvious. The Senate Finance Committee started asking much tougher questions than had been asked in the House, questions that suggested the House never fully understood the ramifications of the legislation (or, perhaps, that some members understood the bill all too well). A clear hint of the outcome is obvious in this exchange at a meeting of the committee on April 30, 1970, the participants (in order of appearance) being Sen. John J. Williams, Delaware; Chairman Russell B. Long, Louisiana; HEW Deputy Undersecretary Robert E. Patricelli; and Sen. Clifford P. Hansen, Wyoming:

> *Senator Williams*: Maybe there is no solution. But I am one of those fellows who thinks you can solve any problem if you really recognize it head on and get to doing it. Now, this man with a family of seven, if he works and makes $9,916, he would have $8,768 of income, or $1,439 less than he would if he did not work at all.
>
> *Chairman Long*: That demonstrates that if that recipient goes to work and actually by dint of his own hard work makes $9,916, then as a result of earning almost $10,000, he is then, after all is considered, more than a thousand dollars worse off than he would be if he had not gone to work at all. Is that correct?
>
> *Mr. Patricelli*: Correct.
>
> *Chairman Long*: How can we justify that kind of result, that a person earns $9,900 and he is worse off than he would be if he had never gone to work at all?
>
> *Senator Williams*: That is based on the bill which is before us assuming we approve it without an amendment. . . .
>
> *Chairman Long*: Is this how the bill would work?
>
> *Mr. Patricelli*: This is how the bill would work. The situation under existing law is worse.
>
> *Chairman Long*: If you are going to spend $4 billion to change the existing law, why does it work out that way? Can't you spend $4 billion better than that? . . . Why not junk the whole thing and start over again.
>
> *Senator Hansen*: I would like to offer my bipartisan support to do just that.

Next day the Senate committee voted to call off the hearings and send the bill back to the White House drawing board. Basically, what the committee wanted was legislation integrating into FAP other programs for the poor—food stamps, medicaid, and housing, in particular—since it was the value of these that made the basic FAP provision of $1,600 worth more than $10,000 in some cases (a family of seven in New York, for example). Said the committee, in effect: Let's have everything out on the table, so we know what we're talking about. Additionally, Long and some of the others questioned HEW cost estimates, observing that the current medicaid appropriation was $3.5 billion, five times what HEW had originally projected.

Revised legislation was introduced the following year and given top priority as bill number HR-1 of the 92nd Congress. It was a measure that set basic FAP assistance at $2,400 for a family of four, and also incorporated changes in social security, medicare, and medicaid. It made its way to a vote in the House of Representatives on June 22, 1971, and approval by the now wider margin of 288 to 132. The Senate, however, took its time again—15 months—and then substituted another, more comprehensive, bill.

When House and Senate differences were resolved in conference, the result was an omnibus bill, approved by both houses on October 17, 1972, that: provided for a federal takeover of welfare assistance to the blind, aged, and disabled, effective in 1974 (known as Supplemental Security Income, or SSI); broadened medicare and medicaid coverage; increased social security payments for most recipients; and raised the social security tax rate and maximum wage base for all taxpayers. FAP went in the wastebasket.

The Family Assistance Plan was the victim both of liberals who complained it was too conservative (California Rep. Ron Dellums: a "feeble and ludicrous response to the plight of the poor") and conservatives who complained it was too liberal (Louisiana Rep. John R. Rarick: "No one reminds the people at home where the money will come from. Santa Claus will write the checks"). There was furthermore the simple reality that a Democratic Congress had a gnawing discomfort about giving a Republican administration—Nixon's above all—credit for out-Great-Society-ing the Great Society.

RECENT YEARS

In the absence of the Family Assistance Plan, which, at least, would have produced some degree of simplification, the overloaded machine continued to shake and wheeze as it had in 1969 when Nixon pronounced it a "colossal failure."

Inadequacies, however, were hardly the result of insufficient funding. Between 1960 and 1970—a period spanning the New Frontier and the Great Society—federal social welfare expenditures increased 210 percent (from $24.9 billion to $77.3 billion). Nor was there a lack of diversity. In 1974 the Joint Economic Committee of Congress compiled a list of all federally funded Income Security Programs. That list, by category, as contained in the committee's 1974 report:*

---

*U.S. Congress, Joint Economic Committee, Subcommittee on Fiscal Policy, *Public Welfare and Work Incentives: Theory and Practice* (Studies in Public Welfare, Paper No. 14, Washington, April 1974).

No Limit on Income

1. Medicare; 2. Compensation to Veterans for Service-Connected Disability; 3. Dependency and Indemnity Compensation to Veterans' Dependents for Service-Connected Death; 4. Veterans' Housing Loans; 5. Veterans' Hospital, Domiciliary, and Medical Care; 6. Veterans' Educational Assistance; 7. Vocational Rehabilitation for Veterans; 8. War Orphans' and Widows' Educational Assistance; 9. Federal Civil Service Retirement; 10. Military Retirement; 11. Social Security Special Benefits for Persons Age 72 and Over; 12. Federal Employees' Compensation (Job-Related Illness and Injury); 13. Meals for the Elderly.

Wage-Tested

14. Old-Age Insurance; 15. Survivor's Insurance; 16. Disability Insurance.

Wage and Benefit-Tested

17. Railroad Retirement, Disability, and Survivors' Benefits; 18. Federal-State Unemployment Insurance; 19. Railroad Unemployment Insurance; 20. Trade Readjustment Allowances (for Workers Displaced by Imports); 21. Black Lung Disability and Survivors' Benefits.

Cash Aid

22. Aid to Families with Dependent Children; 23. Supplemental Security Income; 24. Emergency Assistance; 25. Assistance to Cuban Refugees; 26. General Assistance to Indians; 27. Pensions for Veterans; 28. Pensions for Survivors of Veterans (Non-Service-Connected Death); 29. Death Compensation for Survivors of Veterans (Service-Connected Death); 30. Black Lung Survivors' Benefits.

Food Benefits

31. Food Stamps; 32. Food Commodities (for Families, School Children and Needy in Institutions); 33. School Lunches; 34. School Milk; 35. Special Supplemental Feeding (For Pregnant and Lactating Mothers); 36. Special Supplemental Feeding for Women, Infants, and Children.

Health Benefits

37. Medicaid; 38. Veterans' Hospital, Domiciliary, and Medical Care (Non-Service-Connected Disability); 39. Comprehensive Health Services; 40. Dental Health of Children; 41. Health Care of Children and Youth; 42. Intensive Infant Care Project; 43. Maternity and Infant Care Projects; 44. Crippled Children's Services.

Housing

45. Low-Rent Public Housing; 46. Home-Ownership for Tenants of Public Housing ("Sweat Equity" Accrued through Tenant Doing Maintenance); 47. Home-Ownership Loans; 48. Rent Supplements; 49. Interest Subsidies for Rental Housing; 50. Mortgage Insurance for Low and Moderate-Income Families; 51. Mortgage Insurance for Low and Moderate-Income Families (Condominiums); 52. Mortgage Insurance for Families Who Are Special Credit Risks.

Housing (Rural or Special)

53. Rural Housing Loans; 54. Low-Income Housing Repair Loans; 55. Rural Rental Housing Insured Loans; 56. Farm Labor Housing; 57. Rural Self-Help Housing Technical Assistance; 58. Rural Housing Site Loans; 59. Indian Housing Improvement Program; 60. Indian Housing Technical Assistance; 61. Appalachian Housing Program.

Education (College and Other Post-Secondary)

62. Basic Educational Opportunity Grants; 63. Supplemental Educational Opportunity Grants; 64. College Work-Study; 65. National Direct Student Loans; 66. Interest-Free Guaranteed Loans; 67. Nursing Education Loans; 68. Medical Education Loans and Grants.

Education (Primary and Secondary)

69. "Head Start"; 70. "Follow Through"; 71. "Upward Bound"; 72. "Talent Search"; 73. Special Services for Low-Income and Physically Handicapped Students in Post-Secondary Schools; 74. Vocational Education Work-Study.

Jobs and Training

75. Neighborhood Youth Corps; 76. Operation Mainstream; 77. Senior Community Service Employment; 78. Job Corps; 79. Work Incentive Projects; 80. Public Service Careers (On-the-Job Training); 81. Concentrated Employment Program (Job Referral in Poor Neighborhoods); 82. Manpower Development and Training; 83. Job Opportunities in the Business Sector ("JOBS"); 84. Senior Companions; 85. Foster Grandparents; 86. Career Opportunities Program; 87. Vocational Rehabilitation Services.

Social Services

88. Services to Needy Families on Welfare (Counseling, Day Care, Homemaker Services, Health Care); 89. Services to Needy Aged, Blind, or Disabled (the same); 90. Legal Services for the Poor.

Business Aid

91. Economic Opportunity Loans.

Clearly evident is the enormous diversity of these programs; and furthermore, the vast number of people potentially reached — a number far beyond that envisioned when social security was passed in 1935, and Roosevelt, promising only "some measure of protection to the average citizen," declared, "We can never insure 100 percent of the population against 100 percent of the hazards and vicissitudes of life."

Yet it would seem, judging by the 1974 report of the Joint Economic Committee of Congress, that nearly every citizen ought now to be eligible for something, at some time or another. And indeed, there is statistical justification for suggesting that income security, or social welfare (what started out as public charity) is for all. The report of the Joint Economic Committee included an estimate of beneficiaries, program by program. If those estimates are added together, the total comes to 201,089,614. The estimated 1974 population of the United States was 211,389,000.

To be sure, there are a great many duplications, a great many among the 201 million who were recipients of public support under different categories, and a great many among the 211 million who never required or never received any form of public assistance. Yet the sheer numbers make their point.

That so diverse an assortment of programs evolved ought not to be surprising in light of the enormous increase in funding. In the half-century between 1933 (the beginning of the New Deal) and 1983, federal social welfare expenditures increased from $1.3 billion to $365.5 billion. The increases have been constant and substantial, as is evident in the following table:*

Federal Social Welfare Expenditures

Year	Expenditures	Increase
1933	$1.3 billion	—
1940	$3.4 billion	$2.1 billion
1950	$10.5 billion	$7.1 billion
1960	$24.9 billion	$14.4 billion
1970	$77.3 billion	$52.4 billion
1983	$365.5 billion	$288.2 billion

---

*U.S. Census Bureau, *Historical Statistics of the United States* (Washington, 1975); and Federal Budget, Fiscal Year 1983, Estimated Outlays.

For the great cost, there has been something to show. At the beginning of the War on Poverty in 1964, it was estimated that 20 percent of the population of the United States could be considered in poverty. In 1977 the Department of Health, Education and Welfare estimated the incidence of poverty at 12.3 percent. That was enough to show progress and yet also suggested a need to keep poverty-fighting fully staffed and amply appropriated. But was this a fair estimate? The question arises because the calculating did not take into consideration in-kind benefits: medicaid, food stamps, housing subsidies, school lunches, and the like. Only cash benefits were used in HEW's calculations, whereas it appeared to many an observer that a dollar in food stamps, or a dollar in paid-up medical bills, or a dollar in paid-up rent was no different than a dollar in cash, particularly in a credit card society. The Congressional Budget Office made its own survey, taking into consideration in-kind benefits as well as cash, and determined that the incidence of hard-core poverty in 1977 was 4.2 percent. Some estimates placed the figure at between 3.6 and 6.5 percent. Computations in the recession-plagued early 1980s suggested a rate of anywhere from 10 to 15 percent. Because criteria have varied so widely, however, comparisons are difficult, and the poverty rate remains an elusive entity.

"The welfare system is too hopeless to be cured by minor modifications. We must make a complete and clean break with the past." So declared President Jimmy Carter in August 1977, half a year into his presidency. No complete and clean break would be coming, however. A major reform (substituting a flat cash grant for AFDC, SSI, and food stamps for those who could not work) never made it out of committee. In 1979 a less sweeping proposal passed the House but died in committee in the Senate. Meanwhile, heating assistance for the needy, taking into account a tremendous increase in fuel costs during the 1970s, was approved, with funding of $1.6 billion. In 1980 the Department of Health, Education and Welfare (that monster-sized department that started hatching with Harding in 1920 and was born under Eisenhower in 1953) came to an end. On May 4, by act of Congress, HEW became two new cabinet-level departments: Health and Human Services (HHS) and Education (ED). HHS, which assumed responsibility for the social welfare programs administered by the old HEW, started life as a department of 140,000 employees, with a budget of $226 billion.

In 1981, following the election of President Ronald Reagan and a Republican Senate, there came the belt-tightening that had been a promise of the Reagan campaign. Food stamp eligibility was narrowed, with the result that more than 1 million persons were taken off the program (still leaving roughly one person in every ten across the country receiving food stamps). There were also cuts in AFDC for working parents. Further reductions in these programs and SSI came in 1982. Social security reform legislation in 1983 sought a partial reform of medicare as well by establishing fixed payments for a wide range of medical procedures.

Despite these periodic reforms, the one universally accepted fact about social welfare is that no one is really satisfied with the way it works.

At the 1976 National Governors' Conference, welfare reform was the overriding issue. It produced still another call for consolidation of services and a federal minimum standard of payment to stop the migration of the poor from one state to another in search of ampler benefits. More important, perhaps, was an observation by Washington Governor Daniel J. Evans: "Many of the nation's poor who need help don't get it, and many who do get it don't really need it."

Sometimes it is the result of confusing and absurd regulations. In Michigan, a man and woman, both blind, preparing to get married in 1979, were informed by the government that, as man and wife, they would be entitled to $363 a month in benefits whereas if they lived together unmarried they would be eligible for $502 monthly.

Sometimes it is the result of easy-to-get-around regulations. Housing assistance is a good example. In New Jersey an elderly and relatively wealthy widow sold her house and transferred all her assets to her son; then she applied for a housing subsidy that would pay 75 percent of the cost of an apartment. The subsidy was granted. Soon after, the woman left for a six-month vacation in Europe, paid for by her son. Sometime thereafter, another woman of the same age, recently widowed, applied for a similar subsidy. She had worked at menial jobs all her life and had managed to build only a small savings account. It was wiped out by her husband's terminal illness, which left her virtually destitute. A housing subsidy? She had never heard of one until someone told her. By the time she applied, the allotment was full. Her name went onto a long waiting list.

She may not have been knowledgeable about welfare benefits, but others among the poor sometimes know the system better than those who run it. Chicago's "Welfare Queen" used a score of aliases to claim $150,000 in welfare in one year. A Pasadena woman, with 38 nonexistent children, collected more than $300,000 before she was caught, by then having used her illegal benefits for such luxuries as a Rolls-Royce and a Mercedes. Food stamp fraud (some of it the result of forgery, some of phony claims) was estimated at $35 million in New York City alone in 1979. The city had 1.1 million persons receiving food stamps.

Others who know how to work the system are some of those working for it. As his "share of the wealth," one New York doctor had medicaid billings totaling $571,972 in one year; the 20 top medicaid physicians in the state collected an average of $242,908 each.

It is not surprising the taxpayer remains decidedly unhappy about the state of welfare. Surely so was the worker coming home after a hard day's work to read, in his evening paper, that the average welfare family in New York received more than $18,000 in total benefits, and the average wage-earner $14,032 in taxable income. Those were the averages reported by the Albany *Times-Union* in August 1980, after an examination of statistics of the state Social Services Department. Surely so was the taxpayer who read in March 1976 that the son of U.S. Senator James Abourezk of South Dakota was getting food stamps at college. When surveyed, in 1978, as to whether "too much," "too little," or "about the right amount" was being spent on welfare, six out of ten respondents said "too much."*

Often unhappy is the welfare caseworker, who is crushed under mountains of paperwork (3 billion sheets a year in New York State), bogged down in swamps of often vague rules and regulations, and overloaded with assignments in which he or she must be father, mother, doctor, psychiatrist, friend, and adviser, often for less in salary than what a client family is getting in benefits.

Government is unhappy. The loss in inefficiency, bureaucratic bungling, and error runs into the billions a year, and outright fraud even more. No one knows how much. The U.S. Department of Health, Education and Welfare, in 1980, estimated that errors, just in AFDC payments, were running close to $1 billion a year. Other estimates have placed social security fraud at $6 billion—almost twice the federal social welfare budget in 1940.

Meanwhile, the entire social security system has been creaking and groaning. There is irony in recalling that the original Social Security Act of 1935 included provisions for improving the health of the nation's citizens. Those and many such measures, coupled with myriad breakthroughs in medical science, have resulted in a level of life expectancy considerably greater than was the case in 1935, when the actuarial formulas of social security were first devised. People have been outliving the formulas, and perhaps the solvency of the fund itself. But there is more than that to the crisis that surrounded social security in the late 1970s and early 1980s. Also significant has been the continual broadening of coverage to embrace more and more of the population. In 1950, 15 years after social security was established, there were fewer than 3 million beneficiaries. By the early 1980s the total was 36 million, or one in every seven persons, receiving monthly benefits of some sort. Meanwhile, Congress had amended the Social Security Act in 1956 to permit women to retire at age 62, and in 1961 for men to do likewise. The result: more social security

---

*U.S. Census Bureau, *Social Indicators III* (Washington, 1980), p. 368.

retirees were leaving work before 65 than were staying, further increasing what the system paid out while decreasing what was paid in.

Of even greater impact, however, was 1972 legislation tying increases in benefits to the cost of living index, effective in 1975. This set off a series of annual explosions in the federal budget, so that by January 1983 it was calculated that the Old Age and Survivors Insurance Trust Fund, the largest of three funds making up the social security system, was paying out $47.5 million *a day* more in benefits than it was taking in. Notwithstanding periodic social security tax hikes and a temporary bail-out of the old-age fund in 1982 through the borrowing of $17.5 billion from two smaller trust funds, social security appeared headed for bankruptcy.

Early in 1983 a rescue plan, talked about in one form or another for years, finally emerged. It was the product of a 15-member, bipartisan President's Commission on Social Security Reform, appointed by President Reagan in 1981. Essentially what the commission proposed, Congress speedily turned into legislation that was signed by Reagan in March 1983. The reform measure accelerated revenues and slowed down benefits to assure solvency for what proponents believed would be as long as 75 years. The short-term expectation was an additional $165 billion over seven years to assure, at the very least, that social security's 36 million beneficiaries would be guaranteed their monthly checks for that long. The means: speeding up already scheduled payroll tax increases; increasing the self-employment tax; delaying a scheduled cost-of-living allowance for six months; taxing social security benefits of high-income recipients for the first time; and, most significantly, raising the retirement age for full benefits from 65 to 67 by the year 2027.

Even as social security reform began going into effect, there were new warnings about medicare: that payments were rising far faster than revenues, and bankruptcy would be inevitable if major (and politically precarious) reforms were not instituted. The most dire warning: medicare would be $1 trillion in the red by A.D. 2005.

Thus concludes this study as matters stood.

A BRIEF EPILOGUE

The observations of astronomers and historians are alike in this regard: Those who trace the movement of celestial bodies through telescopes must account for the fact that the earth, also, is moving. In looking back at history, we must remember that we do so likewise from an ever-moving vantage point, for human life is a process of continual change.

From that moving vantage point we call "now," we may look back and observe society's response to the needy over the ages. Finding precise parallels with the present in those observations can sometimes be risky; finding none at all, riskier still.

SOURCE NOTES

CHAPTER 1

ATHENS (pp. 1-6): Aristotle, *Athenaion Politeia*, 26, 49; M. Cary, *History of the Greek World from 323 to 146 B.C.* (London, 1932), pp. 302-06; G. B. Grundy, *Thucydides and the History of His Age* (Oxford, 1911/1948),* vol. I, pp. 66-69, 91-95, 176-83; N. G. L. Hammond, *History of Greece* (Oxford, 1967), pp. 530-32, 552, 565; A. R. Hands, *Charities and Social Aid in Greece and Rome* (Ithaca, 1968), pp. 95-100; Isocrates, *Areopagiticus*, 20, 21; Lysias, *Oration on the Question of a Pension for an Invalid*; Plutarch, *Pericles*, 9, 11, 12, 37; ____*Solon*, 13, 15; L. Whibley, *A Companion to Greek Studies* (1904/Cambridge, 1931), pp. 452-56, 492-93.

THE ROMAN REPUBLIC (pp. 6-11): Appian, *Civil Wars*, I, 21; II, 120; Cicero, *Ad Atticum*, IV, 1; *Orations on the Agrarian Law*, II, 6; ____ *Pro Sestio*, XXV; ____ *Tusculan Disputations*, III, 20; M. Cary and H. H. Scullard, *History of Rome* (London, 1935/1975), pp. 265-69; Dio Cassius, *History*, XLIII, 21; Florus, *Epitome of Roman History*, II, 2; Hands, op. cit., pp. 101-05; Livy, *History*, II, 41; IV, 12; P. Louis, *Ancient Rome at Work: An Economic Study*, tr. E. B. F. Wareing (1927/New York, 1965), pp. 20, 157-61; T. Mommsen, *History of Rome*, tr. W. P. Dickson (New York, 1891), vol. II, p. 408; vol. III, pp. 269-70, 430-31; vol. IV, pp. 227, 591-97; M. P. Nilsson, *Imperial Rome* (New York, 1926), pp. 246-47; Plutarch, *Coriolanus*, 16; ____*Lucullus*, 20; R. Rostovtzeff, *Social and Economic History of the Roman Empire* (Oxford, 1926/1957), pp. 13, 23-27; Suetonius, *Caesar*, 41; R. Syme, *The Roman Revolution* (Oxford, 1939), pp. 37, 357; Velleius, *History*, II, 6.

THE ROMAN EMPIRE (pp. 10-20): J. Carcopino, *Daily Life in Ancient Rome* (New Haven, 1940/1960), pp. 65, 173, 182, 202-03; Cary and Scullard, op. cit., pp. 425-33, 489-503, 517-35; Dio Cassius, op. cit., LV, 10; LIX, 2; LX, 11; LXXII, 36; Diocletian, "Edictum de Pretiis"; T. Frank, *Economic Survey of Ancient Rome* (Baltimore, 1933-40), vol. V, pp. 4-12, 36-56 passim, 65-67, 67-88, passim, 88-90, 218-19; Fronto, *Letters*, "To Lucius Verus, A.D. 165" (Principia Historiae), 17; Hands, op. cit., pp. 105-15; A. H. M. Jones, *The Later Roman Empire* (Oxford, 1964), pp. 695-705, 1053-58; ____ *The Roman Economy: Studies in Ancient Economic and Administrative History* (Oxford, 1974), pp. 190-202, 207-13; *Justinian Code*, Digest, 5.1.52, 34.1.14; Juvenal, *Satires*, X, 78; Lactantius, *De Mortibus Persecutorum*, 7; ____*Divinae Institutiones*, VII, 15; N. Lewis and M. Reinhold, eds., *Roman Civilization* (New York, 1951), vol. II, pp. 138-40, 150-53, 344-47, 464-73, 482-84; Louis, op. cit., pp. 20, 231, 239; Nilsson, op. cit., pp. 247-51, 334; Pliny the Younger, *Letters*, II, 1; ____*Panegyricus*, 62; Plutarch, *Cato the Younger*, 26; Procopius, *Anecdota*, XXVI, 28, 29; Rostovtzeff, *Roman Empire*, op. cit., pp. 449-50, 357, 394, 512-17; Seneca, *De Beneficiis*, IV, 28; Suetonius, *Augustus*, 40-43; ____*Caesar*, 39; ____*Claudius*, 20; ____*Domitian*, 4; ____*Nero*, 11; ____*Vespasian*, 18; Spartianus, *Hadrian*, 7; Tacitus, *Annals*, XII, 43; *Theodosian Code*, 11.27.1-2, 13.3.8-9;

---

*Where two publication dates are given, as shown, the first indicates the original year of publication and the second the date of the edition used.

199

F. W. Walbank, *The Awful Revolution: Decline of the Roman Empire in the West* (Liverpool, 1969), pp. 63-68; J. Watson, *The Medical Profession in Ancient Times* (New York, 1856), chap. 13 passim.

CHAPTER 2

THE MIDDLE AGES (pp. 22-27): *Ancient Laws and Institutes of England* (London, 1840), "Athelstan," "Ethelred"; F. L. Attenborough, *Laws of the Earliest English Kings* (Cambridge, 1922), "Athelstan"; M. Bloch, *Feudal Society* (Chicago, 1968), chap. 13, 19, passim; J. Froissart, *Chronicles*, tr., Sir J. Bourchier, Lord Berners (1523-25/London, 1901), ccclxxxi, ccclxxxiiii; J. Godfrey, *The Church in Anglo-Saxon England* (Cambridge, 1962), pp. 324-25, 327; passim; W. Langland, *The Vision of Piers Plowman*, B-Text, Passus VI, line 220; C-Text, Passus XIII, lines 253-36; H. R. Loyn, *Anglo-Saxon England and the Norman Conquest* (Oxford, 1962/New York, 1963), pp. 254-56; Sir F. Madden, tr., ed., *Layamons Brut, or Chronicle of Britain* (London, 1847), vol. II, p. 400, lines 19630 ff.; A. J. Robertson, *Laws of the Kings of England from Edmund to Henry I* (Cambridge, 1925), "Ethelred," "Canute," "Edgar"; K. de Schweinitz, *England's Road to Social Security* (Philadelphia, 1943), pp. 14-19; *Statutes of the Realm* (London, 1810), vol. I, "Edward III"; F. M. Stenton, *Anglo-Saxon England* (Oxford, 1943/1955), vol. V, chap. 10, passim.

THROUGH ELIZABETHAN TIMES (pp. 27-37): F. Aydelotte, *Elizabethan Rogues and Vagabonds* (Oxford, 1913), pp. 56-75; Sir S. D'Ewes, *Journals of All the Parliaments during the Reign of Queen Elizabeth* (London, 1682), dates and legislation cited; Sir F. M. Eden, *The State of the Poor* (London, 1797), chap. 3, passim; Appendix, vii; G. R. Elton, *England under the Tudors* (London, 1955/1974), pp. 79-81, 206-07, 259-61, 418-19; *Grafton's Chronicle* (London, 1569; reprinted, London, 1809), Vol. II, pp. 529-31; T. Harman, *A Caveat for Cursetors* (London, 1566; reprinted, London, 1814), pp. 33, 70; *Holinshed's Chronicles* ([London, 1587]; reprinted, London, 1807), vol. I, pp. 307ff; vol. III, pp. 1060-62; W. K. Jordan, *Edward VI: The Threshold of Power* (London, 1970), chap. 7, passim; E. M. Leonard, *Early History of English Poor Relief* (Cambridge, 1900), chap. 1, 2, 5, 6, passim; *Middlesex Sessions' Rolls, Middlesex County Records* (London, 1886, J. C. Jeafferson, ed.), vol. I, date cited; Sir T. More, *Utopia* ([1516]; Oxford, 1751, G. Burnet, trans.), pp. 17-18; A. F. Pollard, *The Reign of Henry VII* (London, 1914), vol. II, p. 176; J. G. Ridley, *Nicholas Ridley: A Biography* (London, 1957), pp. 284-89; *Statutes of the Realm*, op. cit., vol. II-IV: 11 Henry VII, chap. 2, 12; 22 Henry VIII, chap. 12; 27 Henry VIII, chap. 25; 1 Edward VI, chap. 3; 3&4 Edward VI, chap. 12; 5&6 Edward VI, chap. 2; 5 Elizabeth, chap. 3; 14 Elizabeth, chap. 5; 18 Elizabeth, chap. 3; 39 Elizabeth, chap. 4; 43 Elizabeth, chap. 2; R. L. Storey, *The Reign of Henry VII* (London, 1968), p. 129; J. Stow, *Annales of England* (London, 1592), "Edward VI"; H. Townshend, *Historical Collections* (London, 1680), p. 333; H. D. Traill and J. S. Mann, eds., *Social England* (London, 1909), Vol. III, pp. 352-66, 750-63; G. N. Trevelyan, *English Social History*, London, 1944/1958), pp. 111-23; *Vitellius Chronicle* (in *Chronicles of London*, C. L. Kingsford, ed., Oxford, 1905), "Year 1502."

CHAPTER 3

SOUTH CAROLINA (pp. 40-42): *Columbian Herald*, Charleston, Sept. 16, 1785; J. H. Easterby, "Public Poor Relief in Colonial Charleston," *South Carolina Historical and Genealogical Magazine*, April, 1941; A. Hewat, *Historical Account of South Carolina and Georgia* (London, 1779) in *Historical Collections of South Carolina* (New York, 1836), pp. 503-09; E. McCrady, *History of South Carolina under Royal Government* (New York, 1899), p. 326; chap. 29, 30, passim; J. T. Main, *Social Structure of Revolutionary America* (Princeton, 1965), p. 156; [T. Nairn], *Letter from South Carolina* (London, 1718), pp. 38, 51; D. Ramsay, *History of South Carolina* (Charleston, 1809), vol. II, p. 481; W. J. Rivers, *Sketch of the History of South Carolina* (Charleston, 1856), p. 231; G. C. Rogers, Jr., ed., *Papers of Henry Laurens* (Columbia, 1976), vol. V, pp. 238n, 647; M. E. Sirmans, *Colonial South Carolina*

(Williamsburg, 1966), pp. 97, 161ff., 229, 250, 317; *Statutes at Large of South Carolina* (Columbia, 1837-40), legislation cited; D. D. Wallace, *History of South Carolina* (New York, 1934), vol. I, p. 268; vol. II, p. 16; vol. III, p. 49; _____, *Life of Henry Laurens* (New York, 1915/1967), p. 129; L. B. Wright, *South Carolina: A Bicentennial History* (New York, 1976), pp. 113, 126.

ASSISTANCE TO THE POOR IN GENERAL (pp. 42-47): G. L. Beer, *The Old Colonial System, 1660*-1754 (New York, 1912), p. 29; C. F. Bishop, *History of Elections in the American Colonies* (New York, 1893), p. 91; C. Bridenbaugh, *Cities in Revolt: Urban Life in America, 1743*-1776 (New York, 1955), p. 122; _____, *Cities in the Wilderness: The First Century of Urban Life in America, 1625-1742* (New York, 1938/1964), chap. 3, passim; J. D. Butler, "British Convicts Shipped to the American Colonies," *American Historical Review*, Oct., 1896; C. Chauncy, *The Idle-Poor Secluded from the Bread of Charity by the Christian Law* (Boston, 1752); M. Chute, *The First Liberty: A History of the Right to Vote in America* (New York, 1969), p. 289; M. Creech, *Three Centuries of Poor Law Administration: A Study of Legislation in Rhode Island* (Chicago, 1936), chap. 2, passim; W. Griffith, *Eumenes* (Trenton, 1799), p. 35; H. Jones, *The Present State of Virginia* (London, 1724), app., p. 114; Main, op. cit., chap. 4, passim; Maryland, *Laws*, 1773, chap. 30, "An Act for the Relief of the Poor within the County of Baltimore"; Rhode Island, *Records of the Colony* (Providence, 1856), vol. I, p. 184; P. T. Stafford, *Government and the Needy: A Study of Public Assistance in New Jersey* (Princeton, 1941), p. 30; chap. 2, passim; Virginia, *Statutes at Large* (Richmond, 1819), vol. IV, p. 475.

MEDICAL ASSISTANCE AND FUEL (pp. 47-50): Bridenbaugh, *Cities in Revolt*, op. cit., p. 124; Boston, *Records from 1660 to 1701* (Boston, 1881), "Nov. 29, 1671"; *Columbian Herald*, Charleston, Sept. 14, 1786; A. Deutsch, "The Sick Poor of Colonial Times," *American Historical Review*, April, 1941; *Diary of Viscount Percival (Manuscripts of the Earl of Egmont)* (London, 1920-1923), vol. II, p. 370; S. A. Green, *History of Medicine in Massachusetts* (Boston, 1881), p. 42; R. J. Hunter, "Benjamin Franklin and the Rise of Free Treatment of the Poor by the Medical Profession of Philadelphia," *Bulletin of the History of Medicine*, March-April, 1957; *Independent Chronicle*, Philadelphia, March 20, 1784; *Newport Mercury*, Dec. 14, 1767.

THE FIRST YEARS OF INDEPENDENCE (pp. 50): J. Belknap, *History of New-Hampshire* (Boston, 1792), vol. III, p. 282; *Independent Chronicle*, Boston, April 8, 1784); *New Hampshire Mercury*, Portsmouth, March 8, 1786; April 12, 1786.

CHAPTER 4

BOSTON (pp. 52-55): *Columbian Centinel*, Boston, April 24, 1822; O. Handlin, *Boston's Immigrants* (Cambridge, Mass., 1959), p. 18; *Independent Chronicle and Boston Patriot*, Boston, May 4, 1822; Massachusetts, *Report of the Commissioners on the Pauper Laws* (Boston, 1833), p. 31; *Massachusetts Register, 1801* (Boston, 1800), p. 177; *Overseers of the Poor of the City of Boston to their Constituents* (Boston, 1823); E. Quincy, *Life of Josiah Quincy* (Boston, 1867), p. 394; J. Quincy, *Municipal History of the Town and City of Boston* (Boston, 1852), pp. 34-40, 46-54, 88-96, 103-06, 138-47, 165-75; *Report of the Committee on the Subject of Pauperism* (Boston, [1821]).

NEW YORK (pp. 55-57): New York, *Messages from the Governors* (Albany, 1909), vol. II, p. 914; New York State Senate, *Journal*, 47th session (Albany, 1824), pp. 101, 105; app. pp. 51, 64; *Report of a Committee of the Humane Society* (New York, 1810), passim; *Report to the Managers of the Society for the Prevention of Pauperism in New York by their Committee on Idleness and Sources of Employment* (New York, 1819), pp. 7, 12; D. M. Schneider, *History of Public Welfare in New York State* (Chicago, 1938), vol. I, pp. 212-15, 221-28, 235-38; J. G. Wilson, *Memorial History of the City of New York* (New York, 1893), vol. III, p. 118; chap. 8 passim. *Note*: Monetary equivalents in this section are based on the value of the pound in New York at the time as quoted in *A Money Table* (T. & J. Swords, New York, 1801).

PHILADELPHIA (p. 57): E. S. Abdy, *Journal of a Residence and Tour in the United States* (London, 1835), vol. III, pp. 165-66; *Report of the Committee Appointed by the Board of Guardians of the Poor of the City and Districts of Philadelphia* (Philadelphia, 1827), passim.

CHICAGO (pp. 57-58): Chicago *Tribune*, June 12, 1879, p. 7; U.S. Census Bureau, *Census of 1870*.

THE WEST (pp. 58-65): H. H. Bancroft, *History of California* (San Francisco, 1888-90), vol. VI, pp. 221, 225, 465; vol. VII, p. 105; W. D. Blackburn, *Southern Nebraska* immigrant guide (Brownville, Neb., 1870), p. 1; S. P. Breckinridge, *The Illinois Poor Law and Its Administration* (Chicago, 1939), pp. 13, 62; G. A. Browning, *Development of Poor Relief Legislation in Kansas* (Chicago, 1935), pp. 9-10; California, *Assembly Journal* (San Francisco, 1852-1853; Sacramento, 1855, 1861), 3rd sess., p. 825; 4th sess., p. 413, documents 21, 51, 55; 6th sess., pp. 420-23; 12th sess., app., exhibits A, C, D (1st-11th Fiscal Years), documents 18-22; California, *Statutes* (San Francisco, 1852-53; Sacramento, 1855-83), 3rd sess., pp. 78, 137; 4th sess., p. 281; 6th sess., pp. 47, 67, 120; 16th sess., p. 214; 25th sess., pp. 303, 380; W. Crafts, *Oration on the Occasion of Laying the Corner Stone of the Lunatic Asylum* (Charleston, 1822); J. S. Hittell, *History of the City of San Francisco* (San Francisco, 1878), p. 366; E. Iles, *Sketches of Early Life and Times* (Springfield, Ill., 1883), p. 61; Indiana, *Senate Journal* (Indianapolis, 1826-27), 10th sess., pp. 26-27; 11th sess., p. 39; *Iowa State Register*, Des Moines, April 1, 8, 1868; *Jefferson Era*, Jefferson, Iowa, April 8, 15, July 22, 1868; [Mississippi] Historical Record Survey, *Sargent's Code: A Collection of the Original Laws of the Mississippi Territory* (Jackson, 1939), p. 71; Missouri Territory, *Digest of the Laws of the Missouri Territory* (St. Louis, 1818), p. 325; New York, *Colonial Laws, 1664*-1775 (Albany, 1894), vol. I, p. 348; Northwest Territory, *Laws, 1788*-1800 (Springfield, Ill., 1925), p. 217; Oregon Territory, *Statutes of a General Nature* (Oregon City, 1851), 2nd sess., p. 186; A. Shaffer and M. W. Keefer, *The Indiana Poor Law* (Chicago, 1936), pp. 30, 112; F. Soulé, J. H. Gihon, and J. Nisbet, *Annals of San Francisco* (San Francisco, 1855), pp. 388, 450; Western Historical Co., *History of the State of Nebraska* (Chicago, 1882), pp. 637, 692, 696, 1040; J. P. Young, *San Francisco: A History of the Pacific Coast Metropolis* (San Francisco, 1912), vol. I, p. 252.

INDOOR VERSUS OUTDOOR RELIEF (pp. 66-70): W. W. Baldwin, *County Pauperism: Remarks . . . before a Convention . . . held at Burlington, October 20, 1903* (Chicago, [1903]); Conference of Charities,* *Proceedings*, 1878, pp. 32, 77-79; De Schweinitz, op. cit., pp. 72-78; D. Fraser, *Evolution of the British Welfare State* (London, 1973), pp. 33-34; S. Low, "Out-Door Relief in the United States," Conference of Charities, *Proceedings*, 1881, pp. 144-61; ____ "The Problem of Pauperism in the Cities of Brooklyn and New York," Conference of Charities, *Proceedings*, 1879; S. Mencher, *Poor Law to Poverty Program* (Pittsburgh, 1967), chap. 14, passim; *Report of the Commission on the Treatment of the Poor* (Boston, 1878), passim; *Report of the Committee Appointed by the Board of Guardians of the Poor of the City and Districts of Philadelphia* (Philadelphia, 1827), p. 24; Schneider, op. cit., vol. I, p. 250; F. Wayland, "Report on Out-Door Relief," Conference of Charities, *Proceedings*, 1877, pp. 46-59.

WORK RELIEF (pp. 70-73): *American Labor Legislation Review*, June, 1915, p. 183; D. D. Lescohier and E. Brandeis, *History of Labor in the United States* (New York, 1935), pp. 169-171, 178-81; Mencher, op. cit., pp. 296-301; New York Association for Improving the Condition of the Poor, *32nd Annual Report*, 1875, p. 62; New York State Employers' Liability Commission, *Third Report on Unemployment* (Albany, 1911), p. 13; New York *Times*, Nov. 16, 1873, p. 5; New York *Tribune*, March 16, 1877, p. 4; Schneider, op. cit., vol. II (with A. Deutsch), pp. 35-41.

MEDICAL AID TO THE POOR (pp. 73-76): Conference of Charities, *Proceedings*, 1877, pp. 31-46; New York *Evening Post*, Feb. 11, 1824, p. 2; New York *Tribune*, April 13, 1877, p. 8; R. Park, "Medical Charities of Cook County, Ill.," Conference of Charities, *Proceedings*, 1880, p. xlix; H. E. Pellew, "Out-Door Relief Administration in New York City, 1878," Conference of Char-

---

*The first conference was 1874, as Conference of Boards of Public Charities. Thereafter: Conference of Charities, 1875-79; Conference of Charities and Correction, 1880-81; National Conference of Charities and Corrections, 1882-83; National Conference of Charities and Correction, 1884-1916; and subsequently, National Conference of Social Work. The place of publication of the *Proceedings* varied.

ities, *Proceedings*, 1878, p. 66; W. H. Taylor, "Medical Charities in Cincinnati," Conference of Charities, *Proceedings*, 1878, pp. 45-46; U.S. Census Office, *9th Census* (1870), vol. III, p. 550; H. B. Wheelwright, "Medical Out-Door Relief in Massachusetts," Conference of Charities, *Proceedings*, 1878, pp. 32-53.

VAGRANTS, VAGABONDS, AND TRAMPS (pp. 76-78): Conference of Charities, *Proceedings*, 1877, pp. 102-33; Lescohier and Brandeis, op. cit., pp. 59-60; H. D. Nottingham, "Pauperism and Vagrancy," Association of County Superintendents of the Poor and Poor Law Officers of New York State, *Proceedings of the 39th Annual Convention* [Watertown, New York], 1909), p. 111; Portland, Oregon, City Board of Charities, *Annual Report*, 1890 (Portland, 1890), pp. 48-49.

THE ALMSHOUSE (pp. 78-86): Abdy, op. cit., vol. I, p. 187; Anonymous, *Relating to Pauper Children* (n.p., n.d.); *Atlantic Monthly*, June, August, 1881; Will Carleton, *Farm Ballads* (New York, 1873); Connecticut, Department of Public Welfare, *Report for 1921-22*, cited in U.S. Bureau of Labor Statistics, *Cost of American Almshouses* (Washington, D.C., 1925, Bulletin No. 386), p. 31; D. L. Dix, *Memorial to the Legislature of Massachusetts* (Boston, 1843); A. Johnson, *The Almshouse: Construction and Management* (New York, 1911), pp. 7, 126, 173; R. W. Kelso, *Poor Relief in Massachusetts* (Boston, 1922), p. 118; W. P. Letchworth, *Address Made at the State Convention of Superintendents of the Poor* (Buffalo, 1885); Massachusetts, Commonwealth, *Report of Hearings before the Joint Standing Committee on Public Charitable Institutions [on] Mismanagement of the State Almshouse at Tewksbury* (Boston, 1883), pp. 505-06, 1289, 2895, 3007, 3010, 3021; Michigan, State of, *Abstract of the Annual Reports of the County Superintendents of the Poor* (Lansing, 1873), p. 51; *The Nation*, March 23, 1876, p. 199; New York State Association of County Superintendents of the Poor, *Proceedings*, 42nd Annual Convention (1912), pp. 150-53; New York, State of, *Report of the Special Committee of the State Board of Charities* (Albany, 1899); *Public Papers and Addresses of Franklin D. Roosevelt* (New York, 1938), vol. I, p. 43; South Carolina, State Board of Public Welfare, *Fourth Annual Report*, 1923, cited in *Cost of American Almshouses*, op. cit., p. 35; U.S. Census Bureau, *Paupers in Almshouses, 1904* (Washington, D.C., 1906); _____, *Paupers in Almshouses, 1910* (Washington, 1915); _____, *Paupers in Almshouses, 1923* (Washington, 1925); *Cost of American Almshouses*, op. cit., pp. 1-9.

CHAPTER 5

ALEXANDRIA (pp. 88-91): D. D. Dana, *The Fireman: The Fire Departments of the United States with a Full Account of All Large Fires* (Boston, 1858), pp. 23-26, 162-63, 358-65; *National Intelligencer*, Washington, Feb. 20, 23, 1812; Jan. 20, 25, 1827; *National Journal*, Washington, Jan. 20, 23, 1827; *Richmond Enquirer*, Jan. 23, 25, 1827; U.S. Congress, *Register of Debates*, 19th Cong., 1st sess., April 10, 11, 1826; *United States Telegraph*, Washington, Jan. 19, 22, 24, 1827.

CHICAGO (pp. 91-92): *Chicago Evening Journal Extra*, Oct. 9, 1871; *Chicago Tribune*, Oct. 12, 13, 14, 18, 19, 1871; *Congressional Globe*, 42nd Cong., 2nd sess., Jan. 23, March 19, 20, 1872.

THE KLONDIKE (pp. 93-94): *Congressional Record*, 55th Cong., 2nd sess., Dec. 16, 18, 1897; *New York Times*, Sept. 15, Dec. 14, 1897.

SAN FRANCISCO (pp. 94-95): *Congressional Record*, 59th Cong., 1st sess., April 19, 24, 1906; *New York Times*, April 19, 21, 1906.

AGRICULTURE (pp. 95-98): *Congressional Record*, May 9, 1916; *Farm Journal*, March, 1916; *New York Times*, May 8, 22, July 12, 21, 1916; W. D. Rasmussen, ed., *Readings in the History of American Agriculture* (Urbana, Ill., 1960), pp. 253-55; *Washington Post*, May 11, 1916.

CHAPTER 6

PANIC OF 1819 (pp. 100-105): *Aurora and General Advertiser*, Philadelphia, Oct. 5, 23, 1819; M. Carey, *Address to the Farmers of the Nation*, quoting Samuel Hopkins (Philadelphia, 1821), p. 12; *Detroit Gazette*, Sept. 17, 1819; J. Flint, *Letters from America*, (Edinburgh, 1822), pp. 31, 202-03,

211; *Franklin Gazette for the Country*, Philadelphia, Oct. 15, 1819; T. W. Griffith, *Annals of Baltimore* (Baltimore, 1824), p. 231; J. Lambert, *Travels through Canada and the United States* (London, 1814), vol. II, p. 65; *Long Island Star*, Brooklyn, Sept. 29, 1819; New York *Advertiser*, June 11, 1819; New York City, *Minutes of the Common Council 1784*-1831 (New York, 1917), vol. IV, pp. 699, 702, 714; New York *Evening Post*, June 15, 1819; *Niles' Weekly Register*, July 24, Aug. 7, Oct. 23, 1819; Sept. 30, 1820; Pennsylvania, House of Representatives, *Journal*, (Harrisburg, 1821-22), 32nd sess., p. 17; S. Rezneck, "The Depression of 1819-22, a Social History," *American Historical Review*, Oct., 1933, p. 28; M. N. Rothbard, *The Panic of 1819: Reactions and Policies* (New York, 1962: Columbia University Studies in the Social Sciences, No. 605), chap. 1, 2, passim; pp. 191-95; Schneider, op. cit., vol. I, p. 166; *The Southern Patriot*, Charleston, Sept. 16, 1819, quoted in *Aurora and General Advertiser*, op. cit., Sept. 25, 1819; U.S. Congress, *Statutes at Large* (Boston, 1846), vol. III, p. 612; Wilson, *Memorial History*, op. cit., vol. III, p. 306.

PANICS OF 1837 and 1857 (pp. 105-106): F. Byrdsall, *History of the Loco-Foco* (New York, 1842: reprinted, 1967), p. 100; *Chicago Weekly American*, May 6, 1837; R. C. McGrane, *The Panic of 1837* (New York, 1924/1965), pp. 130-31, 142-43; "By Members of the New-York Press," *A Brief Popular Account of all the Financial Panics and Commercial Revulsions in the United States from 1690 to 1857* (New York, 1857), pp. 9, 16, 21, 27, 29, 39, 57; New York City, Board of Commissioners of the Central Park, *First Annual Report* (New York, 1858); *New Yorker*, Oct. 7, 28, Dec. 30, 1837; Jan. 20, March 31, 1838; *Niles' Weekly Register*, Sept. 16, 1837; Schneider, op. cit., vol. I, pp. 258-62, 274-78, 289-91; G. W. Van Vleck, *The Panic of 1857* (New York, 1943/1967), pp. 74-76.

THE GREAT RAILROAD STRIKE (pp. 107-110): Baltimore *American*, July 18, 1877, quoted in the New Orleans *Daily Picayune*, July 23, 1877; *Chicago Tribune*, July 27, 28, 1877; R. T. Ely, "Recent American Socialism," *Johns Hopkins University Studies in Historical and Political Science*, April 1885 (vol. III, pp. 291-92); W. M. Grosvenor, "The Communist and the Railway," *International Review*, Sept., 1877 (vol. IV, p. 585); Mobile *Daily Register*, Aug. 3, 1877; New Orleans *Daily Picayune*, July 27, 28, 1877; New York *Herald*, July 26, 28, 31, 1877; New York *Sun*, July 22, 25, 1877; New York *Times*, July 25, 26, 1877; St. Louis *Dispatch*, July 23, 1877.

PANIC OF 1893 (pp. 110-111): J. Addams, *A Centennial Reader* (New York, 1960), pp. 27-28; C. C. Closson, Jr., "The Unemployed in American Cities," *Quarterly Journal of Economics*, July, 1894 (vol. VIII); L. H. Feder, *Unemployment Relief in Periods of Depression* (New York, 1936), pp. 79-82, 158; New York *Times*, May 14, 1893, p. 5; Schneider, op. cit., vol. II, chap. 3, passim.

EARLY COMMUNISM (pp. 111-114): Ely, "Recent Socialism," op. cit., pp. 294-97; P. S. Foner, *History of the Labor Movement in the United States* (New York, 1947/1962), vol. I, pp. 446-47; Grosvenor, "Communist and the Railway," op. cit.; *The Nation*, May 9, 16, 1878; New Orleans *Daily Picayune*, Aug. 4, 1877; New York Association for Improving the Condition of the Poor, *31st Annual Report* (1874), p. 58; New York *Times*, Nov. 16, Dec. 12, 1873; New York *Tribune*, Jan. 14, 1874; July 25, Aug. 13, 1877; R. R. Palmer, *History of the Modern World* (New York, 1951), pp. 586, 589; *Truth, a Journal for the Poor*, as quoted in Ely, "Recent Socialism," op. cit., pp. 262, 291-92, 295; *Woodhull & Claflin's Weekly*, New York, Dec. 30, 1871.

THE LABOR MOVEMENT (pp. 114-117): American Federation of Labor, *American Federation of Labor: History, Encyclopedia, Reference Book* (Washington, 1919), p. 391; M. Carey, *Essays on the Public Charities of Philadelphia* (Philadelphia, 1830), p. 7; *Chicago Tribune*, Dec. 12, 15, 16, 17, 1893; J. R. Commons and J. B. Andrews, *Principles of Labor Legislation* (New York, 1916/1936), chap. 5, passim; H. U. Faulkner and M. Starr, *Labor in America* (New York, 1944), pp. 180-84; H. U. Faulkner, *The Quest for Social Justice, 1898*-1914 (New York, 1931; vol. XI, *History of American Life*, 1937), pp. 66-67, 75-80; Foner, op. cit., vol. I, pp. 70-71, 98-99, 100-05; J. D. Greenstone, *Labor in American Politics* (Chicago, 1969/1977), pp. 27-33; Leschier and Brandeis, op. cit., p. 575; *Memoirs of John Quincy Adams* (Philadelphia, 1878), vol. V, p. 128; Mencher, op. cit., pp. 268-71, 281; U.S. Commissioner of Labor, *Second Special Report: Labor Laws of the Various States* (Washington, 1892), pp. 363, 407, 564-66, 595.

REFORMERS, CRITICS, AND VISIONARIES (pp. 117-122): J. Addams, "The Objective Value of a Social Settlement," *Philanthropy and Social Progress* (New York, [1893]), pp. 55-56;

[M. Cary], *A Plea for the Poor* (Philadelphia, 1836), pp. 3-5, 10-11; M. D. Conway, *Writings of Thomas Paine* (New York, 1894), vol. II pp. 245, 484; E. Denison, *Work Among the London Poor: Letters and Other Writings of the Late Edward Denison*, Sir B. Leighton, ed. (London, 1884), p. 80; Dix, op. cit.; H. George, *Progress and Poverty* (New York, 1880), passim; D. Hunter, *Diseases of Occupations* (London, 1955/1964), pp. 119-23, 411; New Haven *Daily Palladium*, March 7, 1860; New York *Sun*, July 30, 1877; New York *Tribune*, 1864, n.d., quoted in Bremner, op. cit., p. 7; J. G. Nicolay and J. Hay, eds., *Complete Works of Abraham Lincoln* (Lincoln Memorial University, [1894]), vol. V, p. 360; J. A. Riis, "How the Other Half Lives," *Scribner's Magazine*, Dec., 1889 (vol. VI, p. 657); J. Sparks, ed., *The Works of Benjamin Franklin* (Boston, 1836; 1856), vol. II, p. 358 (quotation is from "On the Price of Corn, and Management of the Poor," originally published in the *London Chronicle*, 1766).

IMMIGRATION (pp. 123-126): E. Abbott, *Historical Aspects of the Immigration Problem: Select Documents* (Chicago, 1926), pp. 596, 606-09, 648-51, 684-87; G. Abbott, *The Immigrant and the Community* (New York, 1917), pp. 166-72; Bremner, op. cit., pp. 7-10; *Chambers' Journal*, London, quoted in *Littell's Living Age*, Boston, Oct. 31, 1846; *Chicago Medical Gazette*, March 5, 1880, quoted in Conference of Charities, *Proceedings*, 1880, p. lv; Chicago *Tribune*, Dec. 18, 1893, p. 7; Conference of Charities, *Proceedings*, 1876, p. 180; M. L. Hansen, *The Immigrant in American History* (Cambridge, Mass., 1948), pp. 108-11; H. A. Hill, "Immigration," Conference of Charities, *Proceedings*, 1875, p. 85; Massachusetts Sanitary Commission, *Report to the Legislature, April 25, 1850*, quoted in E. Abbott, op. cit., p. 596; Mencher, op. cit., pp. 135-37; *Niles' Register*, Jan. 19, 1839; F. B. Sanborn, "Migration and Immigration," Conference of Charities, *Proceedings*, 1886, p. 253; ____, "National Legislation for the Protection of Immigrants and the Prevention of Pauperism," in ibid., 1876, p. 162; Schneider, op. cit., vol. I, pp. 303, 308-15; G. P. Scrope, *Extracts from Letters from Poor Persons Who Emigrated Last Year to Canada and the United States* (London, 1832), p. 19; Society for the Prevention of Pauperism in the City of New York, *Second Annual Report* [1819] (New York, 1820), pp. 17, 66; W. S. Trench, *Realities of Irish Life (London, 1868), pp. 123, 133; U.S. Congress, Foreign Criminals and Paupers: Report from the Committee on Foreign Affairs, Aug. 16, 1856* (34th Cong., 1st sess., House Report No. 359).

EUROPEAN PRECEDENT (pp. 126-132): M. Busch, *Bismarck: Sketches for a Historical Picture*, tr. W. Beatty-Kingston (New York, 1891), vol. II, pp. 217-19, 231-32; ____, *Unser Reichskanzler: Studien zu einem Charakterbilde* (Leipzig, 1884), vol. II, pp. 313, 342; Chicago *Tribune*, July 26, 1908, p. 4; Commons and Andrews, op. cit., pp. 232-34, 259, 266, 273-77, 280, 294-97; W. H. Dawson, *Bismarck and State Socialism* (London, 1890), p. 19; De Schweinitz, op. cit., pp. 199, 204-07; L. K. Frankel and M. M. Dawson, *Workingmen's Insurance in Europe* (New York, 1910, 1911), p. 232; Fraser, op. cit., pp. 135-63, passim; Lescohier and Brandeis, op. cit., pp. 564, 570-75; E. Ludwig, *Bismarck (Bismarck, Geschichte eines Kämpfers)*, tr., E. and C. Paul (Boston, 1927), pp. 548-49; New York *Times*, Nov. 18 (p. 1), Dec. 4, (p. 8), 1881; Aug. 4, (p. 6) 1908; New York *Tribune*, Nov. 18, 1881, p. 1; Palmer, op. cit., p. 534; R. Roberts, *The Classic Slum* (Manchester, 1971; Harmondsworth, 1973), p. 84; San Francisco *Chronicle*, July 22 (p. 6), 1908; L. L. Snyder, ed., *Documents of German History* (New Brunswick, N.J., 1958), pp. 234-35; F. Stern, *Gold and Iron: Bismarck, Bleichröder, and the Building of the German Empire* (New York, 1977), pp. 217-20; *The Times*, London, June 19 (p. 15), 1889; Oct. 10 (p. 12), 1908; June 12 (p. 6), 1911; U.S. Commissioner of Labor, *Fourth Special Report: Compulsory Insurance in Germany* (Washington, 1893), pp. 19-27, 29, 253, 263-75, 286.

CHAPTER 7

HARDING (pp. 134-137): R. C. Downes, *The Rise of Warren Gamaliel Harding* ([Columbus], Ohio, 1970), pp. 510-13; W. G. Harding, *Our Common Country* (Indianapolis, 1921), pp. 197-222; New York *Times* July 21 (p. 7), Oct. 2 (pp. 2, 14), Oct. 19 (p. 2), 1920; Jan. 3 (p. 14), April

206 / WITH CHARITY FOR ALL

22 (p. 24), April 27 (p. 2), May 8 (p. VII-1), May 12, (p. 21), May 13 (p. 12), May 21 (p. 12), 1921; New York *Tribune*, Oct. 2 (p. 1), 1920; F. Russell, *The Shadow of Blooming Grove: Warren G. Harding in His Times* (New York, 1968), pp. 399, 405-06, 412; A. Sinclair, *The Available Man: The Life Behind the Masks of Warren Gamaliel Harding* (New York, 1965), pp. 160-61, 213; *Washington Post*, Oct. 2 (p. 1), 1920.

HOOVER'S COMMITTEE ON SOCIAL TRENDS (pp. 137-139): *Memoirs of Herbert Hoover: The Cabinet and the Presidency* (New York, 1952), pp. 312-13; New York *Times*, Jan. 2 (pp. 1, 2), 1933; *Time*, Jan. 9 (p. 23), 1933; *Washington Post*, Jan. 3 (p. 6), 1933.

THE YEAR 1932 (pp. 139-146): *Atlantic Monthly*, May, 1932, p. 538; D. W. Brogan, *The Era of Franklin Delano Roosevelt* (New Haven, 1950), pp. 11-18; *Business Week*, Oct. 26 (p. 20), 1932; *Chicago Tribune*, Jan. 17 (p. VII-1), July 3 (pp. 1-5), July 17 (pp. 1, 2), 1932; *Current History*, March (p. 832), July (p. 415), Aug. (p. 584), Sept. (p. 718), Nov. (p. 204), 1932; H. U. Faulkner, *From Versailles to the New Deal* (New Haven, 1951), pp. 351-56; *Fortune*, Jan. (p. 41), Sept. (p. 19), 1932; J. T. Hackett, "Franklin D. Roosevelt," *The Forum*, March, 1932, p. 147; M. A. Hallgren, "Mass Misery in Philadelphia," *The Nation*, March 9, 1932, p. 275; Hoover, *Memoirs*, op. cit., *Cabinet and the Presidency*, pp. 312-19, *Great Depression*, pp. 98, 112, 236, 310-17; J. M. Keynes, "The World's Economic Outlook," *Atlantic Monthly*, May, 1932, p. 523; *Literary Digest*, June 11, 1932, p. 20; E. Lyons, *Herbert Hoover: A Biography* (New York, 1964), pp. 282-91; *Milwaukee Journal*, Jan. 6, 1932, p. 1; New York *Herald Tribune*, Oct. 23 (p. 2), Oct. 28 (p. 1), 1928; June 11 (p. 1), June 18 (p. 1), June 25 (p. 1), Oct. 21 (p. 1), Nov. 2 (p. 36), 1932; New York *Times*, Oct. 19 (p. 4), 1931; Jan. 3 (p. 2), April 10 (p. IX-1), May 17 (p. 8), June 7 (p. 18), June 11 (p. 1), June 18 (p. 1), July 3 (pp. 1, 8, 9), July 17 (p. 1), July 18 (p. 1), Nov. 1 (p. 1), Nov. 13 (p. II-1), 1932; *Time*, April 4 (p. 11), May 30 (p. 12), June 20 (pp. 8, 11), June 27 (pp. 11, 15), Nov. 7 (pp. 12, 13, 15), 1932; *Variety*, March 19 (p. 66), April 16 (p. 80), 1930; Aug. 16 (p. 44), Sept. 20 (p. 52), 1932; C. R. Walker, "Relief and Revolution," *The Forum*, Aug., 1932, p. 73; *Washington Post*, Jan. 20 (p. 5), Jan. 23 (p. 1), Jan. 24 (pp. 1, 14), June 16 (p. 1), June 17 (pp. 1, 3), June 18 (pp. 1, 3), July 3 (pp. 1, 2), 1932; W. A. White, "The Men and the Issues," New York *Herald Tribune Magazine*, Oct. 23, 1932, p. 1; W. B. Wolfe, M.D., "Psycho-Analyzing the Depression," *The Forum*, April, 1932, p. 209.

THE BEGINNING OF THE NEW DEAL (pp. 146-149): Akron *Beacon Journal*, March 3, 1933, p. 1; Brogan, op. cit., pp. 94-120, passim; *Current History*, Feb., 1934, pp. 586-89; J. F. Essary, "The New Deal for Nearly Four Months," *Literary Digest*, July 1, 1933, p. 3; *Fortune*, Sept., 1932, p. 84; New York *Herald Tribune*, June 16 (p. 1), June 17 (p. 1), 1933; April 1 (p. 14), 1934; New York *Times*, April 1 (p. 6), April 9 (p. 28), May 2 (p. 2), May 23 (p. 21), June 16 (p. 1), Nov. 9 (p. 1), 1933; Jan. 16 (p. 18), Jan. 23 (pp. 1, 8), Jan. 25 (p. 15), Feb. 12 (p. 2), March 6 (p. 28), March 15 (p. 27), Nov. 10 (p. 2), 1934; *Time*, May 29 (pp. 7, 8), June 19 (p. 14), 1933; Jan. 1 (p. 10), 1934; *United States News*, June 10 (p. 6), June 17 (pp. 1, 2), 1933; *Washington Evening Star*, June 16 (p. 1), 1933.

CHAPTER 8

THE PASSAGE OF SOCIAL SECURITY (pp. 152-156): Alaska Territory, Senate, *Journal*, 1915 ([Juneau], 1915), p. 155; Brogan, op. cit., pp. 108-11; Commons and Andrews, *Principles of Labor Legislation*, op. cit., pp. 278-79; *Congressional Globe*, May 3, 1854, p. 1061; *Congressional Record*, House, Aug. 7 (p. 3698), 1911; April 12 (pp. 5529, 5536, 5547, 5560), 1935; *Fortune*, September 1935, p. 147; *Milwaukee Journal*, Aug. 18 (p. 2), 1935; *Newsweek*, Aug. 17 (p. 5), 1935; New York *Herald Tribune*, April 19 (p. 1), Aug. 16 (p. 1), 1935; New York *Times*, Aug. 16 (p. 7), Aug. 27 (p. 11), 1935; R. F. Nichols, *Franklin Pierce* (Philadelphia, 1931/1969), pp. 549-50; F. Perkins, "The Outlook for Economic and Social Security in the United States," National Conference on Social Work, *Proceedings*, 1935, pp. 54-63; R. B. Stevens, ed., *Statutory History of the United States: Income Security* (New York, 1970), pp. 20-31; 152-53; *Washington Post*, Aug. 18 (pp. 2, 3), 1935.

IMPLEMENTING SOCIAL SECURITY (pp. 156-158): Baltimore *Evening Sun*, Aug. 14 (p. 3), Aug. 15 (p. 21), 1935; Boston *Evening Transcript*, Feb. 1 (p. 3), 1940; *Newsweek*, Aug. 17 (p. 5), 1935; New York *Herald Tribune*, Aug. 15 (p. 1), 1935; New York *Times*, Aug. 15 (p. 1), 1935; Nov. 15 (p. II-1), Nov. 25 (p. 25), Dec. 2 (p. 7), 1936; Feb. 1 (p. 15), Feb. 2 (p. 16), 1940; St. Louis *Post-Dispatch*, Aug. 16 (p. 2-C), 1935; San Francisco *Chronicle*, Aug. 15 (p. 12), 1935.

THE NEW DEAL AT WORK (pp. 158-161): H. E. Barnes, *Society in Transition* (New York, 1935/1968), pp. 587-88; Brogan, op. cit., pp. 95-107; Denver *Post*, April 4 (p. 1), 1935; *Forum*, June, 1935, p. 321; *Literary Digest*, June 1, 1935, p. 3; Milwaukee *Journal*, April 4 (p. 6), 1935; New Orleans *Times Picayune*, April 4 (p. 1), 1935; New York *Sun*, April 3 (pp. 1, 16), 1935; New York *Herald Tribune*, April 3 (p. 1), April 4 (pp. 1, 2), April 5 (p. 1), April 6 (p. 1), May 3 (p. 1), May 6 (p. 17), May 7 (p. 1), May 13 (p. 14), 1935; Jan. 4 (p. 8), 1939; New York *Times*, April 1 (pp. 1, 2), April 4 (p. 1), April 7 (p. IV-1), Oct. 24 (p. 1), 1935; Jan. 26 (pp. 1, 36), March 15 (p. IV-3), July 22 (p. 18), 1936; June 22 (p. 10), 1937; *Punch*, Aug. 14, 1929, p. 192; St. Louis *Post-Dispatch*, April 4 (p. 1), 1935; San Francisco *Chronicle*, April 4 (p. 1), 1935; *Scouting*, March, 1930, p. 65; *Time*, Jan. 9 (p. 14), 1939; Washington *Post*, April 6 (p. 1), 1935.

FOOD STAMPS (pp. 161-162); D. M. Hoover and J. G. Maddox, *Food for the Hungry* (Washington, 1969: National Planning Association, Planning Pamphlet No. 126), pp. 4-7; New York *Times*, April 4 (p. 14), Aug. 9 (p. 3), Sept. 26 (p. 17), 1939; March 1 (p. 11), March 2 (p. 22), 1943; U.S. Department of Agriculture, *Economic Analysis of the Food Stamp Plan* (Washington, 1940), p. 3.

HOUSING (pp. 162-165): R. H. Bremner, *From the Depths* (New York, [1956]), pp. 210-12; *Everybody's Magazine*, Jan., 1907, p. 35; J. Gallatin, *Tenement-House Reform in the City of New York* (Boston, 1881); *Newsweek*, June 30 (p. 24), Nov. 10 (p. 11), 1934; New York *Times*, June 29 (p. 1), 1934; J. Quincy, *Moderate Houses for Moderate Means* (Boston, 1871), p. 6; M. T. Reynolds (American Economic Association), *The Housing of the Poor in American Cities* (London, [1893]), pp. 10, 14, 43-44, 54; *Report of the Committee on the Expediency of Providing Better Tenements for the Poor* (Boston, 1846); *Time*, March 8 (p. 16), Aug. 16 (p. 10), Aug. 30 (p. 14), 1937.

RESETTLEMENT (pp. 165-166): *Matanuska Valley Pioneer*, Palmer, Alaska, Aug. 22 (p. 1), 1935; New York *Times*, May 7 (p. 8), May 8 (p. 21), June 27 (p. 32), Aug. 20 (p. 31), 1935; K. H. Stone, *The Matanuska Valley Colony* (Washington, U.S. Department of the Interior, 1950), pp. 84-86; *Time*, July 1 (p. 14), 1935.

APPRAISING THE NEW DEAL (pp. 166-167): New York *Herald Tribune*, May 6 (p. 17), May 7 (p. 1), 1935; New York *Times*, Oct. 24 (p. 1), 1935; Jan. 26 (pp. 1, 36), 1936; U.S. Census Bureau, *Historical Statistics of the United States* (Washington, 1975), pp. 135, 1102, 1114, 1117; *United States News*, Sept. 2 (p. 1), 1935.

CHAPTER 9

TRUMAN, EISENHOWER, AND KENNEDY (pp. 170-172): *National Observer*, Aug. 2 (p. 2), 1965; New York *Herald Tribune*, Sept. 7 (p. 1), 1945; April 3 (p. 16), April 12 (p. 1), 1953; July 31 (p. 1), 1965; New York *Times*, Sept. 7 (p. 1), Nov. 20 (p. 1), 1945; Jan. 11 (p. 20), June 5 (p. 20), Aug. 3 (p. 2), Oct. 5 (p. 20), 1946; July 31 (p. 1), Aug. 21 (p. 8), 1965; Jan. 2 (p. 7), 1966; Dec. 27 (p. 46), 1972; St. Louis *Post-Dispatch*, July 31 (p. 1), 1965.

JOHNSON AND THE GREAT SOCIETY (pp. 172-180): M. Davie, "A British Editor's Size-Up of President Johnson," *U.S. News & World Report*, Aug. 29, 1966, p. 40; J. W. Fulbright, "The Great Society Is a Sick Society," New York *Times Magazine*, Aug. 20, 1967, p. 30; Los Angeles *Times*, Aug. 13 (p. 2), Aug. 15 (p. 1), Aug. 17 (p. 1), 1965; *Newsweek*, Aug. 17 (p. 32), 1964; July 31 (p. 17), Aug. 21 (p. 15), 1967; New York *Daily News*, July 31 (p. 4), 1965; New York *Times*, Jan. 9 (pp. 1, 16), April 9 (p. 1), April 14 (p. 36), April 25 (p. 1), May 23 (p. 10), July 1 (p. 13), Aug. 21 (p. 1), Oct. 4 (p. 1), 1964; March 22 (p. 17), Aug. 14 (p. 1), Aug. 15 (p. 1), Aug. 16 (p. 29), Aug. 20 (p. 1), Aug. 27 (p. 1), Oct. 10 (Supp., p. 1), Oct. 25 (p. 41), Nov. 2 (p. 17),

1965; April 16 (p. 12), Oct. 24 (p. 35), Nov. 17 (p. 20), Nov. 28 (p. 1), Dec. 12 (p. 65), 1966; A Steinberg, *Sam Johnson's Boy* (New York, 1968), pp. 659-63; *Time*, Jan. 17 (p. 11), Oct. 9 (p. 26), 1964; Aug. 20 (p. 22), Oct. 29 (p. 22), 1965; *U.S. News & World Report*, Aug. 10 (p. 23), Aug. 17 (p. 34), 1964; Sept. 6 (p. 27), Nov. 1 (p. 29), 1965; May 16 (p. 67), 1966; Sept. 25 (p. 46), 1967; Washington *Post*, May 23 (pp. 1, 6), Aug. 21 (p. 2), 1964; April 1 (p. 1), 1968.

NIXON AND THE FAMILY ASSISTANCE PLAN (pp. 181-188): M. Anderson, *Welfare: The Political Economy of Welfare Reform in the United States* (Stanford, Calif., 1978), pp. 78-83; *Congressional Record*, House, Feb. 3 (p. 2322), April 16 (pp. 12043, 12063), April 28 (p. 13327), 1970; Los Angeles *Times*, Aug. 9 (p. 1), Aug. 10 (p. 1), 1969; D. P. Moynihan, *The Politics of a Guaranteed Income* (New York, 1973), *passim*; *National Observer*, Aug. 18 (p. 10), 1969; *Newsweek*, Aug. 18 (pp. 17-19), 1969; New York *Times*, Aug. 8 (p. 1), Aug. 9 (pp. 1, 11, 12), 1969; April 17 (p. 1), May 2 (p. 1), June 19 (p. 30), 1970; *Public Papers of the Presidents: Richard Nixon, 1970* (Washington, 1971), pp. 1124-25; *Time*, Aug. 15 (p. 14), 1969; Oct. 5 (p. 17), 1970; U.S. Congress, Senate, Committee on Finance, *Hearings on H.R. 16311* (Washington, 1970), vol. I, pp. 288-89; *U.S. News & World Report*, Aug. 18 (p. 20), Aug. 25 (p. 26), 1969; Oct. 30 (p. 16), 1972; Washington *Post*, Aug. 8 (p. 1), Aug. 9 (pp. 1, 9), Aug. 10 (p. 1), 1969.

RECENT YEARS (pp. 188-195): Albany *Times Union*, Aug. 3 (p. 8), 1980; *Business Week*, Nov. 14 (p. 46), 1983; *Congressional Quarterly*, Almanac 1977, p. 46E; Almanac 1980, p. 464; March 26 (p. 596), Nov. 26 (p. 2479), 1983; *National Observer*, Feb. 19 (p. 1), 1977; *Newsweek*, Aug. 1 (p. 28), 1983; New York *Post*, Oct. 27 (p. 3), 1979; Aug. 4 (p. 3), Oct. 24 (p. 10), Nov. 17 (p. 35), 1980; New York *Times*, June 19 (p. 30), 1970; July 6 (p. 1), 1976; May 4 (p. 38), 1980; March 26 (p. 1), April 21 (p. 1), 1983; U.S. Census Bureau, *Historical Statistics of the United States* (Washington, 1975), p. 341; U.S. Congress, Joint Economic Committee, Subcommittee on Fiscal Policy, *Public Welfare and Work Incentives: Theory and Practice* (Studies in Public Welfare, Paper No. 14, Washington, April, 1974), pp. 45-54; *U.S. News & World Report*, Feb. 20 (p. 21), 1978; Oct. 17 (p. 91), 1983.

INDEX

Abdy, E. S., 80-81
Accelerated Public Works Act of 1962, 172
actors, and CWA, 148
Adams, John Quincy: as president, 89; as secretary of state, 114
Addams, Jane, 110, 121-122
agentes in rebus, 17
Agricultural Adjustment Act of 1935, 161
Agricultural Marketing Act of 1929, 98
agricultural workers, 103; and minimum wage, 177, 179
agriculture, 95-98
Aid to Dependent Children (ADC), 153, 154, 156 (*see also* Aid to Families with Dependent Children, *alimenta*)
Aid to Families with Dependent Children (AFDC), 172, 181-182, 183, 192, 194; imbalance of benefits, 182 (*see also* Aid to Dependent Children, *alimenta*)
Akron *Beacon Journal*, 146
Alaska Rural Rehabilitation Corp., 165
Alaska, territory: old age assistance, 154; resettlement, 165-166
Albany *Times-Union*, 194
Alexandria, Va., 88-91
Alger, Russell A., secretary of war, 93
alimenta, 14-15, 19
almshouse, 60, 65, 103, 105, 125; bodies from, for dissection, 83; Boston, 52-55; Chicago, 57-58; in colonial America, 44, 47, 49; as entertainment for visitors, 83; in general, 78-86; Iowa, 60-61; Nebraska, 61-62; New York (city), 55-57, 73-74; as opposed to outdoor relief, 68-70; other names for, 80; Philadelphia, 57; as place for insane, 81, 84, 120; population, by government estimate 85-86
American Federation of Labor, 137, 148, 164, 186; demands on government, 115-116

American Labor Legislation Review, 72
Andrews, John B., 72
Antoninus Pius, Roman emperor, 14
Appian, 7, 9
archiatri populares, 13-14
Aristotle, *Athenaion Politeia*, 2, 4
Arizona: old age assistance, 154; aid to dependent children, 154
Athelstan, king of the English, 22-23; King Athelstan's Ordinance, 22-23
Athens, ancient, 1-6; abolition of debts, 7; *cleruchs*, 5; *epidoseis*, 4; land redistribution, 7; *poleos argurion*, 2, 4; Theoric Fund, 4; work relief, 3-4
Atlantic Monthly, 81-82, 145
auction system, 50, 56
Augustus, Roman emperor: grain distribution, 10-12, 19; state assistance for children, 14, *tesserae frumentariae*, 12-13
Aurelian, Roman emperor, 13, 20

Babylonia: housing regulation in, 162
Bailey, Rep. Joseph W., 94
Baldwin, Rep. Henry, 104
Baldwin, W. W., 68
Ball, John, 26
Baltimore, 46, 70, 100, 103
Baltimore *American*, 108
Barnard, Charles, 74
Bedford-Stuyvesant (section of Brooklyn, N.Y.), 175
Belknap, Jeremy, 50
Bellevue Hospital, 49, 74
Berger, Rep. Victor L., 153-154
Bismarck, Chancellor Otto, von, of Germany, 127-129
"Bonus Expeditionary Force," 140-141
boondoggles, 160-161; origin of word, 161
Boston, 68, 69-70; colonial, 43, 45, 48; Committee on the Expediency of Providing Better Tenements for the Poor, 164; poor law reform, 1820's, 52-55; housing conditions, 1840's, 163-164

Boston *Evening Transcript*, 157-158
Boston *Independent Chronicle*, 56
Boston *Mercantile Advertiser*, 105
"bread and circuses" (*see panem et circenses*)
Brooklyn, N.Y., 69-70, 175; naval yard, 102
Brougham, Lord, 67a
Burlington, Iowa, 68, 71, 111
Butler, Governor Benjamin Franklin, 83

Caesar, Julius: distribution of grain, 8-10; *congiaria*, 10; land reform, 9
Cairo, Ill., 91
Calhoun, John C., secretary of war, 114
California: poor relief, mid-19th century, 62-65; State Marine Hospital, 63-64, 80; home loans for veterans, 164
California Emergency Relief Administration, 165
Caligula, Roman emperor, 12
Cambreleng, Rep. Churchill, 90
Canada, government of, relief of U.S. prospectors in the Klondike, 94
Cannon, Rep. Joseph W., 94
Caracalla, Roman emperor, 19-20
Carey, Matthew, 118-119
Carleton, Will, "Over the Hill to the Poor-house," 78-79
Carson, Rep. Samuel, 90
Carter, President Jimmy, 192
Cassius Spurius, 7
Cato, 19
Caveat for Cursetors, 30
Census Bureau, U.S., 84, 85, 125
Chamber's Journal, 124
Chandler, Senator Zachariah, 92
Charleston, S.C., colonial: poor relief, 40-42
Charleston *Columbian Herald*, 49
Chattanooga, Tenn., 71, 111
Chauncy, Reverend Charles, 45
Chicago, 110, 115, 139-140; free medical care, 75; Panic of 1837, 105-106; Great Fire, 91-92; poor law reform after Great Fire, 57; World's Fair of 1893, 110

Chicago *Tribune*, 58, 109, 132, 139
Chicago *Weekly American*, 105
child welfare, 136 (*see also* Aid to Dependent Children; Aid to Families with Dependent Children; *alimenta*)
children, indentured as apprentices, 46
China, 56, 154
Churchill, Winston, and England's Old Age Pension Act of 1908, 130-131
Cicero, 8, 9
Civil Works Administration (CWA), 148-149
Civilian Conservation Corps (CCC), 147-148; and WPA, 159
Cincinnati, 69, 75-76; Cincinnati Hospital, 76
Claudius, Roman emperor, 16
Clayton Anti-Trust Act, 116
Clinton, Governor De Witt, 55-56
Cold War, effect on social legislation, 171
Commodus, Roman emperor, 17
Communism, 107, 109; effect on social legislation, 111-114
Communist Manifesto, published in English, in New York, 112
Community Action Program (CAP), 174, 176, 178
Conference of Charities (also called National Conference, etc.: *see* Source Notes, p. 363), 67, 68, 73, 74, 75, 83-84, 125, 143
congiaria, 10, 12, 16, 19
Congress: debates in, on matters of relief and social welfare: 88-91, 92-93, 93-94, 140-141, 153-154, 160, 186-187
Congressional Budget Office, 193
Connecticut Department of Public Welfare, 84
Constantine, Roman emperor, 12, 15, 16, 20
constitutional questions relating to evolution of social welfare: 89-91, 91-92, 93-94, 120-121, 154-155
contract system for caring for the poor, 56
Cook County, Ill., 75, 81-82
Coriolanus, 6-7

cost of living index, and public benefits, 195
Cotta, 8
Council of Economic Advisers, 171
county asylum (*see* almshouse)
County home (*see* almshouse)
Cox, Reverend James R., 141
Crafts, William, 60
Crédit Foncier, France, 96
Current History, 145

Danvers, Mass., almshouse, 81
Dayton, Ohio, 71, 110
Dellums, Rep. Ron, 188
Delos: free grain, 6
Demonstration Cities, neighborhood renewal program, 177
Demosthenes, 4
Denver *Post*, 160
Depression, Great (1929–), 98, 138, 141-149 passim, 152-167 passim; historical effect of, at the polls, 145-146; significance of, in particular, 144-155, 164, 167
depressions (*see* Panic of . . .)
Detroit, 71, 111, 179
Detroit *Gazette*, 101
Dexter Asylum, 80
Dio Cassius, 17
Diocletian, Roman emperor, 17, 18
Dirksen, Senator Everett McKinley, 185
Dix, Dorothea, 81; *Memorial to the Legislature of Massachusetts*, 120
Dixmoor, Ill., 175
dole: ancient Rome, 8-13; medieval England, 22; United States, as something to be avoided: Hoover on, 143-144; New Deal policy on, 147; Roosevelt on, 158; Johnson on, 174
Domitian, Roman emperor, 12, 15-16

Eastern State Hospital, 49
Economic conditions, as factor in evolution of social welfare: United States, generally, nineteenth-early twentieth centuries, 70-73, 100-111, 111-114, 114-117; agriculture, early twentieth century, 95-98; Great Depression, 141-142
Economic Opportunity Act of 1964, 173-175, 176
Economic stagnation of 1808-09, 101-102
Eden, Sir Frederic Morton, 25
Edgar, king of the English, 23
Edward VI, king of England, 33-34
Egypt, ancient, peasant strikes, 6
eight-hour day, 116
Eisenhower, President Dwight D., 171-172
Elizabeth I, queen of England, 35, 36-37
Elizabeth, N.J., 175
Ely, Richard T., 114
Embargo of 1807, 70, 101
Employment Act of 1946, 171
Engel, Rep. Albert J., 153
Engels, Friedrich, 112
England: *Medieval through Elizabethan times*: almshouse, 37; enclosure, 28-29, 31; free legal aid, 31; inflation, 29, 31; monasteries, and the poor, 29; poor law generally, 32-37; poor law, as applied to children, 32, 33, 36; poor relief at home, 35, 36; poor as victims of economy, 29; Statute of Apprentices, 36; Statute of Laborers, 25-26; unemployment, 31; vagabonds and beggars, 29-30, 31-32, 33, 34, 35-36; workhouse, 34-35, 36; *Eighteenth-nineteenth centuries*: export of poor, 124; Poor Law Amendment Act of 1834, 67; Speenhamland Act, 66-67; *Modern times*: National Insurance Act, 131; Old Age Pension Act, 131; reaction to, in U.S., 132; social insurance generally, 130-132
Essary, J. Frederick, 146
Ethelred, king of the English, 23
European precedents for U.S. social legislation, 126-131
Evans, Governor Daniel J., 193
Everybody's Magazine, 163

Fair Deal, 171

Family Assistance Plan (FAP), 183-188
famine, among Klondike miners, and federal response to, 93-94
Farm Journal, 95
Farm Loan Act of 1916, 95-97
farm relief, 98
Federal Emergency Relief Administration (FERA), 147
federal government, evolution of its role in social welfare up to the New Deal, 88-98, 104, 120-121, 138, 145, 167; in aftermath of Great Railroad Strike of 1877, 108-110; through public works, 72; as seen by Harding, 135-137; under Hoover, 143-144; New Deal proposed, 140; New Deal begins, 146-149
Federal Home Loan Bank System, 164
Federal Housing Authority (FHA), 164-165
Federal Resettlement Administration, 166
Federal Surplus Commodity Corporation, 162, 171
feorm, 22-23
Ferris, Rep. Scott, 96
fires (*see* natural disasters)
Flint, James, *Letters from America*, 100-101
floods and flood relief (*see* natural disasters)
food, free or subsidized, 74, 102 (*see also* food stamps; grain distribution; *panem et circenses*; school lunch program; soup kitchens; *tesserae frumentariae*)
food prices, 61, 93-94, 94, 96, 105
food stamps, 181, 186, 187, 192; origin of program, 161-162; fraud, 193 (*see also tesserae frumentariae*)
Ford, Rep. Gerald Ford, 185
Fortune, 146
"43rd Elizabeth," 37
Forum, 145, 161
Franklin, Benjamin, 49, 118
Froissart's Chronicle, 26
frontier, as a factor in policy toward the poor, 42-43, 58-59, 105-106, 165-166

Fronto, 11
Frost, Robert, 79
fuel, free or subsidized, 49, 192; Cincinnati, 69; New York, 74, 110
Fulbright, Senator J. William, 179-180
full employment, proposed, 170

Gallienus, Roman emperor, 20
gardens, as a relief measure, 111
Garner, Senator John Nance, 144
Genesee County, N.Y., Agricultural Society, 101
George, Henry, *Progress and Poverty*, 121
Georgia, colony, 48
Germany: Accident Insurance Act, 129; export of poor, 124-125; Invalidity and Old Age Insurance Act, 129; *Reichstag*, 126-127; Sickness Insurance Act, 129; social insurance, in general, 126-129; U.S. and British reactions to social programs of, 129-130
Glass, Senator Carter, 166
Gompers, Samuel, 115, 137
Gracchus, Gaius Sempronius, 7-8
Gracchus, Tiberius, 7
grain distribution, ancient Rome, 7-10
Grant, President Ulysses S., 92
Great Seal of the United States, on one-dollar bill as symbol of New Deal, 152
Great Society, 175, 179; proposed, 173; generally, 173-180; criticized, 179-180
Greece, ancient: abolition of debt, 6; land redistribution, 6; medical care, 13-14 (*see also* Athens, ancient)
Greeley, Horace, 106
Griffith, Thomas, *Annals of Baltimore*, 103
Griffith, William, *Eumenes*, 46-47
Grosvenor, W. M., 111-112
guaranteed annual income, 155, 183

Hadrian, Roman emperor, 14
Hall, Gertrude, 83-84
Hansen, Senator Clifford P., 187
"Happy Days Are Here Again," song: origin, 140; used by Democrats, 139, 140; used by Republicans, 140

Harding, Warren G., senator and president: proposal for Federal Department of Public Welfare, 134-137
Harlem, 174
Harman, Thomas, *Caveat for Cursetors*, 30
Harper's, 144
Hartford, Conn., 78
Havemeyer, Mayor William, 70-71
Health, Education and Welfare, Department of (HEW), 178, 184, 187, 194; established, 172; superseded by Health and Human Services, 192
Health and Human Services, Department of (HHS): established, 192
Helena, Mont., 71, 111
Henry VII, king of England, 28, 30-31
Henry VIII, king of England, 28, 31, 33
Hiester, Governor Joseph, 103-104
Hobby, Oveta Culp, 172
Holinshed's Chronicles, 27-28, 33-34
Home for the aged (*see* almshouse)
Home Owners' Loan Corporation (HOLC), 164
Hoover, President Herbert, 73, 98, 142-144, 167; renominated, 140; Research Committee on Social Trends, 138-139; position on federal role in relief, 143; Reconstruction Finance Corp., 144; on 1932 election as referendum on social policy, 145
"Hoovervilles," 141, 143
Hopkins, Harry, 147-148, 159, 160
housing: public assistance for, generally, 162-165; for the poor, proposed for Massachusetts, 1871, 163-164; New York (city), 1870's, 74; public housing, 171, 175, 181; subsidies, 178, 181, 192, 193
Housing Act of 1937, 165
Housing Act of 1949, 171
Humphrey, Vice-President Hubert H., 180, 185

Ickes, Harold L., 148
Idaho, 72
Iles, Elijah, *Sketches of Early Life and Times*, 58

Illinois, territory, 58
immigration and evolution of social welfare, 123-126
income security, as defined by Joint Economic Committee of Congress, 188-191
Indiana, early poor relief, 59-60, 80
indigent insane, 120
indoor relief: examples, 44, 52, 74; as opposed to outdoor relief, 52, 53, 56-57, 60-61, 66-70, 74, 102
infant mortality rate, 136
inflation: Rome, ancient, 18-20; England, sixteenth century, 29, 31; United States, 102, 105
in-kind benefits, 192-193
International Review, 111-112
Iowa: poor relief, 60-61; "welfare cycle," 68
Iowa State Register, 60
Ireland, export of poor, 124
Isocrates, *Areopagiticus*, 5-6

James I, king of England, proclamation of, 43
Jersey City, N.J., 175
Job Corps, 174, 176
Johns Hopkins University Studies, 114
Johnson, Alexander, 83; *The Almshouse*, 84
Johnson, President Lyndon B.: his administration generally, 172-180; medicare, 170-171; War on Poverty, 173-180; Great Society proclaimed, 173-174; declines to seek another term, 180
Joint Economic Committee of Congress, 188
Jones, Reverend Hugh, 43
Jones, Jesse H., 159
Justinian, Roman emperor, 13
Juvenal, *Satires*, 12

Keith County, Neb., 85
Kennedy, President John F., 172, 173
Kentucky, 159
Klondike gold rush, 93-94
Krock, Arthur, 159

Labor, Department of, 72, 137, 180
labor, organized, 114-117 (*see also* American Federation of Labor; Gompers, Samuel)
labor, organizing, 102, 105-106, 107-110
Labor Statistics, Bureau of, 85, 86
Lactantius, 16-17, 18
La Follette, Senator Robert M. Jr., 144
Lambert, John, *Travels*, 102
Landon, Alf, 166
Landrecht, Prussia, 128
Landschaften, Germany, 96, 97
Langland, William, 27
Laurens, Henry, 41, 42
Layamon's Brut, 22
Leach, Henry Goddard, 161
Legal aid to the poor: England, under King Edgar, 23; under King Henry VII, 31; United States, proposed in California, 1853, 63; under Johnson, 1965, 176
Letchworth, William P., 83
Lex Clodia, 9
Lex Iuliae Agraria, 9
Lex Sempronia, 8
Licinian Laws, 7
Lincoln, Abraham, 119
Lister, Thomas, 124
Literary Digest, 146
Littel's Living Age, 124
Livy, 7
Lloyd George, David, 130-131
Long, Senator Huey, "Share the Wealth" plan, 155
Long, Senator Russell B., 187
Long Island Star, (Brooklyn, N.Y.), 101
Lord, Henry W., 67
Los Angeles *Times*, 176-177
Low, Seth, 69
Lundeen, Rep. Ernest, and the Lundeen Plan, 155
Lysias, "Oration on the Question of a Pension for an Invalid," 2

McCormack, John, Speaker of the House, 174
McKinley, President William, 94

magicians, and the CWA, 148
Mahon, Rep. George H., 179
Maine, 178
Manpower Development and Training Act (MDT) of 1962, 172
Mansfield, Sen. Mike, 186
Marcus Aurelius, Roman emperor, 14, 17
Martinsburg, W. Va., 108
Maryland: colony, 46; state, 80
Marx, Karl, 112
Massachusetts, 53, 71, 77-78, 81, 82-83, 85; colonial, 45; immigration, 125; medical aid to poor, 75; Joint Standing Committee on Public Charitable Institutions, 82; old age assistance, 154; housing for the needy, 164
Massachusetts General Hospital, 49
Matanuska Colony (Alaska), 165-166
Matanuska Valley resettlement, 165-166
Maternity death rate, 136
medical care for the poor: Greece, ancient, 14; Rome, ancient, 13-14; colonial times, 47-49; *1820s*: Connecticut, 73; *1850s*: California, 62-64; *1870s and 1880s*: Chicago, 75, 125-126; Cincinnati, 75-76; Massachusetts, 75; New York (city), 73-75 (*see also* medicare and medicaid; occupational hazards; Harding, proposed Public Welfare Department, as related to public health)
medicare and medicaid; 172, 175, 181, 182, 188, 192, 193; first proposed, by Truman, 170; signed into law, in Independence, Mo., 170; take effect, 178; abuse of, 193; warnings of bankruptcy, 195 (*see also* medical care for the poor)
mensae oleariae, 19
Michigan, 80, 178, 192
Milwaukee *Journal*, 152, 161
Miner, Rep. Charles, 89
minimum wage, 171, 177; established, in Massachusetts, 116
Mississippi, territory: poor law adopted before laws for highways and ferries, 58

Missouri, territory, poor law, 59
Model Cities program, 180
Mondale, Senator Walter F., 186
Monroe, President James, 104
More, Sir Thomas, *Utopia*, 28-29
Morgenthau, Henry, Jr., secretary of the Treasury, 152
Moynihan, Daniel P., 181, 185
Musicians, and CWA, 148; and WPA, 159

Nairn, Thomas, 40
Nation, 114, 126
National Association of Manufacturers, 186
national debt, 159, 167
natural disasters, and evolution of federal role in social welfare, 88-93, 94-95
National Governors' Conference, 193
National Industrial Recovery Act (NIRA), 148, 152
National Labor Relations Board, 152
National Recovery Administration (NRA), 149
National Welfare Rights Organization, 186
Nebraska: poor relief, mid-nineteenth century, 61-62, 85
Neighborhood Youth Corps, 174, 179
Nero, Roman emperor, 12, 18
Nerva, Roman emperor, 14, 15
New Amsterdam, 162
Newark, N.J., 178-179
New Deal: in general, 146-153, 154-155, 155-162, 164-166; proclaimed, 140; the One Hundred Days, 146-148; criticism of, 166; 1936 election, as a referendum on, 166-167; summarized, 166-167
New Frontier, 172, 188
New Hampshire, 50, 79-80; Board of Charities, 79-80
New Hampshire *Mercury*, 50
New Jersey: colony, 46, 47; state, 178, 193
New Mexico, 85-86, 178
New Netherlands, 48

New Orleans *Daily Picayune*, 109, 110, 112
Newport, R.I., 43, 44, 49
Newsweek, 152, 157
New York *Advertiser*, 104-105
New York Association for Improving the Condition of the Poor, 72, 74, 112
New York (city), 78, 85, 91, 102, 148; colonial, 45, 47; relief the largest item in 1800 budget, 55; relief expenditures generally, 106, 110, 126; Panic of 1837, 105; Panic of 1857, 106; work relief, late 1800s, 70-72; housing conditions, 1880s, 162-163; and WPA, 159-161; promotion of medicaid, 178
New York City Council of Hygiene and Public Health, 163
New York City Home for the Aged, 85
New York *Daily News*, 176
New York Dispensary, 74
New Yorker, 106
New York *Evening Post*, 73
New York *Herald*, 108
New York Hospital, 74
New York, Humane Society of, 55-56
New York Public Health Association, 73-74
New York Sanitary Aid Society, 162-163
New York (state), 69, 72, 78, 83-84, 86, 103, 181; as colony, 59; poor law reform, 1820s, 55-57; immigration, 125; old age assistance, 154
New York State Association of County Superintendents of the Poor, 78, 83-84
New York State Board of Charities, 83-84
New York *Sun*, 107, 120
New York *Times*, 71, 97, 107, 132, 135, 136, 140, 142, 149, 159, 161
New York *Tribune*, 73-74, 106, 111, 134
Niles' Weekly Register, 100, 102, 105, 123
Nixon, Richard M., president, 182-186, 188; Family Assistance Plan,

183–188; Nixon administration, 182–188
North Dakota, old age assistance, 154
Northwest Territory, poor law, 59
"notch," problem of the, 182, 184
Nottingham, H. D., 78

occupational hazards, 119
Odoacer, 20
Office of Economic Opportunity, 176–177, 179, 184
Ohio, 68, 69, 80
old age pensions, 138, 153, 181; adopted by states, prior to Social Security Act of 1935, 153–154; proposals counter to Social Security Act of 1935, 155; under Social Security Act of 1935, 156–158
Old Age and Survivors Insurance Trust Fund, 195
Oregon, territory, poor law, 59

Paine, Thomas, *The Rights of Man*, 117–118
panem et circenses, as public policy in ancient Rome, 11
Panic of 1819, 100–101, 102–105; of 1837, 105–106, 146; of 1857, 106, 146; of 1873, 146; of 1893, 71, 146
Paris, the Commune, 111–112
Park, Dr. Roswell, 75
Paterson, N.J., 175
Patricelli, Robert E., 187
pauper insignia, 46
Pennsylvania, 79, 103; public works construction of bridges and turnpikes, in wake of depression of 1819, 70, 103–104; old age pensions, 79
Pennsylvania Hospital, 49
Pericles, 3
Philadelphia, 125, 148, 175; colonial, 45, 49, 69–70; depression of 1819, 100–101, 103; poor law reform in the 1820s, 56–57; unemployment in wake of Panic of 1837, 105; during the Great Depression, 142
Philadelphia *Aurora-General Advertiser*, 100, 101

Pierce, President Franklin, 120–121, 154–155
Pinckney, Charles, 43
Pingree, Mayor Hazen S., 111
pioneers, and poor relief, 58–59
Piso, 8
Pittsburgh, 109, 111–112
Plutarch: *Pericles*, 3, 4, 5; *Cato*, 19
poleos argurion, 2, 4
poorhouse (*see* almshouse)
poor law, English, as applied in America, 32–33, 43–44, 56, 59
Poor Law Amendment Act of 1834, 66–67
Portland, Me., 92
Portland, Ore., City Board of Charities, 77
Portsmouth, N.H., 50
Post, Wiley, 166
poverty cycle, 33, 68
poverty, estimates of, in U.S., 192
praefectus alimentorum 14
presidential election: of 1920, 134–137; of 1928, 143; of 1932, 139–140, 145–146; of 1936, 166; of 1940, 167
President's Commission on Social Security Reform (Reagan), 195
President's Research Committee on Social Trends (Hoover), 138–139
Procopius, 20
Project Head Start, 176
Providence, R.I., 80–81
Prussia, poor law, 128
public assistance (federal, as established under the Social Security Act of 1935, for the blind, aged, and disabled), 152, 153, 156, 181; under FAP, as proposed, 186; superseded by SSI, 188 (*see also* Supplemental Security Income)
public health, 136, 153, 156, 162–163
Public Health Service, 172
public lands, relief for purchasers of, 104, 120
Public Interest, 181
Public Welfare, Federal Department of, proposed 1920, 135–137
Public Works Administration (PWA), 148

public works employment (*see* work relief)

Quincy, Josiah, 53–55
Quincy, Josiah Phillips, 163–164
Quincy, Mass., 91

Railroads, as factor in economic and social unrest, 107–110
Railroad Strike of 1877, 107–110
Raleigh, Sir Walter, 36
Rarick, Rep. John R., 188
Ray, Governor James B., 59–60
Reagan, President Ronald, 192, 195
reclamation (*see* Civilian Conservation Corps; work relief)
Reconstruction Finance Corp. (RFC), 143–144, 147
Reed, Senator David, 144
Reform, 50, 83, 86, 182, 193; *quinqueviri*, ancient Rome, 15; England, late 1700s and early 1800s, 66–67; United States, *1820s*: Boston, 52–55; New York, 55–57, 69; Philadelphia, 57; *1870s*: Boston, 69–70; Brooklyn, 69; Chicago, 57–58; Cincinnati, 69; major eastern cities generally, 70; reform and reformers generally, 117–122; as proposed under FAP (Nixon), 182–188; social security reform, 1983, 194–195
Reichstag, Germany, 126–127
relatives, liability for support of the poor, 41
resettlement, as a relief measure, under Pericles, 5; under F. Roosevelt, 165–166
Reuther, Walter, 178
revolution, in United States, seen as possibility in 1932, 144–145
Rhodes, ancient, free grain, 6
Rhode Island, colony, 44, 45
Richard II, King of England, 26
Richmond, Va., 80
Ridley, Nicholas, 33
Riis, Jacob, *How the Other Half Lives*, 122
Rinehart, Mary Roberts, 134–135

Ring, Thomas F., 68
riots and demonstrations: New York City, 1800s, 102, 105; Great Railroad Strike of 1877, 107–110, 113; "Bonus Expeditionary Force," 140–141; U.S., 1960s, 174–180
Robin Hood, 27
Rochester, N.Y., 175
Rome, ancient: *Republic*: *congiaria*, 10; grain distribution (dole), 7–10; land redistribution, 7; *Empire*: *agentes in rebus* (secret police), 17; *alimenta* (aid to dependent children), 14–15, 19; *archiatri populares* (medical care of the poor), 13–14; bureaucracy, 19, 20; *coloni*, 17; Colosseum, 15; *congiaria*, 12, 16, 19; free meat, 20; free salt, 20; grain distribution (dole), 18–20; inflation, 18–20; *mensae oleariae* (free oil), 19; *panem et circenses*, as policy, 11, 15; *panes gradiles* (free bread), 19–20; *praefectus alimentorum*, 14; taxation, 17; *tesserae frumentariae* (food stamps), 12–13, 17; wine, subsidized, 20; work relief, 15–16
Romney, Governor George, 179
Romulus Augustulus, Roman emperor, 20
Roosevelt, President Franklin D., 73, 135, 139–140, 145–149, 154, 165, 166–167; on poor law reform, as candidate for governor, 86; pledges "new deal," 139–140; on 1932 election as referendum on social change, 145–146; on role of federal government in social welfare, 139–140, 149, 154, 156, 156–157, 158, 167; Roosevelt administration, generally, 146–149, 152–167 (*see also* New Deal)
Roosevelt, President Theodore, 97
Roosevelt, Theodore, Sr., 73–74
rural population, decline of, 95
Russell, Charles Edward, 163

St. Louis, Mo., 71, 110
St. Louis *Post-Dispatch*, 157, 160
Sanborn, F. B., 125
San Francisco, 62–65; earthquake, 94–95

San Francisco *Chronicle*, 132, 157, 161
Sanilac, Mich., poorhouse, 80
Saturninus, Apuleius, 8
school lunch program, 171, 181, 192
Scribner's, 122
Sears, Roebuck, and Co., 142
Seneca, 13, 16
Severus, Alexander, Roman emperor, 19
Severus, Septimius, Roman emperor, 12, 14, 19
Shakespeare, William, 6, 27; on enforcement of Elizabethan vagabond laws, 33
"Shanty in Old Shanty Town, A," song, 141
shantytowns, 141
Shouse, Rep. Jouett, 96
sieckentroosters, 48
Sinclair, Upton, EPIC, 155
six-day week, 116
slaves, in Rome, not eligible for dole, 9
slum clearance, 165, 171
Smith, Governor Al, 166
Social Security Act of 1935, 152-158, 167, 177, 181; immediate precedents for, adopted or proposed, 153-156; contents of act, 156; debated in Congress, 153-154; vote on, in Congress, 153; reactions to, in press, 157; takes effect, 157-158; commemorated, on one-dollar bill, 152
social security (subsequent to of Social Security Act of 1935): amendments of 1950, 171; amendments of 1954 and 1956, 172; amendments as alternative to FAP, 1972, 188; reform act of 1983, 194-195
Social Security Administration, 172
socialism, 132
Socialist Party, 153; platform of 1932, compared to Hoover Research Committee on Social Trends, 138
Solon, 2
soup kitchens, 102, 103, 115
South Carolina: colony, poor relief, 40-42; state: Department of Public Welfare, 84

Speenhamland Act, England, 66-67
Springfield, Mass., 77-78
Steagall, Rep. Henry, 95-96
stock market crash of 1929, 98, 146
Stow, John, *Annales*, 33-34
Stuyvesant, Peter, 45
Suetonius, 10, 11, 15
suffrage laws, with regard to paupers, 46-47
Sulla, Lucius Cornelius, 8
Sullivan, Mark, 166
Supplemental Security Income (SSI), 188, 192 (*see also* public assistance)
Sweeney, John D. Jr., first social security card, 157
Syracuse, N.Y., 178

Taft, President William Howard, 97
Talmadge, Governor Eugene, 166
Taylor, Dr. William H., 75
tesserae frumentariae, 12-13, 17
Tewksbury, Mass., almshouse, 82-83
Thackrah, Charles Turner, 119
Themistocles, 3
Theodoric, king of the Ostrogoths, 20
Theodosian Code, 13, 15
Thomas, Norman, 145
Tiberius, Roman emperor, 12
Times (London), 129-130
Tousey, Sinclair, 77
Townsend, Dr. Francis: Townsend Plan, 155
Trajan, Roman emperor, 13, 14
Truman, President Harry S., 170-171; Fair Deal, 171
Truth, a Journal for the Poor (San Francisco), 113

unemployment, 114-115, 124, 138, 172; England, 31, 66-67; United States, generally, 1800-1920, 70-73; Panic of 1819, 100, 102-104; Panic of 1837, 105-106; Panic of 1857, 106; Panic of 1873, 107-108, 110; Panic of 1893, 110-111; Great Depression, 141-142, 147, 148-149, 158-161, 166-167; 1960s, 179, 180, 181
unemployment compensation and relief,

unemployment compensation and relief *(continued)*
  138, 155, 170–171; England, late 1700s, 66–67; U.S., 1932, 144; New Deal, generally, 146–149, 152; first state unemployment compensation laws, 154; under Social Security Act of 1935, 156–157 *(see also* work relief)
United Auto Workers, 178
United British Emigrant Society, 103
Urban population increase in, 95
Utah, 154
Utopia, 28–29

vagabonds and vagrants, United States: 53; colonial period, 43–44, 47; late 1800s, early 1900s, 76–78; and almshouses, 79–80, 84–85 *(see also* England)
Valentinian I, Roman emperor, 13, 20
Verginius, Proculus, 7
Vespasian, Roman emperor, 15–16
veterans' bonuses, 140–141
Vietnam War, 179–180
Virginia, colony, 43, 46, 47, 52; state, 88; Board of Charities, 79
Volunteers in Service to America (VISTA), 174

Wages, 100, 103, 106, 108, 110, 142, 148–149
Wagner, Senator Robert F., 144
Wallace, Governor George, 185
Wallace, Henry, secretary of agriculture, 162
War on Poverty, 173–180, 184, 192
Washington, D.C., 70, 80, 91, 148; widows' and children's assistance, 154
Washington *Post*, 138, 143, 153, 173, 183
Washington (state), unemployment compensation, 154
Watts District (Los Angeles), riot of 1965, 177
Wayland, Francis, 68
Weeks, Paul, 176–177
welfare caseworkers, 194
welfare cycle, as perceived in 1903, 68

"welfare," defined, 181, 188–191
welfare fraud and abuse, 182, 184–185, 193–194
Wendte, Reverend Charles W., 69
West, U.S., poor relief in, during nineteenth century, 58–65
Wheelwright, Dr. Henry B., 66, 75
White, William Allen, 146
widows' laws, 181
Wilbur, Dr. Ray Lyman, secretary of the interior, 142–143
Wiley, George, 186
Willett, Mayor Marinus, 102
William I, emperor of Germany, 126–127
Williams, Senator John J., 187
Wilson, President Woodrow, 95, 97; and labor, 116
Wisconsin, 68, 125; first state unemployment compensation law, 154
Wood, Mayor Fernando, 106
Woodhull & Claflin's Weekly (New York), 112–113
women's rights, 136
"workfare," so called, 182, 183; in concept, 35, 36, 66–67 *(see also* work relief)
workhouse *(also called* bridewell, house of correction, house of industry), 44, 52, 80; England, 34, 35, 36; Boston, 53–55
workhouse test, 67
work incentive, 184–185
workman's compensation, 116
Work Projects Administration (WPA), 158–161
work relief: ancient Athens, 3–4; ancient Rome, 15–16; England, 1500s, 35, 36; New York, early 1800s, 102; Pennsylvania, 1820s, 103–104; New York, 1850s, 106; U.S. generally, nineteenth-early twentieth centuries, 70–73, 110–111; Great Depression, 143–144; under Roosevelt, 152, 158–161; Kennedy, 172; Johnson, 175; as proposed under Nixon, 184–185 *(see also* Job Corps)

Works Progress Administration. *See* Work Projects Administration
work-study program, 174
World War I, 97
World War II, 167

Wright, Rep. Hendrick B., 110

Yates, John V. N., 56
Youngstown, Ohio, 141

ABOUT THE AUTHOR

MERRITT IERLEY is an author and former journalist with extensive background in government from the municipal level to the federal (as one example, legislative assistant to N.J. Senator Fairleigh Dickinson, Jr.). It is background that proved invaluable to the writing of *With Charity for All*.

His first book, *The Year That Tried Men's Souls*, appeared in 1976. A journalistic reconstruction of the world of 1776, with an introduction by the former director of the American Press Institute, it was published in both the United States and England.

Ierley is also a composer, primarily of choral music. Works of his have been performed around the country, among other places at the New York Cultural Center, the College of William and Mary, and the Memorial Arts Center in Atlanta.

A native of New Jersey, Ierley is an alumnus of William and Mary and still calls Williamsburg, Virginia, a second home.